TOWARDS ONE WORLD?

TOWARDS ONE WORLD?

International Responses to the Brandt Report

EDITED BY THE

FRIEDRICH EBERT FOUNDATION

TEMPLE SMITH ·LONDON

First published in Great Britain in 1981
by Maurice Temple Smith Ltd
Gloucester Mansions, Cambridge Circus,
London WC2

© Friedrich Ebert Foundation 1981

ISBN 0 85117 218 0 ✓

Photoset by Robcroft Ltd
Printed in Great Britain by
The Camelot Press Ltd

Towards one world.
   1. Independent Commission on International
   Development Issues.
   North-South, a programme for survival
   2. Equality of states
   3. Economic development
   I. Friedrich Ebert Foundation
   330.9   HD82

CONTENTS

INTRODUCTION

Alfred Pfaller, Michael Hofmann, Michael Dauderstädt

The Report of the Independent Commission on International Development Issues was submitted by the Commission's chairman, Willy Brandt, to the Secretary-General of the United Nations in February 1980. Since that occasion, the Report has been the subject of worldwide discussion. It has been criticized in reputable daily newspapers as well as popular and specialist journals, deliberated at international conferences, 'acknowledged' by governments, and adopted by the institutions of the UN family as an important working document. The original English version of 'North-South: A Programme for Survival' has now been translated into more than ten languages; other translations are in preparation. Accordingly, it can safely be assumed that the reader will himself have read the Brandt Report or at least be familiar with its content. The following observations are therefore intended to serve merely as an aide memoire for placing the commentaries presented here in their proper context.

As the terms of reference under which the Commission commenced its work explain, its mandate was to provide orientation aids for political action: 'It should seek to identify realistic and desirable directions for international development policy in the next decade, giving attention to what in their mutual interest both the developed and the developing countries should do.'

The Report proceeds from the assumption that, in view of the grave economic problems afflicting both the developing and the industrial countries, the existing structures of the world economy no longer do justice to both parties. Without disputing the existence of antagonisms, the Report contends that it is nonetheless possible to fashion mutual interests from the controversies which have plagued international negotiations for many years. It argues that interdependence between states has increased so rapidly that the social challenge of our time can be met only by means of jointly supported international solutions. The Commission maintains that only if long-term, well-understood self-interests are accorded priority over short-term, defensive measures can the world economy be revitalized and discrimination against the developing countries overcome. This would imply a positive adjustment of the industrial structure instead of protectionism; well-functioning commodity agreements instead of a unilateral decline in purchasing power induced by price changes; long-term investment to safeguard energy supplies instead of short-term squandering of non-renewable energy resources; and finally, more power-sharing in international finance institutions to facilitate medium-term adjustment policies. These are merely some of the issues examined in the Report.

Of overarching significance is the interest in terminating the arms race in order to liberate resources for purposeful development action and thus safeguard the survival of mankind. And an ever more urgent imperative of global policy is that of placing international solidarity in the service of overcoming absolute poverty so that a self-sustaining development process is rendered possible in even the poorest regions of the world.

The Commission was very much aware that many of its proposals are not realizable overnight and, in fact, represent tasks for the 1980s and 1990s. Yet in view of the profound crisis embracing both North and South, the Commission considered it pertinent to set out an Emergency Programme, to be initiated immediately, for the period 1980 to 1985. This programme, incorporating a large-scale transfer of resources to developing countries, an international energy strategy, a global food programme and a start on some major reforms in the international economic system, is to be understood as a package deal implying a fair measure of give-and-take for all parties.

The Brandt Report is intended to be a political action document, the dimension of which is the future; for this reason, issues of historical guilt are deliberately excluded. It is addressed in the first instance to the decision-makers of political life, calling upon them to take action, but also to the interested public, for, as Willy Brandt states, 'the shaping of our common future is much too important to be left to governments and experts alone.'

For the authors of the Report and all those who identify themselves with its objectives, the question now assuming priority importance is: What are they doing, those who were called upon to act? To what extent are they turning the Report's recommendations into reality?

This question is likewise the point of departure for this collection of commentaries. Yet a direct answer can be given only through actions. Thus the observer as well as the committed citizen will raise the additional question: What can induce political decision-makers to act in line with the recommendations of the North-South Report?

The political effectiveness of a document such as the Brandt Report does not depend on the charismatic force of its appeal. It must be measured rather by the extents to which it can open the eye to menacing developments and transmit the conviction that the measures it recommends are in the interest of those who are meant to introduce them. The Commission's appeal for political action is inevitably also an appeal for reflection. The arguments advanced in the Report must be weighed against other demands placed on political action. Will they withstand the selection imposed by political reality? Can they themselves influence this political reality?

This book was born of a quest to stimulate and bring to the public that reflection which shapes and accompanies political action. It presents viewpoints of those who are primarily called upon to act, as well as commentaries by experts who, like every committed observer, raise the question: How sound are the theses of the Report? What are their prospects of being transposed into reality?

The central idea of the Report is that a massive promotion of the economic development of the South is in the best interests of the rich countries of the North. And it is in respect of this core thesis, on which the political thrust of the Report depends, that the commentaries presented here show profound differences. While one line of thought sees in it the basis for a purposeful – although perhaps bitterly resisted – reshaping of international economic policy, other commentators display an attitude of undisguised scepticism.

The first group can be subdivided according to the manner in which its various adherents approach the implementation of the new North-South policy:

> economic arguments and political appeal on one side;
> examination of the conditions of political feasibility, on the other.

The attitude of intrinsic scepticism is expressed:

> in a pragmatic approach which subscribes less to a comprehensive programme of North-South solidarity than to concrete bargains in line with prevailing economic conditions (and power relations);
> in a view which, while acknowledging a Brandtian North-South policy to be purposeful in principle, regards with pessimism the ability of the North to moderate its short-term aspirations;
> in a view, which unambiguously denies the mutuality of

interests between North and South postulated by the Commission.

Given the variety of analytical dimensions expressed in the commentaries and the many differences between the various positions adopted, a classification into groupings is necessarily somewhat arbitrary and tentative. But it may be expedient for the limited purpose of orienting the reader. On the basis of the criteria mentioned above, the commentaries are therefore presented in six sections. They are explained and correlated in terms of their conceptual linkages below.

1. The Way Out of the Crisis: Solidarity plus Reflation

As in the Report of the Commission itself, two parallel basic motives can be identified among its advocates:

> solidarity among peoples, derived in the last instance from ethical reasoning;
> economic cooperation between North and South for the benefit of both.

The significance of the first in the attainment of the second is emphasized in the contributions by **Mário Soares**, **Claude Cheysson**, **Léopold Senghor** and **Barbara Ward**. Other commentators, such as **Paul Streeten**, who consider a North-South policy based on mutual economic interest to be more a matter of case-by-case procedure, or, as with **Ralf Dahrendorf**, who even views it with fundamental scepticism, nevertheless consider the solidarity motive to be important.

However, the message of the Report is also understood as a policy programme indicating a way out of the present world economic crisis. The central component of this programme is the stimulation of demand on a worldwide basis by means of massive financial transfers to the countries of the Third World. The Report's line of argument in this respect is explicitly put forward once more by **Angelos Angelopoulos** and **Michael Lipton**, the latter's contribution stating clearly that the economic concept advanced is one which is diametrically opposed to the austerity policy currently prevailing in the western world. In the contribution by trade union representative **Carl Wright** (and, to a somewhat lesser extent in that by the Federal German trade union leader **Heinz-Oskar Vetter**), the global reflation recommended by the Commission is presented even more clearly as an alternative political programme, which must be enforced against tough interest-based resistance. That **Orville Freeman** too, as spokesman for transnational entrepreneurship unambiguously supports the global growth policy advocated by the Commission reveals the potential of this policy as the basis for a 'class-bridging' coalition of interests.

Whereas the North's representatives among the commentators of this group emphasize the issue of 'expansive growth policy versus deflationary stabilization policy', the Commission's followers from the South perceive the Programme for Survival primarily as a cooperative strategy of long-term rationality which is beginning to take shape in the North as a political alternative to the defence of short-term vested interests pursued to date (see the contribution by **Luo Yuanzhen** and the interview with **Raúl Prebisch**.) This point of view is also reflected in the commentaries by **Jan Tinbergen**, **Claude Cheysson** and **Barbara Ward**. It should be noted, however, that a due measure of scepticism can be found among the representatives of the South (especially on the part of **Adebayo Adedeji**, **Carlos Andrés Pérez**, **Carlos Rafael Rodrıguez**, and **Benjamin Udogwu**) regarding the implementation prospects of this concept. That the attitude toward the Commission's North-South Programme is determined also by the strategic interests of specific countries or groups of countries (a point especially made by **Johan Galtung**) emerges clearly from the contribution by **Luo Yuanzhen**.

A more technical economic aspect to which the 'positive' commentaries (especially that of **Michael Lipton**) pay special attention is the debt issue, where – irrespective of economic standpoint – the immediate interest of the North in averting acute crises is being seen. This attitude is also shared by some of the commentators (like **Andre Gunder Frank**), who view as illusory the intrinsic interest of both North and South in a global growth policy asserted by the Commission and its followers.

2. Mutual Interests: The 'Pragmatic' Approach

The commentaries of the first group leave no doubt that the Brandt Report should be understood as an appeal for a decisive change of course in the policy pursued by the industrial states vis-à-vis the Third World. It is precisely this demand, however, that is played down, if not directly rejected, by the commentators of the second group, among whom – significantly enough – we find the heads of government of Great Britain and the Federal Republic of Germany, **Margaret Thatcher** and **Helmut Schmidt**, and the former Assistant Secretary of Treasury in the Carter Administration, **Fred Bergsten**. Instead of subscribing to Brandt's thesis on the necessity of reforming North-South relations, they implicitly or explicitly focus their attention on the usefulness of the existing order. Instead of political turnabout, they recommend specific improvements in cooperation between industrial and developing countries, to be introduced on the basis of specifiable mutual interests.

In the contribution by **Fred Bergsten**, the capacity of the prevailing order to accommodate such improvements is put forward as an apologetic antithesis to the demand for a new world economic order. This approach is also explicitly supported by the British Prime Minister, **Margaret Thatcher**. **Helmut Hesse** underlines the superior efficiency of the existing market economy as compared with the bureaucratic tendencies inherent in the Commission's proposals. The concept of development assistance advanced by **Karl-Heinz Sohn**, which is rather representative of official Western thinking on the topic, ties in with this line of thought.

To some extent, the observations made by **Paul Streeten** try to confirm the adaptability of the present system. However, he goes beyond the identification of concrete areas of cooperation (an approach similar to that adopted by **Michael Lipton**) to point out the system's overarching interest in a generally accepted international order. That the endangered functional efficiency of the world economy might in fact require a closer reintegration of the South into the existing order (alleged by critics such as **Pavel Khvoinik** to be the tacit purpose of the entire exercise) is an aspect which can also be found in the contribution by **Helmut Hesse**, although he finds the Report's arguments on this point unconvincing.

The key economic argument of the Report, namely impulses to global growth through an accelerated development of the South, is rejected by the commentators of this group who thus reflect the prevailing economic policy view (and meet with the politically opposing view advanced by **Andre Gunder Frank**).

Another theme putting the Commission's concept of an all-embracing North-South development alliance into perspective is that of the limited capability of the North to aid the South (a theme emphasized by **Helmut Schmidt** in particular). This leads, on the one hand, to a greater emphasis on the responsibilities of the countries of the South and of OPEC and, on the other, to the fear (explicitly voiced by **Fred Bergsten**, but also discernible in the contribution by **Luo Yuanzhen**), that the Brandt Report, by awakening unrealistic hopes, might relegate the North-South dialogue to the level of sterile rhetoric. The assumption that the North can do little to assist the South in the solution of its development problems – an assumption emphatically opposed by **Michael Lipton**, for example – is given credence by a number of Third World commentators (including **Pérez**, **Adedeji**, and **Tévoédjrè**) who likewise believe the key to progress in their countries to reside in their own national efforts.

Altogether, the pragmatic attitude of influential politicians in the North signals an implicit dissociation from the spirit of the Brandt message. They basically consider the situation of the poor countries to be not radically improvable within the foreseeable future, but they do not betray any apocalyptic fear which might call for a 'programme for survival'.

3. How to Make 'Survival' Politically Feasible

To a certain extent it is the attitude discernible in the commentaries of the second group which the Commission in its Report (and in particular Willy Brandt in his foreword) seeks to discredit. Just how the Commission could succeed in so doing and incorporate the long-term rationale of its viewpoint into the policies of the North (beyond the mere reconciliation of isolated concrete interests) is taken as the main subject for reflection in a number of contributions. **Norman Girvan** takes the raw materials issue to illustrate the fundamental political problem of the North-South programme proposed by the Commission. **József Bognár** and **Helio Jaguaribe** phrase it in theoretical terms as a contradiction between 'structure-bound' and 'structurally independent' rationality or between 'operational' and 'regulatory convenience' (concepts which are also distinguishable in the contributions by **Dahrendorf**, **Streeten**, and **Ward**). Among the conditions which set the 'regulatory convenience' of a comprehensive North-South development alliance at variance with the 'operational convenience' of down-to-earth politics, **Curt Gasteyger** and **József Bognár** single out the East-West conflict.* Others (**John P. Lewis**, **Norman Girvan**, but also **József Bognár** and **Karl-Heinz Sohn**) emphasize the present worldwide economic difficulties. A certain resignation vis-à-vis these inauspicious preconditions alternates with a search for means to overcome them. The social mechanisms on which hopes are places in this connection are:

> initiatives of political persuasion to change attitudes and generate majorities, of which the Brandt Report itself is one example (see **Girvan**, **Lipton**, **Angelopoulos**);
> proceeding from preparatory persuasion campaigns:

---

* Bognár views this also as a decisive obstacle to greater commitment to the cause of Southern development – appealed for by the Commission – on the part of the socialist countries of the North.

meetings of responsible decision-makers at which operational priority is attributed to the fight against Southern underdevelopment (see in particular **Aurelio Peccei**, but also **József Bognár**);

greater pressure exerted by the South on the North (a point which, although touched on by **Norman Girvan** and **Jan Tinbergen**, is emphasized by commentators such as **Carlos Andrés Pérez** and **Silviu Brucan** who anticipate no voluntary change in the North's policy towards the South).

Typically, a summit meeting such as the Commission proposes is regarded as a useful step on the path to a new North-South policy by those to whom the higher rationality of such a policy is obvious and who (like **Silviu Brucan**) view the conventional, 'pragmatic' form of bargaining as short-sighted. Yet it awakens but few positive expectations among those commentators who cast doubt (like **Fred Bergsten**) upon the premises of the Report and hence upon the value of politicizing the issue of development cooperation, or (like **Carlos Rafael Rodrıguez**) upon the disposition of the Northern politicians to give up short-term advantages. Accordingly, the prospects of the planned summit meeting*, one to which **Aurelio Peccei** attributes decisive importance for the establishment of a new North-South policy, depend to a considerable extent on the degree of urgency which the North is prepared to bestow upon the South issue.

4. Mutual Interests – An Illusion?

Are there irrefutable arguments to back up goodwill, enabling it to overcome all political obstacles? To what extent is 'survival' actually at stake? Here, the plea for a comprehensive North-South alliance has to defend itself against the arguments put forward in the fourth group of commentaries. These arguments can be reduced to the three basic theses described below.

1. Whether the peoples of the developing countries are well off or badly off is, in the final analysis, irrelevant to the material well-being of the industrial countries. Events taking place in the South do not exert any decisive influence on those taking place in the North (**Ralf Dahrendorf**).

2. The economic development of the Third World and its progressive integration into a system of global interdependence is more likely to increase conflict than stability. Whereas the powerlessness of the have-nots does not represent a danger to the existing international order, the emergence of new contenders for power and status will

* October 1981 in Mexico.

inevitably breed more competition and disruption (**Robert Tucker**).

3. To assume the existence of a uniform interest throughout the North in economic prosperity and political stability is illusory. The positions taken up by countries as well as by social classes are in fact those of rivals struggling for economic and political power. Their various interests are matched by diverse strategies incorporating diverse sympathies for the various aspirations of élites and peoples in the South. Whereas **Johan Galtung**, **Silviu Brucan**, and also **Immanuel Wallerstein** stress the divergent economic and political positions of various countries and groups of countries, **Constantine Vaitsos** focuses his attention on the conflicting positions adopted by specific groups within the societies of the North. Seen from this angle the programme proposed by the Brandt Commission shows itself as a strategy which, although corresponding to a specific line of interests, in fact runs counter to the dominant preoccupations of the hegemonial powers in East and West or of big capital vis-à-vis other sectors of society. It should be noted that this viewpoint is not entirely absent in some commentaries of the first group (in particular those by **Lipton** and **Wright**), and could find itself confirmed to a certain extent by those of the second group. The same general line of thought is also developed by **Andre Gunder Frank** and other commentators in the sixth group.

It is in the political context emphasized by this group of commentators that the Commission's Programme for Survival would have to assert and establish itself as a relevant strategic alternative. Whereas in a **Dahrendorfian** world the substance of North-South solidarity has only a moral quality, **Tucker**'s scenario could invoke the institutionalization of international solidarity (and authority?) as a countermeasure to increasing global instability. As a project for a new international order (into which it would perforce have then to expand), the Programme for Survival would necessarily find itself in competition with other projects envisaging the consolidation of different distribution structures.

5. *Brandt Helps, but Self-reliance is Essential*

While the North is finding difficulty in bringing itself to grant the South more generous concessions and to accept preoccupation with Third World development as a programme for its own survival, in the South expectations of voluntary concessions by the North are declining. At the same time increasing importance is being attached to the mobilization of the South's own resources.

Whereas the first sentiment leads to the conclusion to build up potential for political pressure by the South (an interpretation put forward in particular by the former President of the OPEC country Venezuela, **Carlos Andrés Pérez**), the second implies a certain retreat from the arena of the North-South conflict (an interpretation developed in the contributions by **Adebayo Adedeji** and **Albert Tévoédjrè**). In contrast to the view of the Commission yet fully in line with that of the sceptics of our second group, the role of aid and trade in improving the living standard in the poor countries is regarded as auxiliary rather than fundamental. Decisive importance is instead attached to developing self-reliance and to orienting production towards the people's needs.

An integral part of this view is criticism regarding the transfer of inappropriate production structures from the North to the South resulting in the Southern economies working in accordance with a world economy which is oriented towards the interests of the North. This perspective is discernible also in the contribution by **Léopold Senghor** and assumes focal importance in the commentaries of the sixth group. Foreign aid is not rejected, but the fixation on it is regarded as a distraction from the real issue at hand (a point made in particular by **Johan Galtung**).

In the political variant of Southern self-reliance (emphasized by **Carlos Andrés Pérez**), the decisive factor would be the South's ability to defy the North and to establish its own position in the world economy. Much significance is therefore attached to the question as to with whom OPEC, as the main support of Southern economic power, will ally itself. Undisguised mistrust regarding the possible advent of a 'Club of the Rich' complemented by the Gulf States emanates from the contributions by **Carlos Andrés Pérez** and **Albert Tévoédjrè**. **Silviu Brucan**, on the other hand, sees real chances for a Southern alliance strategy of OPEC. In the very spirit described by **Tucker** this would reflect the struggle of new élites for status and power in a world once again in motion.

6. *The Limits to Reformism*

The Brandt Report can be seen as a plea for a better place for the Third World in the international economic system. This, it is contended, also corresponds with the interests of the hitherto privileged participants in the international economic system, since the continued functioning of that system would otherwise no longer be guaranteed.

It is this very endeavour to preserve the existing system by way of reforms which the commentators of the sixth group consider to be the fundamental inadequacy of the Report, or, looking at it another way, as its 'true purpose', bespeaking an objective intention to counter the emancipation of the Third World. That which in the commentaries by **Adedeji** and **Tévoédjrè** is portrayed as a shift of emphasis is reason for **Samir Amin** and **Amilcar Herrera** to reject unequivocally the Commission's strategy to integrate the developing countries into the present world economic system since, even assuming the implementation of the Brandt reforms, it would retain its basic (i.e. capitalist) features. And while **Pavel Khvoinik**, and to some extent **Pedro Vusković** and **Samir Amin** warn the Third World against the illusory temptations of the Report (a warning which is also to be found in the commentaries by **Fred Bergsten** and **Helmut Hesse**, albeit presented with politically very different connotations), **Immanuel Wallerstein** and **Andre Gunder Frank** criticize the Brandt proposals as being unrealistic because incompatible with the dictates of real-life interest positions, and furthermore inadequate as a strategy to overcome the problem of underdevelopment. It is contended that more favourable terms in international economic relations and more generous transfers are more likely to bring about a consolidation of the existing system of inequality and of the power relations on which it is based.

Less disposed to compromise than the commentators in the fifth group, those in the sixth group (in particular **Samir Amin**) call for a deliberate break with the economic driving forces inherent in the capitalist world system. **Cardinal Arns**, led by his first-hand experience of the continuous pauperization process in a 'successful' developing country, shifts the focus of attention from the issue 'rich vs. poor countries' to the marginalization of the poor within the Third World countries, and hence from the need for more aid to the need for liberation from the forces of inhumane capitalism. It is **Pedro Vuscović**, one of the architects of the economic policy of the Allende government in Chile, who contrasts most clearly the established, world-market-oriented and dependent development model (which the Commission offers in a slightly reformed version) with the alternative concept of autonomous development which is now increasingly gaining acceptance in the South. Little doubt is left that to achieve such autonomous development, which would not serve the dominant sectors of Southern societies, would require a revolution in existing power relations. Correspondingly, **Wallerstein** is pessimistic about the chances of its being realized within the foreseeable future when he forecasts that 'the next 20 years of

North-South negotiations are not going to be more significant or efficacious than the last 20 years'. Also **Carlos Rafael Rodrıguez'** attitude of qualified disposition to cooperate with world capitalism in the more concessive form envisaged by the Commission, reveals that even countries like Cuba, that have opted for the alternative path of development, realize that they will have to cope with the forces of the old model in the foreseeable future.

In contrast, something resembling a prescience of imminent and drastic change similar to that invoked in the Report is evident in the commentaries by **Amilcar Herrera** and **Mahdi Elmandjra** (to some extent also by **József Bognár**). For both observers, the emergence of a document like the Brandt Report is simultaneously a symptom of change and a futile attempt to bring that change under control and accommodate it without major disruptions. For **Herrera**, the issue at hand is not only how the poor countries can come to share the North's prosperity but that this very prosperity, the manner of its generation and the manner of its consumption, is itself approaching its demise.

The purpose of this introduction is not to take positions in the intellectual controversy surrounding the Report but to mark out provisionally a number of points which might serve as orientation aids for the reader. It is in this same spirit that the following general observations should be understood.

As **Andre Gunder Frank** points out, the political programme of the North-South Commission can be ascribed to various levels of perspective. The same appears to be discernible in the debate presented in the following texts. At the one level the debate takes up the Commission's proposals as concrete recommendations for action to be taken by governments within the existing multipolar, hierarchical, and competitive international system. The cardinal question to be raised in this connection is how far the proposals correspond with the interest constellations moulded by that system and oriented towards its structures.

At the other level the question is, to what extent are the existing structures themselves – which now define what is 'realistic' and what is not – still viable? Here, the Commission's programme is regarded as a draft plan for restructuring the international system and adjusting it to menacing new realities. The focal element of this draft plan, which must necessarily appear as utopian from the 'realistic' perspective of the first level, emerges as the institutionalization of global, i.e. transnational, solidarity. And alongside the question of the functional necessity of such a system change (is it a matter of 'survival'?), there comes another: to what extent do the constraints and necessities of the present world leave room to adjust to those of the future? Reality is preparing the answer. Will it afford politics the right to state its case?

FOREWORD

In an address to the World Affairs Council of Boston in January 1977, I proposed the creation of a private commission of experienced and distinguished individuals, to .be chosen from the developing and industrialized countries, whose purpose would be to assess the critical development issues confronting the world, and to recommend feasible actions to be taken by the rich and poor nations alike.

I stressed that the members of such a group would have the advantage of collaborating not as official representatives of particular countries, or blocs of nations, but rather as international figures of recognized competence and independent judgment. Clearly, the chairman and convener of such a commission ought to be a person of great political experience and stature, and I suggested that Willy Brandt, former Chancellor of the Federal Republic of Germany, and Nobel Laureate, consider serving in that capacity.

Willy Brandt graciously accepted the proposal, recruited an outstanding group of commissioners, gathered together an expert staff, and formally launched the Independent Commission on International Development Issues. Two full years were devoted to the work. The 'Brandt Commission' – as it deservedly came to be known – remained rigorously independent of governments and international institutions, and when the Report was finalized and published the full group of 21 commissioners were in unanimous agreement with the main thrust of its recommendations, and its programme of priorities.

The Friedrich Ebert Stiftung has now usefully brought together in this volume a collection of commentaries on the commission's work from a broad group of observers and scholars around the world.

As one would expect in such comments, there is a very wide variety of views expressed here on the commission's conclusions. Some of the observers feel that the recommendations go too far; others believe they do not go nearly far enough.

But as I cautioned at the outset, 'Such a commission cannot be expected, of course, to provide an instant, comprehensive, all-purpose solution to the problems of development – for none exists.'

What I did believe then, however, and continue to believe now, is that such an independent, high-level, experienced group of commissioners could help point the way to those actions which, in time, can command public and legislative support in rich and poor countries alike, and hence enable the international development community to break out of prolonged deadlock and impasse.

The Brandt Commission has helped point that way. And its conclusions deserve the widest possible consideration and discussion.

Again, as I noted in Boston, 'there will be some critics who say that it is fanciful to suppose that the rich and poor nations – all of them politically sensitive over their own national prerogatives – can come to any meaningful understanding over development issues.'

It is true enough that the world today is divided on a whole spectrum of issues: political, economic, ideological, cultural. It would be naive to pretend otherwise. But it is also true that it is an increasingly interdependent world. And that is why it is clearly advantageous to all to understand better the mutuality of their interests, and to search for those areas of agreement that in the end can benefit all.

The Brandt Commission's task, the international development community's task – indeed the task of all of us into whose hands this volume has found its way – is surely to help move that effort forward.

Robert S. McNamara

ONE

THE WAY OUT OF THE CRISIS: SOLIDARITY PLUS REFLATION

CLAUDE CHEYSSON*

. . . among the industralized countries it is the Europeans who will have to take the initial steps on the paths opened by Mr. Willy Brandt.

The reports which have preceded that of the Brandt Commission are numerous. Some have undoubtedly been remarkable. Yet this quality did not prevent flattering commentaries from being toned down and realistic and orthodox consideration from being raised in their place just a few weeks after their publication and – perhaps unfortunately – before the most audacious of their proposals were to be implemented. The situation seems to be not quite the same in the case of the Brandt Report. Could this be some kind of indication? Is it such as to kindle hope? This may be so, for new and objective reasons which merit examination.

The Commission was composed of eminent personalities with a wealth of experience of politics and devoid for the main part of any ambitions relating to the object of their reflections. They were drawn from North and South, from the political right and the political left. Their intellectual resources enriched the lengthy discussions of the Commission. All thereby discovered or reaffirmed to what extent we people of the world are interdependent and the need for us to join forces to put the world back in order. And it is the conviction which this discovery afforded them which radiates from their simple affirmation of this interdependence, this globality.

Interdependence between North and South: this affirmation is present throughout the Report. Even if it is not yet experienced personally by everyone, it is no longer contested by anyone holding political or economic

* France. Minister of Foreign Affairs

responsibilities of anything more than insignificant standing. Its degree of acceptability is found to increase the more disadvantaged the country, sector or milieu in question is, or the less able it is to overcome its problems. It is thus not surprising that the argument meets with the greatest interest in the European countries which are heavily dependent for their supplies on foreign countries and which owe their economic growth of recent years exclusively to their relations with the countries of the South. That the Report has found a more attentive readership in the Federal Republic of Germany or in England than in the United States of America reflects a state of interdependence by degrees. This leads us to our first conclusion: among the industrialized countries it is the Europeans who will have to take the initial steps on the paths opened by Mr Brandt.

Interdependence also concerns the subjects to be dealt with. In no previous report has this principle, this fundamental principle been expounded and proclaimed with such force as in that of the former Chancellor of the Federal Republic of Germany and his colleagues.

Some of these colleagues, such as Edward Heath, former Prime Minister of the United Kingdom, dazzlingly highlighted this aspect during subsequent communications destined for the public at large: energy will not be dealt with if the oil-producers are not motivated to cooperate; this implies that the security of financial assets accumulated from the production and sale of oil must be dealt with; which implies that the conditions for the industrialization process to be financed by oil revenue must be dealt with; and this in turn implies that technology-sharing and technology-adaptation must be dealt with. It is the same with access to the world's major markets for the manufactures thus produced, and relations with the members of the multinational economic and industrial community. A word on energy thus reveals the necessity for deliberation on issues monetary, financial, techno-logical, commercial, etc. And, irrespective of the field selected – regularity of food supplies, expansion of commerce, mineral production, demographic growth, development of the developing countries – it is evident that all other fields have to be dealt with simultaneously. All or almost all the major issues are interlinked. And for each of them, one or more groupings in the South, one or more groupings in the North hold decisive responsibilities. Consequently, the problems of the present – economic crisis or poverty and penury, economic revival or development – cannot be broached except from a global view-point and in a global manner.

I am even in favour of going further than Mr Brandt and his group and of pointing out that the changes, the upheavals envisaged in the economic order (is it in any case anything other than economic?) will have implications of such magnitude within each of our societies that we must recognize from the outset that the national order is and will continue to be affected: how can we encourage industrialization in other parts of the world without accepting that the division of labour will be restructured? So, let us acknowledge without delay that policies favouring industrialization and development in the South should be linked with restructuring in the North.

Let us keep vigil to ensure that the enormous benefits accruing to the industrial countries from the economic development of the developing countries serve in the first instance to facilitate an acceptable restructuring process in the industrial countries. Let us acquiesce to evolution, but let us not leave the control and organization of that evolution to large enterprises and national and, above all, transnational economic forces which obviously feel under no obligation to assume responsibility for converting industries and regions or for compensating and reorienting the working man and mankind's communities.

A further conclusion can be drawn at this point: the consequences of this evolution should be observed over a certain period of time, evaluated with our partners in the South, and appraised with the participation of the social and political forces in our own countries. (The Friedrich Ebert Foundation manifests its awareness of this fact by publishing this work; a most welcome aspect is that the trade union movement has thus been drawn into the process from the outset.)

In other words, we are no longer in the position in which

we found ourselves one or two decades ago, at a time when tried and tested ways and means could be used to face and overcome difficulties in accordance with a familiar process. We are now at the turn of an era. Can there remain any doubt of this? We shall not be returning to the sixties, and everyone accepts this fact as regards the energy issue. But the situation is the same in all fields. That a number of strong forces on the market cherish a tacit hope that the task of elaborating and developing new strategies will be left to them is possible, indeed probable. But this cannot be allowed to take place if its price is the prior demise of the weak, the disadvantaged, the handicapped, and the backward in all their guises.

The foregoing clearly indicates the global, fundamental and political nature of both the deliberations and their expression. Since we live in a free democracy, it is imperative that a broad-based debate be initiated among us all. Public opinion should know what is at stake and its representatives should acknowledge their positions via the parliaments, the trade unions, associations of all kinds, and the press.

Negotiation at world, regional, and sectoral level should be resituated within a political framework. Governments should be heard periodically within the United Nations; we should no longer be content to leave debates to specialists and officialdom.[1] During these lengthy and general negotiations, each meeting of political leaders should be used to express political pressure and prevent this major reflection on the turn of an era from becoming transformed into a bartering session on production tonnage or a dispute over the formulation of resolutions. The Commission's proposal for a North-South summit meeting refers to such a political framework and will probably be remodelled in practice into a series of North-South conventions composed of different but probably equally eminent members. The periodic meetings of the prime ministers of Commonwealth countries, of the seven heads of government in the West (pursuant to the Venice summit), etc. will afford further opportunities to consider this or that aspect of change in a manner as authoritative and informal as possible while not compromising the generous dimensions of the debate.

During this period, it is to be hoped that some of the most topical, most difficult or most urgent issues will be made the subject of negotiations distinguished by a display of imagination on the part of those directly involved. Is it conceivable that the oil-producing countries and the industrial countries will pursue their dialogue with flamboyant communiqués and price-increase notifications while – and this was pointed out above – they together dispose of the means to elaborate a genuine strategy? The same is true of the most urgent problems: greater security of food supplies, conclusion of commodity agreements, increase in the investment essential to the survival of certain countries or simply needed for the commercialization of underground resources.

All these dialogues taking place parallel with those of the United Nations are not intended to take the place of world-wide exchange in New York nor that of interregional cooperation (cf. Lomé). However, they concern North and South and North-South and progress within their framework is essential if the proposals of the Brandt Report are to be transposed into reality.

Note

1. The negotiations of Lomé which ultimately led to the association of Europe with 59 developing countries were of a global nature and dealt for the main part with subjects of mutual interest to North and South. Led by specialists and officials, they would never have been successfully concluded if they had not been interspersed with ministerial meetings of a political nature and parliamentary conventions.

ANGELOS ANGELOPOULOS*

> . . . we must aim at the linkage between savings and investment not in one country alone, but on an interational scale.

The Brandt Report on the North–South problems is an historic document of fundamental importance. It opens new vistas and new possibilities for the implementation of a new development strategy on an international scale. But it also serves as a serious warning to leaders throughout the world to face up to their responsibilities. It is a 'cri d'alarme' for the future of humanity, which looks uncertain and bleak. For the whole problem of development on a world scale is, in the final analysis, a political problem. The responsibility rests with the political leaders who continue to apply a myopic policy of limited goals, and who are not in a position to cope with these big problems that demand international solutions.

Perhaps the Brandt Report will contribute to a change in the politicians' way of thinking and coping with the problems of our time. For what Albert Einstein - who opened the path to the atomic era - stressed half a century ago, is still valid:' The sector which determines the future of the nations,' he said , 'has been political men without brakes and without responsibility.'

The greatest danger today stems from the arms race between industrial countries and the continuous militarisation of the Third World. This is the consequence of the ceaseless competition in armaments that takes away from the productive process the enormous amount of $500 billion per year, at a time when the rate of growth in the OECD has, since 1974, slowed down to around 2½ per cent per year from about 5 per cent earlier; at a time when the gap between rich and poor countries grows continuously and assumes alarming proportions; and at a time when a significant part of the world's population – almost 800 million – is undernourished and lives under conditions of misery and poverty.

Should we perhaps remind ourselves that two fifths of total research expenditure is on the military sector, and that persons serving in the armed forces are twice as numerous as doctors, nurses and teachers put together? Or that even during the period 1945-79, considered a 'peaceful period' ,

*Greece. Former Governor of the National Bank of Greece. Leading theoretician of worldwide economic growth through Third World development. Author of 'For a New Policy of International Development'

there were 130 civil or regional wars, involving 80 countries, mostly in the Third World?

All this indicates how humanity stumbles to castastrophe, instead of walking towards progress and properity. Instead of creating those moral, economic and cultural values that are the preconditions for Man's creative activity, humanity is led to make weapons that threaten its very existence.

The need, therefore, to change the policy implemented so far is imperative. 'The next two decades will be decisive for the North-South relations and for the future of humanity in general', stressed Willy Brandt, when he presented his Commission's Report to the United Nations Secretary-General Kurt Waldheim.

To disregard the fundamental principles on which the new development strategy proposed in the Report is based would lead to a further deterioration of the present recession. The most important principles are the following:

First, the recognition of the close interdependence among all the economies of the world is the fundamental precondition for economic and social progress. Without progress for the countries of the South, there will be no prosperity for the countries of the North. Indeed, balanced development on a worldwide scale is the only way to ease international tension and conflict. The creation of economic cooperation among nations is a precondition for a climate of trust, for strengthening détente and for gradual disarmament.

Second, economic development is the precondition for monetary stability in every country. On this point, the Commission's proposals for the reform of the international monetary system (in the framework of the proposed economic policy on a world scale) are employment opportunities created and monetary stability secured only in conjunction with a whole-hearted drive to foster economic development.

Third, the transfer of economic aid, capital and technology from the developed to the developing countries, within a framework of a rational management and code of conduct are, as the Report rightly stresses, a necessary part of an effective policy of economic cooperation, with useful results for both North and South.

In the framework of these proposals, the Report puts forward a series of recommendations for the preparation and implementation of a global plan for the mobilization of the world's potential resources, with the ultimate aim of gradually reducing the gap between rich and poor countries, as well as removing the poverty and misery that the greatest part of earth's population suffers.

But, in parallel with this long-term programme, the Report stresses specifically the need to draw up an emergency programme for the quinquennium 1980-85. In view of the recent deterioration of the international economy, this is of fundamental importance. To this effect, the Report proposes a summit meeting of world leaders to examine urgently the measures for this emergency programme: 'the present deadlock is so serious, and the need to break through is so evident that nothing should delay discussion and negotiation at the highest level.' (p. 281)

The need for an immediate programme is especially urgent since the present situation will be aggravated by two factors:

> The first is that the huge increase in oil prices in 1979 and 1980 has placed an enormous burden on non-oil producing countries. Their deficit in 1980 is estimated at $50 billion, and is expected to grow in the next few years.

> The second, and related, factor is the over-indebtedness of the developing countries, whose debt, according to OECD estimates, will, at the end of 1980, reach $450 billion, with an annual service charge in the order of $88 billion[1]. Without new policies this will lead sooner or later to a financial crash worse than that of 1929, as the bankruptcy of the Third World countries will also severely test the viability of the big Western banks, which are important lenders to these countries.

To cope with the immediate economic problem of the less developed countries, I would make two proposals. These ideas were explained in greater detail at a recent conference

(April 1980) at the Royal Institute of Foreign Affairs at Chatham House in London[2].

Briefly these proposals are focused on two main points:

First, the granting of long-term loans from the industrialised to the less developed countries of the order of $30 billion per annum, about 0·5 per cent of the GNP of the O C E D countries. These loans would be interest-free for the first five years.

Second, the suspension for five years of the obligation to pay the service charges of the old debts of the less developed countries, which will be in the order of $75 billion.

These policies are interdependent and should be applied simultaneously. If the suspension of service charges for the old debts does not materialize, then any aid or financing under favourable terms will benefit only the creditors who will collect these sums as interest for the older loans.

The extension of such favourable credit would generate effective demand from the Third World countries and so contribute to the steady recovery of industrial production in the developed countries, and encourage new productive investment. Entrepreneurs today hesitate to invest because they are not certain that consumers will be found for their products. The consumers, therefore, must be sought in the Third World countries, where the need for capital goods and appropriate services is great. In other words, we must aim at the linkage between savings and investment not in one country alone, but on an international scale. This is the only way that Keynesian policy, which secured full employment for twenty years after the Second World War, can be successfully implemented.

The burden of the proposed financing (the interest on the loans for the first five years, which is expected to be in the order of $4-5 billion per annum) could be covered by allocating a certain percentage of oil export revenues to this scheme.

The present situation whereby the price of oil is set in an uncontrolled and arbitrary way cannot continue without seriously disturbing the workings of the world economy. The industrialized countries should therefore seek to conclude a permanent agreement between oil-producing and oil-consuming countries that would aim at the annual readjustment of the price of oil on the basis of OECD inflation, the changes in the effective rate of the dollar, and the rate of growth in the OECD.

Approximately 3 per cent of the revenues generated by this price should be applied to finance the World Development Fund proposed by the Brandt Report. In view of the fact that the total revenue of OPEC countries amounts to approximately $300 billion per year, this 3 per cent would produce an annual income of $9 billion. This is more than sufficient to cover the interest payments of the interest-free loans of the five-year period, with some left over to finance limited suspension of banks' service charges on existing loans.

The Development Fund could also be assisted through a small contribution from the appreciation in the value of official gold holdings, a part of which, as I have suggested in the past, ought to be given to the poorer countries[3]. It should be pointed out that the value of gold reserves was of the order of $40 billion in 1965, while its value today is estimated at $750 billion. In other words there appears a difference of some $710 billion.

The policy proposed by the Report, along with the additions suggested here, offers a way of leading the international economy out of the present impasse. Only a policy which relies on the implementation of Keynesian theory on a world scale for a rational redistribution of world income between rich and poor countries would contribute to the fight against the international economic crisis[4]. The continuation of the present policy would inevitably lead to a series of new recessions, and risk violent reactions that would ultimately threaten world peace.

References
   1. See 'Statistiques de l'endettement exterieur des pays en development' O C D E, Paris juillet 1980
   2. See also my book *For a new policy of international development*, by Guido Carli, Praeger Publishers, New York 1977, and the German edition *Zu einer nach-Keynesiamshen Weltworkschafts Politik*, worwort Willy Brandt, (Gabler-Verlag, Wiesbaden 1978).
   3. See my book: *Gold in the service of the developing countries*, Nagel, Geneva 1970.
   4. See also my address to the Royal Institute for International Affairs.

LÉOPOLD SÉDAR SENGHOR*

> If the developing countries were to try to reproduce the development model pursued by the industrial countries, countless centuries would not be enough and they would ultimately lose heart.

The Brandt Report is a work which, despite the problems encountered in its preparation, excels by its positive approach. Is it in fact possible to make any original observations on North-South relations? So many bodies have convened at so many conferences for so long to discuss this issue and have already advanced an abundance of proposals. Reports and books written on the subject would fill a library. There is now a plethora of literature on North-South relations. This notwithstanding, the Report of the Brandt Commission has found scope for a number of innovations.

There is evidence of innovation firstly in the fact that the problem is approached from a moral viewpoint: 'One should not give up the hope that problems created by men can also be solved by men. This calls for understanding, commitment and solidarity - between peoples and nations'. The problem is one of morality because it is one of civilization.

The present international economic order, the artefact of men, is unjust and, as such, the vehicle of grave threats to peace. Should we – men, nations, and states – be sufficiently intelligent and responsible to face up to and satisfactorily solve a problem which is not only a stain on but also a mortal threat to our civilization? This is a question of fundamental importance, for history has shown that a civilization, even a civilization of material abundance and comfort, which is incapable of solving its major problems is condemned to perish.

* President of the Senegal from 1960 to 1980. Advocate of the revival of African cultural heritage ('Negritude').

This approach probes beyond the classic notion of aid being transferred from industrial countries to developing countries. Both North and South must be made to realize that the issue cannot focus on charity, on non-repayable donations, on loans granted in a spirit of generosity on favourable terms, or on assistance, even technical assistance, being passed from a superior to an inferior. The choice is between a world of peace based on justice and solidarity and a world of chaos leading to hatred and the end of our civilization. We, all of us together, must build the Universal Civilization by juxtaposing the unique contributions which can be rendered by each people and each nation. If the developing countries were to try to reproduce the development model pursued by the industrial countries, countless centuries would not be enough, and they would ultimately lose heart. They must develop themselves by creating something different and making an original and prodigal contribution to the treasury of humanity. This is precisely what has begun to happen in the twentieth century insofar as Black Art – to cite merely the case of Africa – has left its mark on contemporary aesthetics.

The Report of the Brandt Commission also displays innovation by viewing the issue of North-South relations in a practical and functional manner. An accurate comprehension of the simple, long-term interests of North and South should induce both industrial and developing countries radically to change their attitudes in favour of working in cooperation in order to erase the major curses afflicting humanity. This implies an increase in the goods and services originating in Third World countries, and a situation in which men would no longer die of hunger, disease would no longer wreak such devastation, and the labour of the populations of the Third World, as well as the raw materials located there, would command a just price. At the same time, the economies of the industrial countries would be stimulated by the emergence of a veritable purchasing power in the developing countries, as well as by the fact that their unemployment would be very substantially relieved, their inflation would be stifled, their pollution would be reduced, and a greater volume of funds – the increase deriving primarily from a reduction in military spending – would be available for allocation to spiritual and cultural life. Given all this, we could live together on this earth, a world of peace, without the threat of a third world war. Given all this, we would be able to devote ourselves fully to works of creativity and beauty.

Yet the Report of the Brandt Commission does more than innovate. It is a work of practical use. Concrete proposals are advanced which, if adopted, would improve North-South relations and solve some of the major problems confronting humanity: hunger, disease, education, raw materials, energy, pollution, unemployment, disarmament, desertification, population growth. In short, the Report proposes establishing a new international order in both the cultural and the economic spheres, based on the values which would be the quintessence of the Universal Civilization: justice, brotherhood, solidarity and progress for all, and, lastly, a genuine freedom which derives its genuineness from the fact that mankind would have been delivered from his 'animal instincts'. The Report is a useful work because its proposals incorporate a programme and a time schedule which can be considered to be realistic.

The Report of the Brandt Commission thus confirms that which we already knew: solutions to our problems do exist because the means to solve them exist. If we genuinely desire to do so, we may have vanquished the major curses of humanity by the year 2000. From now until the year 2000, twenty years or approximately the term of a generation – this is the time for a generation of men of good-will to prove that it can radically change the course of history. The Report is a useful work, finally, because the members of the Brandt Commission were drawn from all quarters, from developing countries and industrial countries alike, from all the continents, from all races and from all creeds; and they profess ideologies ranging from socialist to liberal. They have thus demonstrated that, if they so wish, men with such differences can reach agreement on an action programme to save our civilization.

From this point on, the discourses heard within the various international institutions on the historical responsibilities of this or that ideology for under-development, the present disequilibrium within the world, its injustices and the establishment among mankind of the law of the jungle whereby the strongest imposes his will on the weakest – all these discourses will have no more than academic value. They can no longer serve as an excuse for lethargy. For the man who is dying of starvation, it is of little consolation that the historic responsibility for his state is attributable to this or that ideology. For him, that which matters is that mankind, his brothers, whoever and wherever they may be, are determined to take action, with him, to change the situation. As for the countries of the Third World, one cannot ignore the fact that if the deterioration in the terms of trade is a capitalist phenomenon, the countries described as socialist benefit from it likewise. A number of elements of triangular commerce – such as were observed at the time of the slave trade – are clear proof of this: raw materials or semi-processed products are purchased from a Third World country to be sold subsequently on the world market at a higher price.

The final question is whether we possess the political will to accept the challenge. The members of the Brandt Commission propose that a limited summit conference be held in 1981 to trigger off action at political level. The idea is a good one and deserves to be borne in mind. It could generate a salutary shock.

However, despite the fact that time is pressing, this will be a lengthy process. To face together the issues of our time presupposes mutual confidence among nations, a world free of the fear which drives nations to stockpile arms. It presupposes the unswerving observation of a number of simple principles listed in, inter alia, the United Nations Charter, the Charter of the Organization of African Unity, and in the final act of the Conference on Security and Cooperation in Europe concluded in Helsinki. It presupposes that throughout the world there prevails a spirit of respect for the rights of man and that the battle on ideology is channelled into the improvement of the living condition of all mankind.

To have the political will and to act accordingly, this is the only option remaining to mankind in our times. By halting the trend which is leading inexorably to chaos, mankind must prove the validity of our civilization and, by extension, that of the Universal Civilization: one of all mankind, one of each and every individual.

MÁRIO SOARES*

The problem has to be formulated as an issue of solidarity; only thus will it become possible to establish a new international order and only thus will the industrial countries . . . find ways and means of overcoming the intransigent world economic crisis.

The Brandt Commission Report constitutes a political occasion of lofty significance. Not because the relevant specialist public could await important revelations or original recommendations, but because the Report, incorporating the authority of its signatories, personalities of different ideological attitudes and geographical origin, and of undisputed international standing, commands the attention of the world with dramatic precision and conviction and directs it towards the major challenge which the survival of mankind now represents and with which humanity, all of humanity, finds itself confronted in the remaining two decades of the twentieth century.

Although the disparity between the developed and the developing countries is tending to become broader day by day, the dialogue between North and South has still not succeeded in arresting this trend or even finding a minimal amount of positive expression. There is evidence that the work of finance institutions and the various initiatives undertaken elsewhere to aid the Third World (e.g. by way of technology transfer), have not succeeded in creating the conditions necessary for allowing the poorer countries to overcome, within a reasonable period of time, the state of backwardness in which they find themselves. This is the

* Prime Minister of Portugal from 1976 to 1978. Founding Member and President of the Socialist Party of Portugal. Author of several books on Portuguese politics.

most modest assessment of the situation. In fact, their predicament has worsened to such a degree that it can no longer be remedied. This is why, despite evidence of growing general awareness and a corresponding reorientation of world policy, the situation has become genuinely explosive.

For it can be nothing more or less than the survival of mankind which is at stake when, each day, no fewer than 12,000 individuals die of hunger in the world in which we live. The problem is one of safeguarding the equilibrium of our planet in terms of its ecology and demography and their implications for the exploitation, conservation, and distribution of food and energy resources; and one of safeguarding the health, education, advancement and well-being of all human beings, irrespective of country of birth.

We have to recognize that this is an unprecedented expression of sympathy combined with a force to persuade and sensitize public opinion which we cannot afford to ignore.

Yet the problem cannot be formulated in terms of charity, or even of simple, disinterested and humanitarian aid, afforded to the poor and underdeveloped countries, irrespective of whether or not they are oil-producers, by the wealthy countries. The problem has to be formulated as an issue of solidarity; only thus will it become possible to establish a new international economic order and only thus will the industrial countries, by virtue of the aid granted to the less developed countries, be able to find ways and means of overcoming the intransigent world economic crisis which has confronted them since 1973.

The fact is that the industrial countries of the North include the two politico-military blocs which dominate the world. The crisis which affects them both in equal measure, albeit in different forms and conditions, has to do, in both instances, with the terrible difficulties to which the so-called Third World finds itself exposed. It now appears certain that there neither will nor can be a real North-South dialogue in an atmosphere of rising tension between the super-powers, at a time of crisis in the policy of détente, and stalemate in endeavours to bring about an effective armaments control embracing both nuclear and conventional weapons, and in the absence of a minimum of consensus regarding the rights of small countries and human rights in all countries.

It has been said that there is no alternative to détente since a world war in this nuclear age would jeopardize the survival of humanity. However, détente presupposes a minimum of confidence and trust which, even given the precarious progress made at the Helsinki Conference, is not easily built up. We now know that détente cannot be restricted in its terms of reference to the security of Europe alone, however important this may be. Its dimension must be worldwide. Accordingly, détente between East and West is a precondition for the successful continuation of the North-South dialogue; yet the North-South dialogue, for its part, will undoubtedly influence détente insofar as détente affects the countries of the Third World, of which many belong to the non-aligned movement. It is therefore imperative that we move in both directions simul- taneously – even with only modest steps as long as these are resolute – in the knowledge that the North-South dialogue and East-West détente are mutually comple- mentary and mutually influential.

Disarmament, peace and international solidarity thus reveal themselves to be three forceful factors of one and the same problem, the most critical of our times: the challenge confronting mankind with respect to mankind's own survival – in the West, East, North, and South of our planet, and with the very unequal living conditions, the very different levels of development, and the very diverse socioeconomic and cultural systems which characterize the world of today.

It is incontestable that the state of economic and monetary crisis in which the world now finds itself (and for the solution of which no international political will has to date been manifest) will tend to become more acute and, in view of the currently heightened tension in world relations, will predicate ever more dangerous consequences.

However, only in a context of détente is it possible to create the preconditions for dialogue between industrial and developing countries. The countries of Eastern Europe cannot excuse themselves from participating in this dialogue on the grounds that they did not count among the colonial powers of the past. These countries belong to the industrial countries of the world, they participate in world trade just as the others do, acknowledging that their participation takes place under the same conditions. It is therefore neither reasonable nor tolerable that they should disavow in the North-South dimension the international responsibility which they claim in the East-West dimension. Similarly, the People's Republic of China must also be persuaded to assume the important role which is incumbent on it in this dialogue as the largest developing country of the world.

Meanwhile, it is becoming more than clear that it is not possible to approach these problems with conviction as long as there exists no political will to reexamine the concept of development on which are founded the societies of the developed world, both the western capitalist model and the bureaucratic model adopted in the totalitarian states of the East.

The consumer society, which it was possible to establish in the 1960s on the basis of virtually unlimited economic growth (which, for its part, presupposed inexhaustible resources, cheap energy and constantly expanding markets for its continuation), no longer exists. The energy crisis has caused this legendary society to be replaced by one in which the traditional mechanisms of economics are no longer under control. We cannot now escape from our obligation to reflect on the functioning of this development model which, since 1973, has been in an unconcealable state of crisis, and which has proved, on an international plane, to be incapable of levelling off the fearful disparities evident between the developed and the developing countries.

Placing the economy at the service of mankind is a highly topical issue as much for the industrial as for the developing countries. Other issues which likewise can no longer systematically be brushed aside include those of the quality of life, the redistribution of wealth, and national and international solidarity. Redistribution of wealth is a practice more frequently found in the countries of the

North than in certain underdeveloped countries, where ruling politico-economic oligarchies, allied with or represented by a professional military, enjoy privileges and distinctions which are the more scandalous, the crasser the poverty in which their peoples live.

To restructure society in the spirit of greater social justice and liberty, to elaborate new concepts of development which are not quantifiable exclusively in terms of the gross national product – these imply a quest to respect that which Willy Brandt terms the 'quality of growth'. The developing countries themselves must contrive to apply those development models which, measured against the concept of 'quality of growth', are found to be best suited to their cultural and socioeconomic conditions. The indiscriminate adoption of imported economic and cultural models always entails sinister consequences if such models were originally developed for and tested on fundamentally different situations.

As I make these observations on a text of such richness and profundity as the Brandt Report, I do not forget that I count myself, in ideological terms, among the followers of democratic socialism. Accordingly, I find it in keeping to emphasize here the value and significance of international solidarity.

In fact, it will perhaps be the socialists who, on account of their ideological terms of reference, will be in the best position to understand that the old struggle between the privileged and the disadvantaged within a national society has now assumed an international dimension in the form of the struggle between the rich and the poor countries. The socialists could not react otherwise than to proclaim their solidarity with the latter. And by way of major structural reforms adopted at international level (just as their counterparts at national level) on the strength of the values of solidarity and justice, solutions will be found which will be capable of bridging the great divide, surmounting the antagonism between rich and poor countries which is menacing world equilibrium and world peace.

Furthermore, it will come as no surprise that I, a Portuguese, do not neglect to point out that the boundaries between North and South are singularly indistinct.

Backwardness is manifest in the southern periphery of Europe in comparison with central and northern Europe which can be explained largely by the political instability which countries such as Spain, Greece, Turkey, and Portugal experienced before recently emerging from their cruel dictatorships. Among these, Portugal and Spain in particular are interested in full integration into the EEC. But all concur in their belief that the North-South dialogue must find positive expression within Europe itself in the form of aid given in a spirit of solidarity by the countries of the North to the countries of the southern periphery.

At a time when the international communist movement is giving clear indications of malaise and irreconcilable contradictions – as the events in Poland testify – the answers to the great questions of the world cannot be found by recourse, whether brutal or subtle, to the age-old recipes of capitalism. A coordinated and appropriate strategy must be devised for successfully meeting the major challenges of our times. The Brandt Report points out paths which we cannot refuse to tread. The Programme of Priorities and the Emergency Programme for the years 1980 to 1985 contained therein are orientation aids of decisive importance. But these do not suffice for closing the file on this issue. There remains the necessity of mounting a major campaign to mobilize public opinion throughout the world in favour of urging governments to initiate appropriate action. In this respect, democratic socialism has an important role to play: a role to play in the mobilization of will, in the struggle against routine, in changing attitudes, and in pointing out paths which must be trodden if mankind is to succeed in measuring up to its great challenge. Merely technocratic solutions are not adequate. What is required is political will and readiness to work in the service of peace, liberty, the safeguard of human rights, and international solidarity – values which are inseparable in the mind of every socialist. For, as Willy Brandt stated 'The shaping of our common future is much too important to be left to governments and experts alone.' The issue immediately at hand is not to allow hope to be extinguished and to act while there is still time.

RAÚL PREBISCH*

It is imperative that the developed countries look much further beyond their immediate problems with a marked sense of historic foresight which hitherto they have not displayed.

FRIEDRICH EBERT FOUNDATION: The Brandt Commission in fact proposes many of those changes in international economic relations which the countries of the Third World have been demanding for some years now. The Commission argues (a) that these changes are necessary if economic development in the South is to be accelerated and (b) that a more rapid development of the South is essential if the North is to be able to maintain its level of prosperity and its security. Will these arguments convince political leaders and public opinion in the North?

RAÚL PREBISCH: I am completely in agreement with the Brandt Report as regards points (a) and (b) of this question. Political leaders and public opinion in the North have been reluctant to accept similar arguments, but given the prestige and authority of Mr Brandt and the marked interest now being displayed, it is to be hoped that a positive effect will be forthcoming.

FRIEDRICH EBERT FOUNDATION: The Brandt Report implies that in a similar way the well-being and the security of the socialist sphere also depend on progress in North-South relations. Will the political leaders of the East be convinced?

RAÚL PREBISCH: The same could be said of the political leaders of the socialist countries, particularly given the respect which Mr Brandt commands among them.

FRIEDRICH EBERT FOUNDATION: The Brandt Report gives the impression that a simple advance in the North-South dialogue is no longer sufficient and that what is lacking is prompt and drastic action. Are we on the brink of disaster? Or are we at the beginning of a long march towards a new

---

* Argentina, Former Secretary General of U.N.C.T.A.D. Famous for his ideas on the Third World's deteriorating terms of trade

international economic order?

RAÚL PREBISCH: The Brandt Report is largely accurate in stating that the long-term measures proposed are not sufficient and that emergency action is required. It is necessary first and foremost to ward off the disaster which would undoubtedly ensue if the industrial countries and the oil-producing countries with an excess of financial resources were to fail to reach agreement with the developing countries on important emergency measures.

FRIEDRICH EBERT FOUNDATION: The Brandt Commission appeals to the foresight and goodwill of those responsible in the North to induce them to adopt a more cooperative attitude towards the Third World. Others believe that international inequality has its own dynamic and that only the negotiating power of the South can change the aims pursued in the International economic relations. What would be the prospects of the South in this respect

RAÚL PREBISCH: I consider that the grave problems of the South do not depend only on international factors, but also on internal factors operating within these developing countries. It is for this reason that I believe that converging action by North and South is necessary.

FRIEDRICH EBERT FOUNDATION: The countries of the North are trying to protect their interests by way of specific agreements with those countries of the South which are of particular interest on account of their raw materials, their opportunities for investment, etc. Would this practice be prejudicial to the cause of the South? Does it show a lack of foresight on the part of those responsible in the North inasmuch as they think only of their most immediate interests?

RAÚL PREBISCH: Some specific agreements can be very useful but they will not resolve the big problems of world inequality. It is imperative that the developed countries look much further beyond their immediate problems with a marked sense of historic foresight which hitherto they have not displayed. That a mutual interest exists throughout is a factor which is strongly emphasized in the Brandt Report.

FRIEDRICH EBERT FOUNDATION: Let us suppose that those responsible in the North realize that they have a vital interest in the stabilization of the economy of the South – because they fear the negative repercussions which economic crises in the South could have on the world economy. Would this lead to fundamental improvements for the peoples of the Third World? Or does the mutual interest postulated by the Brandt Commission restrict itself instead to the smooth functioning of the world economy?

RAÚL PREBISCH: I believe, like the Brandt Commission, that there is a mutual interest in reciprocal cooperation between North and South. Consequently, I consider to be of vital importance all that is recommended in the Brandt Report as regards commercial, financial and technological cooperation, within the scheme presented. To allow the countries of the South to drift will have negative consequences not only on the world's economic order but also on its political order.

FRIEDRICH EBERT FOUNDATION: The Brandt Report calls for a 'development based on the genuine needs of man and not on the transfer of development models which have machines and equipment at their centre.' Does this correspond to the aspirations of the peoples of Latin America? Are there forces which guide the economic process in the opposite direction?

RAÚL PREBISCH: I am also in agreement with the Brandt Report on this point. I am convinced that the developing countries cannot simply copy the experience of the developed countries but must elaborate their own forms of development, profiting thereby from that experience. In recent years this problem has begun to be better understood in the South.

FRIEDRICH EBERT FOUNDATION: Which are the recommendations of the Report which will most likely meet with sufficient consensus to be implemented?

RAÚL PREBISCH: The Brandt Report is characterized by a marked spirit of unity and any selection of recommendations could weaken this feature. Nevertheless, may I underline first and foremost the recommendations relative to international trade, not only between North and South but also between the developing countries. At the same time it is also necessary to emphasize the importance of the measures for international financial cooperation.

FRIEDRICH EBERT FOUNDATION: What would be the appropriate action for the South to take in order to make the greatest possible use of the political potential of the Brandt Report? What should be the next steps to achieve practical results?

RAÚL PREBISCH: In the sense indicated, it seems to me that the summit meeting of heads of state suggested by Mr. Brandt has great importance and should not be delayed for too long.

FRIEDRICH EBERT FOUNDATION: The Brandt Report also appeals to the political leaders of the South to bring about a better distributuon of wealth within their countries and to ensure that the benefits of economic growth primarily accrue to the poor. What could motivate the élite of the developing countries to take this exhortation seriously?

RAÚL PREBISH: The Brandt Report has done very well in stating to the countries of the South the need for internal measures to remedy blatant social inequalities. The élites of these countries are showing the same lack of foresight as the leaders of the North. And there is not much that we can hope for in this respect. If they do not react in time and fail to effect major economic and social changes, these changes will come fatally by other means.

LUO YUANZHEN*

Perpetuating mutual confrontation will result in nothing but the deterioration of the international economic situation which will in turn undermine political stability.

After long and thorough research the Brandt Commission has published its report, which has aroused great attention and widespread comment throughout the world. Covering as it does more than just the basic principles and demands put forward by the Third World for the establishment of a new international economic order, the Report deals systematically and objectively with a number of the major problems confronting the world at present and in the future. It carries 'enlightened' views on the North-South relationship, as held by the noted statesmen and economists of the Brandt Commission. A valuable and well researched document of practical significance, the Report could well serve as the basis for a new international economic order and for the improvement of North-South relations.

The Report aims at an overall exploration of the fundamental means of improving these relations, rather than the mere solution of a number of specific questions important to both sides. We highly appreciate this attempt by the Commission as one which is both bold and meaningful. The end of World War II was followed by a series of profound changes in the international political situation. One after another, the former colonies, semi-colonies and dependent countries freed themselves from colonial rule; and together these countries now constitute an independent, vital factor in world affairs. Concurrently, the post-war 'golden era' which had lasted more than two decades in the West gave way, in the mid-seventies, to an unstable period of slackened growth. The decline of U.S. dominance in world affairs, combined with difficulties and disagreements among Western nations, made it possible for the Soviet Union with its expanded military might to attempt, whether in its own right or through surrogates, to invade or dismember some of the Third World countries and to launch direct or indirect attacks on the West in order to weaken it. Events have shown that the USSR is now the source of current crises in many parts of the world. It has as its ultimate aim the subjection of the whole world to its control. In the face of this particular state of international affairs, the importance of improving and readjusting the

* China. Director of the Institute of World Economy in Beijing. Occupied important positions in the Chinese state administration.

North-South relationship can no longer be restricted just to the redistribution of the world's wealth, but unquestionably involves the strategic significance of an overall settlement. This means that unless the developing countries and the West handle their relationship in an appropriate way, and unless North-South cooperation is strengthened, the effective prevention of, or practical resistance against, Soviet infiltration, expansion and aggression will be as unimaginable as a victory in a possible world war. The Brandt Commission undoubtedly displayed a penetrating view when it focussed its attention precisely on the essence of the world solution, pointing out that the North-South relationship is a life-or-death issue.

More and more statesmen as well as far-sighted observers in the West are, to varying degrees, relinquishing their traditional bias against the Third World and their long-held anti-nationalist and anti-democratic concepts. They are beginning to attach due importance to the West's relationship with the developing countries. They stress the facts that the outstanding trend in world politics is the development of the relationship between developing and industrialized countries, that economic cooperation with the Third World has become the 'decisive demand of the age' and that the Third World constitutes a 'great partner of the modern world'. Thus they advocate the inauguration of a new international economic order based on 'dialogue' instead of confrontation. In 1979, the 'seven-power summit conference' in Tokyo affirmed that 'a positive North-South relationship is imperative for world economic development'. In this evolution in Western strategic thinking is the desire for a better relationship and enhanced cooperation with the Third World. The problem now laid before the North and the South, however, is no longer a question of desire, but the realization of a workable solution.

It was precisely for this purpose that the Brandt Report, in its 'Emergency Programme 1980-85' and 'plan for long-range reforms', presented a specific detailed layout. However, the fact that most Western countries were formerly the metropolitan powers of the Third World nations means that the latter are instinctively wary about the former. Moreover, the Western powers, though rich economically and endowed with advanced science and technology, 'lack space and resources'. Self-reliant only to a limited extent in natural resources, they depend largely on the developing countries for raw materials, particularly strategic materials. On the other hand, the developing countries, forging ahead in their industrialization, need capital and technology from the West. As is observed in the Brandt Report, there is now greater interdependence and more need for cooperation than before between the North and the South regarding the expansion of exports, continuation of supplies and stabilization of the international monetary system. Yet, in North-South economic transactions, the economic rights of the developing countries are still to some extent infringed by the West, which has always enjoyed significant extra benefits at the expense of Third World partners. Such a relationship, contradictory as it is to the principles of interdependence, has come to be the major source of confrontation between the North and the South, resulting in a worsening of that relationship.

The nations of the world are now living in an 'internationalized community'. This is due to the increasingly clear trend of internationalization of production and trade, or, as the Brandt report puts it, because 'the world is a system in which each part affects the others'. Thus, the best solution is gradually to bridge the gulf between the North and the South through dialogue and to work for the relaxation of tensions, thereby achieving a better relationship, and closer cooperation between both sides. Perpetuating mutual confrontation will result in nothing but the deterioration of the international economic situation which will in turn undermine international political stability, ultimately providing more freedom of action for the Soviets. The International Economic Cooperation Conference held in 1975 in Paris and attended by delegates from 24 nations, representing both the developing countries and the Western powers, marked the transition from confrontation to dialogue. Despite its failure to obtain considerable or substantive results, this particular conference was nevertheless something to be welcomed in international affairs.

The central issue now is the inauguration of a new international economic order since this is the essential prerequisite for a better North-South relationship. It is consequently appropriate to affirm that such a new order and the anticipated better North-South relationship are inextricably inter-related. The old international economic order, benefitting just one side or one bloc of nations, can only give rise to more serious North-South confrontation. It should not be perpetuated. Inevitably it must be altered. The new international economic order proposed by the Third World is aimed at defending national independence and sovereignty, resisting hegemonies, all forms of plunder, exploitation or control and promoting economic cooperation and development among the nations of the world on the basis of equality and mutual benefit. It is obvious that the establishment of such an economic order is to the advantage of the countries of both the North and the South. Better North-South relations can only be based on such a new order. As we have observed, the Brandt Commission in its report accords due respect to and correct evaluation of the struggle for this new international order.

Ever since the sixth special session of the UN General Assembly, consultations and joint efforts have been made between the North and the South. These have resulted in achievements of varying dimensions in a number of fields in connection with the inauguration of this new order. But there remains much to be done before the eventual attainment of that goal. Moreover, serious attention must be paid to the fact that the negotiations between both sides on this issue are dragging on without result, although not without hope. The introduction of this new order has long been a basic desire of the developing countries, which look forward to an early breakthrough that might serve as an impetus to a change in the economic relations among different nations of the world. Proceeding from this aim, the Group of 77 took the initiative for a new round of 'global negotiations' within the framework of the UN for a package solution covering such problems as raw materials, energy sources, trade, development, the monetary system and finance. It gave special emphasis to institutional reforms in the international monetary system. On the other hand, the West, defending its own economic interests, is reluctant for a new round of North-South negotiations for the reform of the international economic order. The Brandt Report embodies proposals that could achieve a breakthrough in the deadlock between the North and the South. In our opinion, there are four problems which demand immediate solution.

1. The North-South Dialogue

The Report puts forward a useful proposal when it urges the convening, at the earliest possible date, of a summit conference to be attended by 25 world leaders from both industrialized and developing nations. The meeting should give careful consideration to the Report and to the means for realizing some of its proposals, especially the emergency programme. In keeping with our desire for the strengthening of cooperation between the North and the South, we have always been in favour of efforts for such dialogue within, or outside, the framework of the U.N. We give our support to endeavours aimed at holding dialogues and signing agreements for economic cooperation between the European Economic Community on the one hand and the African, Caribbean, Pacific or the ASEAN countries on the other. It has been our aim to encourage contacts and consultations on a regional scale between the developing countries and the West as well as the wide-ranging interrelations between Western Europe on the one hand and the Arab and African nations on the other.

2. Appropriate handling of North-South differences and the need for compromise between them.

A number of agreements were reached in the seventies between the two sides as a result of consultation, discussion and compromise. There remain numerous important problems, which must be settled during this next decade, particularly those concerning the establishment of a new international economic order. Necessitating a radical change in the interrelations of the different nations, such a development would be possible only after a long and complicated process involving both discussion and compromise. There is no easy solution. Inflexible adherence by each side to its own principles will not facilitate a transformation of the international economic order, let alone improve the North-South relationship. Despite this simple truth, we see that, following the first petroleum crisis, recriminatory exchanges between the North and the South have recurred with ever greater intensity. While the developing countries hold the industrialized West responsible for their deteriorating economic situation, the developed nations have imputed the global recession to be due to the arbitrary raising of oil prices by the petroleum exporting countries and have tried to form an alliance with the non oil-producing developing nations against those exporting it. It is beyond doubt that a vicious circle of attacks and counter-attacks has not, and will not, contribute to any satisfactory solution. The only conclusion that can be drawn from this is that a global package deal between the North and the South offers the best remedy, and is required urgently.

3. The drafting of a plan of operation based on the actual conditions, and acceptable to both the North and the South.

Just as the Chinese saying 'one hand makes no clapping' indicates, the effort for a new international economic order must be a joint venture. The common endeavour of working for progress towards a new order calls for long-term programmes as well as emergency plans based on prevailing conditions and potential for the future. Where no favourable realistic possibilities exist, long-term objectives should be postponed in order to avoid new North-South confrontation. The Brandt Commission, working from an awareness of the successes and failures in the North-South dialogue, put forward quite a practical proposal in the form of an 'emergency programme' plus a plan for 'long-term reforms'. The objectives set for the near future include large-scale transfer of resources to the developing countries, an international energy strategy, and a start on some major reforms in the international economic system and a global food programme. In addition to these, however, the urgently needed reform of the international trade system should be implemented immediately. In particular there should be stabilization of prices for raw materials and primary products imported from the developing countries, as well as the abolition of formal or informal barriers against the Third World manufactured goods. As was pointed out by the Brandt Report, industrialization in the developing countries should not be considered a menace to the industrialized north. Furthermore, special importance should be attached to the reshaping of the world's economic structure and to reforms able to be carried out in the existing international and financial institutions.

4. Co-ordination of 'International measures' and 'National measures'.

A fundamental prerequisite for the establishment of a new international economic order is that the developing countries, whether individually or collectively, develop their potential for steady growth in their national economies. A stronger economy in the developing countries depends chiefly on the presence of appropriate 'national measures' which should be based on the adherence to the important principle of self-reliance or collective self-reliance. Guided by this conviction, we favour and encourage the efforts by the developing countries to improve cooperation amongst themselves. Such efforts include the formation of common markets on the basis of shared economic interests and the foundation of regional banks for development, and of regional financial bodies. These are some of the various means aimed at building up the respective national economies of the countries concerned as well as an integral Third World economic system. In the early sixties the United Nations started its practice of drawing up for the developing countries a 'strategy for international development' for each decade, which provides for 'international measures' that need to be taken for economic advancement. This 'strategy', considered to be important, should be bold enough to set to work all positive national and international factors and, at the same time, prove practically possible. One vital component of a comprehensive plan is, of course, the nature of the international measures to be taken. Therefore, the strategy should in the first place set out clearly what is to be done through international means. But such a comprehensive programme should also pay attention to the necessary measures to be adopted by individual nations. In the absence of the latter, international measures will not be able to produce the desired results. For this reason the Brandt Commission urged the Third World countries to launch such necessary reforms. In addition it must be reiterated that it is equally wrong to overlook or to underestimate the responsibilities to be borne by the international community in dealing with the developing countries. It is important not to interfere in their internal affairs when drawing up plans for individual nations, or to focus on steps to be taken internationally at the expense of the indispensable measures, to be taken by nations themselves.

The current decade has opened up a new era in the North-South relationship. The Brandt Commission has greeted this new era by offering its valuable Report. It is our belief that both industrialized and developing countries will be interested in and accept the positive things contained in this Report and use them as the basis for promoting the future positive development of North-South relations.

BARBARA WARD*

. . . can Northern democracies live with any sense of moral order and decency if they are content to let millions starve, to see malnutrition, illiteracy and unemployment as the inevitable lot of a large number of their fellow human beings, to enjoy their own advantages and basically not to care?

Two questions above all are raised by the Brandt Report. The first is whether it is at all urgent to have a strategy or 'programme for survival' for North/South relations. The second is whether the Report itself is a relevant and satisfactory programme.

There can surely be little dispute about the urgency. There will be six billion human beings on this planet by the year 2000, most of the additional two billion being born in 'Southern' lands. In many of these areas food production does not keep pace with population growth now. The likelihood of devastating and repeated famines must be counted – if anything is – a matter of urgency.

This insufficiency of a basic supply – food – is reinforced by others, above all in the matter of energy. The great increases in oil prices have left some countries – India, Tanzania – expending nearly half their export earnings on oil. At the same time, drastic needs for domestic fuel are leading, in many regions, to a decimation of forests and a potentially irreversible spread of deserts.

But these basic risks do not only affect the South. With the Russians 'grain raid' on America's reserves in 1973, prices tripled for everyone, rich and poor alike. There is no reason to suppose that world food shortages would not have similar effects in the future. Oil price rises are one of the roots of continuing Northern inflation and the extent to which payments for oil are not being sufficiently rapidly reabsorbed by imports and by investment is a main reason why some $800 billions are held outside the United States. They are, as it were, 'loose' in the world monetary system and if quite a small number of dollar sellers were to appear at the same time on a falling market, the kind of collapse that occurred in 1931 could recur. Moreover, even though recession is discouraging price increases for raw materials now, the lack of investment in Third World minerals – and energy – could mean a renewed spurt in primary prices as economies recover. The North, in short, is floundering as well as the South, at however much more prosperous a level.

* United Kingdom, Chairman of the Council, International Institute for Environment and Development; Chairman, Society for International Development. Author of various books on core questions of mankind's future. (Died 1981)

The chief argument for the Brandt approach is that it offers some promise of dealing with all these problems not simply in an orderly and rational fashion but in a way which is of common interest to North and South alike. The central recommendations – contained in its 'emergency programme' – cover a wholly new emphasis on food production in the Third World and sufficient funds from the wealthy Northern and OPEC countries to support the needed agricultural programmes. These funds could be drawn from a larger flow of aid proposed by the Report. At present, the North has undertaken to transfer 0·7 per cent of its Gross National Product and indeed the Scandinavian countries and Holland have already reached this percentage. But others – notably the United States – give less than 0·35 per cent. If they could all double their giving – as the Report suggests – to the promised 0·7 per cent by 1985, aid would rise to some $60 billions a year.

These funds would also be available not only to assist agriculture. They would permit a massive programme of investment in world energy resources – including forestry – and in the dangerous backlog for mineral exploration and development. At the same time, they would both underpin and reinforce the Report's critical proposals for basic reforms in long-term international financing. These reforms include a measure of automatic international taxation – on travel, on seabed resources, on some forms of trade – but they also propose a world development fund which could clearly start its existence as a consolidation of OPEC and other balances in a special 'substitution account', possibly administered by a new affiliate of the International Monetary Fund structured on the lines of the International Fund for Agricultural Development – with representation of North, South and OPEC countries.

But, it will be protested, what interest have the Northern states, already a prey to inflation for the last decade, in increasing the risk of yet further inflation by large-scale aid and investment policies? (One should keep a sense of proportion. The proposed 0·7 per cent, twice present levels of aid, is only $60 billions a year. Military spending runs at some $450 billions.) The short answer is that investment in expanding Third World markets may be the quickest route to general recovery. Some of the really big increases in agricultural productivity can now be obtained in developing countries since the technological limits of growth have been mainly reached among the rich. But between a Korea or a still backward India the difference may be of the order of 3 tonnes of rice per hectare. The yet-to-be explored oil and mineral reserves are largely Southern. Markets in the South already absorb around a third of the North's merchandise exports – for Japan the figure is nearer 50 per cent. Increase their productivity, create new customers and you get a corresponding increase in Northern exports and, in many areas, a cheapening of imports.

This does mean some degree of readjustment in a number of Northern sectors – clothing and leatherware for example. But a whole new range of industries unleashed by the electronics revolution are awaiting development and with a measure of short-term restraint and a commitment to redeployment of capital and skills, developed economies will have much to gain from cheaper imports. At the same time, investment in new sources of energy coupled with really ambitious conservation programmes will enable them to bargain with OPEC for a phased, regular and reliable increase in oil prices – a much greater reassurance against inflation than any other conceivable measure.

Nor should we forget the political implications of the Brandt Report. Within the Third World, in a mere couple of decades, it is impossible to overcome the suspicions and resentments of a century and more of colonial control. Nor is it part of Russia's global policy to see that these memories are forgotten. As hunger, shortages and difficulties increase, regimes become more unstable and more likely to look for external scapegoats. If, on the contrary, it was known, declared and reliable Northern policy to share a part of its overwhelming preponderance in wealth, trade and technology – over 80 per cent for a third of the world's peoples – on a systematic and agreed basis with its Southern neighbours, one at least of the causes of distrust, disorder and collapse of non-aligned Governments would have been removed.

We are not without historical precedents here. The great modern revolutions – French, Russian, Chinese – all took place in societies where the rich were too blind and too greedy to see the growing despair below. Perhaps even more relevant is the contrast of world collapse through economic inaction in 1931 and the astounding postwar recoverly being pursued at national level will form the basis for preparing the Conference of the International Confederation of Free Trade Unions on a new economic and social order, envisaged to take place in early 1981. The work of the Conferce will be VCdesigned to intensify the North-South dialogue, with special consideration being given to the trade unions' role within the development process. The Brandt Report will serve as a valuable point of departure for the conference discussionslly not to care? Such a world 'half slave, half free' would not endure. Nor can we honestly say that it would deserve to do so.

HEINZ-OSKAR VETTER*

> . . . the trade unions in both North and South . . . raise objections when multinational enterprises, taking advantage of low wages and backward social conditions, establish manufacturing plants which they operate exclusively in the interest of exporting to the industrial countries, without social benefit . . . for the developing countries.

More than any other report published in the recent past, that prepared by the Independent Commission on International Development Issues under the chairmanship of Willy Brandt has succeeded in sparking off a worldwide and constructive discussion on the problems of North-South relations. The very composition of the Brandt Commission laid the foundation for its subsequent work in identifying problems and solution approaches which are acceptable to the representatives of industrial and developing countries alike. The Report not only reveals the grave problems confronting the world economy today but also provides concrete proposals for a programme for

* Federal Republic of Germany. Chairman, German Trade Union Federation.

survival by building on the mutuality of interests of all human beings.

According to the trade unions, this clear emphasis on the mutuality of interests between the two groups of countries is one of the most important elements of the Report. At the same time, the Report affirms that the problems of developing and industrial countries can be solved only by way of joint action, stressing that, even then, major changes in international economic relations are unavoidable. Naturally, there can be no such mutuality of interests as long as the status quo is maintained. What is urgently needed is greater involvement on the part of organizations such as the trade unions which, within the framework of their educational work, are able to prepare their memberships for the necessary changes and cooperation.

The Report of the North-South Commission was welcomed by the German Trade Unions Federation and by all independent and democratic trade unions in the International Confederation of Free Trade Unions. According to trade unionist opinion, the growing confrontation between North and South is a serious obstacle to the efficient international cooperation which is a precondition for successfully tackling the problems of our world. With the publication of the jointly elaborated development charter of the International Confederation of Free Trade Unions entitled *Towards a New World Economic and Social Order*, the trade unions of the industrial and the developing countries have already taken an important step in this direction. This trade union charter was submitted to the Chairman of the North-South Commission on the occasion of the Tenth Ordinary Congress of the German Trade Union Federation held in Hamburg in May 1978.

The trade unions were gratified to find that the North-South Report contains some of the most important demands voiced by the international trade union movement. The trade unions consider the greatest merit of this Report to be the inter-linking of the economic and social aspects of North-South problems. For many years they have advocated that the elimination of social distress in the developing countries should not be handled as a by-product of economic development. The past twenty years have shown only too clearly that economic progress does not automatically entail social advancement. The trade unions therefore fully concur with the North-South Commission when it defines the satisfaction of basic needs as an independent objective of development policy.

The elimination of the deplorable distress suffered by the peoples of the Third World is primarily the task of the developing countries themselves. But on the industrial countries in East and West and the oil-producing countries also rests an obligation to support, more effectively than hitherto, the developing countries' endeavours to accomplish this difficult task. The governments of these latter countries must realize that the creation of employment and the development of rural areas must be promoted to be the priority targets of their development policy. The North-South Report clearly points out that the industrial countries are, in fact, well able to provide sufficient food, housing, and clothing for the disadvantaged, as well as important services for the community such as safe drinking water, health care, and educational facilities. However, the practical measures required to realize these objectives present us with major difficulties. Today, as in the past, too little consideration is given within the framework of development aid to the creation of employment, an equitable distribution of income and wealth, and the satisfaction of basic needs. The trade unions would be well able to cooperate in the achievement of such objectives. We believe that their contribution would even be a precondition for an equitable distribution of income and wealth and for economic and social development. It is therefore essential that the governments recognize the rights of the worker and sanction the establishment of free and freely-operating trade unions. We, as trade unionists, would certainly have welcomed a clearer position on this point on the part of the North-South Commission.

The Report deals in great detail with the structure of the international economic and social order. The appeals made in this connection are primarily those voiced by the international trade union movement. For their part, the trade unions of the industrial countries have supported the developing countries' demands for the establishment of national industries. However, the trade unions in both North and South do find cause to raise objections when multinational enterprises, taking advantage of low wages and backward social conditions, establish manufacturing plants which they operate exclusively in the interest of exporting to the industrial countries, without social benefit and with often an only very dubious and short-lived economic effect for the developing countries.

One particular problem in this connection is that of the so-called 'export zones,' which offer, alongside the tax privileges granted to enterprises operating within their confines, poorly developed labour and social legislation with a restrictive or even suppressive attitude towards trade union rights, that is to say, zones which offer advantages to the foreign investors only, most of whom in any case operate merely on a short-term basis.

Industrialization in developing countries must go hand in hand with an improvement of the economic and social conditions of their workers. Adequate wages should enable the people to participate in the economic process. And an increased demand for goods to satisfy basic needs in the developing countries should permit the establishment of domestic and regional markets which could provide important incentives for sustained economic and social development.

The argument frequently raised by entrepreneurs and governments in both developing and industrial countries to the effect that trade union activity in developing countries would merely impede the development process is, in our opinion, not only negative in its tone but also inconsistent with our experience. On the contrary, the development process calls for the cooperation and support of the trade unions, and this not only in the countries of Africa, Asia, and Latin America, but also in those of the industrial world. We should realize that we, too, shall increasingly have to undertake structural changes which are not to be explained by technological developments. It is up to the trade unions of the industrial countries to cooperate in overcoming these structural problems and to see to it that their solutions do not operate to the detriment of the workers whom the trade unions represent.

The Report also meets with trade union approval on account of its tackling problems which are closely related to development problems, such as armament and multi-national undertakings, yet which have hitherto often been examined in isolation. It is with considerable trepidation that the trade unions observe the annual increase in military expenditure. Development aid expenditure amounting to $US 20 billion stands alongside military expenditure amounting to $US 400 billion. Ever since their inception the German trade unions have advocated a process of general and controlled disarmament, firstly to diminish the danger of armed conflict and secondly, to secure social peace. Hunger, poverty, illiteracy, and oppression are the most menacing dangers to stable and lasting peace. The trade unions' objection to military expenditure is thus directed as much to the developing countries as to those industrial countries which are only too keen to offer both weapons and the credit required for their purchase.

The growing influence exerted, as the North-South Report discloses, by multinational enterprises on the economic and social development of industrial and developing countries is also a focal point of international trade union work. In our opinion it is imperative that the decisions taken by enterprises such as these which are able to evade the provisions of national legislation be subjected to an effective control mechanism enforced by the trade unions, governments, and international organizations. The establishment of trade union structures to represent workers' interests at enterprise level should be supplemented by the elaboration of international codices to guarantee the rights of both workers and trade unions. This is particularly true for countries in which the trade union movement is relatively undeveloped or is suppressed by the local power-wielders.

It remains only to reaffirm that the German Trade Unions Federation, both as one entity and in its constituent parts, considers the North-South Report to be a decisive step forward in the discussion on development issues. Together with the other independent and democratic trade unions conjoined in the International Confederation of Free Trade Unions, the Federation of German Trade Unions strongly advocates that the recommendations of the Report be allowed to find greater expression in the development policy concepts of governments and development aid organizations and awaken in those responsible in political and economic life the awareness that hunger, unemployment, housing problems, and illiteracy should no longer be tolerated and can be overcome only by way of joint action.

Moreover, the trade union debate on the Report which is currently being pursued at national level will form the basis for preparing the Conference of the International Confederation of Free Trade Unions on a new economic and social order, envisaged to take place in early 1981. The work of the Conference will be designed to intensify the North-South dialogue, with special consideration being given to the trade unions' role within the development process. The Brandt Report will serve as a valuable point of departure for the conference discussions.

CARL WRIGHT*

In the view of the trade union movement the world community must agree and act upon Brandt's 'Programme for Survival' and in particular the emergency programme.

For almost a decade, the world has been experiencing a deepening economic crisis, a situation which is being accentuated by dangerous political tensions – between 'North' and 'South' and between 'East' and 'West'. Little consensus exists as to the way out of the crisis, and many people display a marked fatalism in the face of the failure of established policy measures. In this context it is therefore

*United Kingdom. Director, Commonwealth Trade Union Council.

remarkable that such a diverse group of Commissioners as those who drew up the Brandt Report – from the Left and the Right, from Business and Trade Unions, from the North and the South – have been able to agree a radical set of policy measures or a 'Programme for Survival', as it is aptly termed.

Underlying the present sorry state of affairs – a far cry from the optimism and 'white-hot heat' of technological advance of the 60's – is a blatant breakdown of the post-war economic and political consensus. In the developing countries, despite the grandiose theories about 'economic take-off', workers have seen few real improvements in the last 35 years. Indeed it can be argued that the situation of ordinary men and women in these countries has deteriorated to a point where some 700 million are living in what the World Bank has termed 'absolute poverty' – a polite way of saying that they are on the brink of starvation. In the developed countries moreover, the decade of the 70's has been one of uncertainty and – in the case of the over 20 million unemployed – a tightening of belts and of hardship. Unemployment levels have reached the proportions of the 1930's and while social security provides some protection, real economic and social distress is taking a heavy toll. Even where advances have been made, the clock of history is being turned back and previous commitments to full employment and social progress are being abandoned.

What has made matters worse has been the response of those in positions of authority. While the 1973-74 oil crisis took many governments by surprise, it merely brought to a head an underlying malaise, which was by no means merely a question of the cost of oil. Certainly the great majority of countries were already facing problems in maintaining full employment, raising real living standards and narrowing income gaps prior to the oil crisis. Rather than developing new policy measures to replace those that had failed, many governments, even those of a social democratic orientation, have adopted or flirted with policies of monetary restraint, associated with the name of the American economist Milton Friedman. This 'love affair' with monetarism is like marrying on the rebound, the old partnership having been deemed hopeless and, instead of seeking a period of reflection and reassessment, plunging recklessly into a new, untried relationship. What makes the preoccupation with monetarism all the more extraordinary is that it represents a lurch into economics of a kind which had been thought dead and buried ever since Roosevelt's 'New Deal'.

It is frightening to realise that the same 'bankers' policies' – balanced budgets, monetary restraint and massive cut-backs in public spending – which helped to bring about the Great Slump of the 30's, are being proposed. The effect of these policies where they have been tried out in practice – for example Britain and Israel – has been disastrous, producing mass unemployment, leading to spiralling price rises, and bringing the economy to a standstill. Even the most dogmatic proponents of the Friedman school must now surely recognize that the modern economy is too intricate and sophisticated to be influenced merely by crude theories about the amount of money in the economy and the rate at which that money circulates.

Trade unions totally reject policies which belong to the days of the Weimar Republic and which have caused untold hardship and suffering for working people and their families and have already once brought about economic catastrophe. Both can be achieved given the right mix of demand management and supply management. Just because traditional 'Keynesian' remedies have not worked does not mean they should be abandoned; they need to be built upon and adapted to changed circumstances, taking into account the real forces that shape the economy, such as market-dominant, multinational, companies.

Mutuality of Interests

The Brandt Report rightly rejects monetarism. Instead, the Report's analysis builds upon the premise that while the world economy is a complex one and cannot be controlled through the application of any one narrow doctrine, its overall management is not beyond the wit of man. More specifically, Brandt advocates a kind of global

'Keynesianism' which is much in line with the thinking of the trade union movement. More than a piecemeal approach is required given the interdependence of the world economy. At past world economic summit meetings – London in 1977, Bonn in 1978, Tokyo in 1979 and Venice in 1980 – the trade union movement has called for bold and imaginative initiatives to revive the world economy. Brandt's call for massive transfer of resources to the developing countries would be a significant way in which a global balance in demand and supply can be restored, at least in the medium-term. There is a great 'mutuality of interest' between developed and developing countries and the fact that, as Brandt points out, one third of US, EEC and Japan exports went to developing countries in 1977 serves to emphasise this point. It is not realized enough that this 'mutuality of interest' means more domestic production and more jobs – already one job in 20 in the USA is for export to the developing countries and this ratio is likely to rise. Workers in developed countries therefore have at least as much to gain from the Brandt approach to economic management as their counterparts in developing countries.

Trade unions are by their very nature internationalist in outlook. This was true of the early workers' movements of the nineteenth century as it is of their counterparts today. Some of the most famous workers' struggles – such as the early London dockworkers' strikes—were assisted by support and donations from fellow workers abroad. In the 1980's the workers' movement is forging even closer links and complex structures of international trade union organizations exist at global, regional and functional level.[1] Particularly important in this regard is the role of international trade secretariats which bring together workers within particular industries, such as the metal workers, or in multi-national companies, and which are seeking to evolve a common trade union position on such questions as health and safety and working conditions.

Trade unions exist above all to defend the material well-being of their members and to ensure that basic standards of living are raised; beyond that they also wish to extend the scope of democracy at the workplace and to safeguard democratic rights and freedoms. In the face of the evident failure of existing policy and practice, the trade union movement has been demanding a major reappraisal. Thus at the First General Session of the newly-established Commonwealth Trade Union Council, which groups trade union bodies in over 40 countries, in June 1980 unanimous backing was given to the Brandt Report. Strong support has also been voiced by other trade union bodies at national and international level.

Economic Reforms

Developing countries provided a policy reappraisal in the Programme of Action for a New International Economic Order issued by the UN General Assembly in 1974. This pinpoints the main areas where major reforms in economic structures are necessary. While it represented the right response, it was somewhat strong on rhetoric and weak on facts. This absence of analysis has however been corrected in a multitude of studies issued since 1974 by the specialized UN bodies such as the World Bank, UNCTAD, UNIDO, and the ILO, and now by the Brandt Report. There is therefore no excuse to delay action. Insofar as there remains a problem, it is the need to translate existing aspirations into specific issues for negotiation, and thereby to lay the foundations for a re-establishment of a consensus for economic and social advance.

One area for reform is the international monetary system. The need for its overhaul was evident well before the formal abandonment of the Bretton Woods system. The value of the Brandt Report is that it points out the priorities for reform, such as the establishment of an efficient mechanism to recycle petro-dollars to over-debted developing countries, and the need to overhaul the policies of the International Monetary Fund. In doing this, the Report does not mince its words – talking of the IMF, it argues that the Fund has formulated its policies 'on the basis of a monetary approach . . . which generates too uniform and rigid conclusions' and that 'the Fund's insistence on drastic measures . . . has tended to impose unnecessary and unacceptable political burdens on the poorest, on occasions leading to 'IMF riots' and even the downfall of governments.' The recent experience of countries like Jamaica, Tanzania and perhaps most disturbing in view of the events of 1980, Turkey, serves to underline this critical assessment.

The system of international trade also requires reform. Much importance has traditionally been attached to the preservation of 'free trade', a concept which is the object of lip-service in bodies such as GATT. Free trade as based on the theory of comparative costs between countries is however largely a myth; in fact, much of international trade is highly managed. Non-tariff barriers such as government procurement and aids and subsidies to industry grossly distort – despite the GATT Tokyo Round – the working of the free market. Regional blocks such as the European Community exclude certain industries – such as agriculture – from normal trade and heavily protect others. Even more significant is the role of transnational corporations in international trade. The Brandt Report has pointed to the fact that such corporations control between a quarter and a third of all world production, that intra-firm trade between the different branches of a TNC makes up over 30% of total world trade.

Trade unions in developed countries are frequently accused of protectionism. It cannot be denied that there are difficult areas, such as trade in textiles, although recent studies have shown that most problems are caused by structural change in the industry, and not by competition from cheap imports from developing countries. The Brandt Report, however, explains the real concern of trade unions, namely that they 'raise questions when they suspect that wages in developing countries are being held down by exploitation of a weak and unorganized labour force, by excessive working hours, or by the use of child labour. They resent it all the more if the competition makes excessive profits – especially if it comes from multinationals, which in some cases may also be their own employers.' Brandt rightly states that ILO fair labour standards – internationally agreed between developed and developing countries – should be adopted 'in order to prevent unfair competition and to facilitate trade liberalisation'. The

Report also points to the long-standing trade union demand, for the inclusion of a 'social clause' in GATT which would aim at helping to generate respect for such labour standards. Such an approach is not protectionist. It seeks to ensure that ordinary people reap the benefits of trade and it has the support of unions from both developed and developing countries.

As well as guaranteeing fair labour standards in the developing countries it is necessary that developed countries pursue active adjustment policies. The Brandt Report notes with concern that the record in this respect is 'not very satisfactory'. Workers faced with redundancy and little hope of a new job will clearly cling on to their job and it is essential that they are offered the prospect of retraining and new employment on at least equivalent remuneration and conditions. Active labour market and regional policies ensuring that work is brought to the workerspolicy entails greater attention to employment-creation, the eradication of poverty and what the World Bank in its 1980 World Development Report termed 'human development'. Such human development is not an alternative to economic growth,   Another area where a new framework has to be created is in respect of the activities of TNCs. This has been recognized by most governments and the rudimentary beginnings of such a framework are presently being evolved, notably in the shape of the proposed UN Code of Conduct for TNCs. The UN Code, once adopted, should provide a major focus for an objective judgement of TNC activities – and the extent to which they are complying with the standards of behaviour expected of them by their host countries. In order to be effective, the UN Code will however need to be a living instrument, not confined to legalistic discussions at the international level, like the already existing OECD Code, which was drawn up by the industrialized country governments. This means that the provisions of the code must be endowed with an effective implementation machinery which is of real meaning not only to government civil servants, but also to management and unions.

The Brandt Report recognizes the importance of giving a practical relevance to international laws and suggests 'an international procedure for discussions and consultations on measures affecting direct investment and the activities of transnational corporations'. This is precisely what the trade unions have sought in their proposal for information and consultation arrangements within a TNC. This concept envisages a formal structure for information disclosure to unions about global – not only local – TNC operations: for example possible closures and transfer of production. It is to be accompanied by provision for consultations with management including those at the level of global TNC headquarters. Such a structure is long overdue, given the transnational nature of modern industry, which has meant that negotiations are often devoid of meaning as a result of being confined to a limited, possibly insignificant, part of the total TNC operations.

The creation of information and consultation arrangements for workers within a TNC would make a significant contribution towards facilitating, through the provision of a meaningful dialogue between workers and management, structural adaptation in the economy. As such it should also help to establish a better understanding between North and South and thereby enhance international relations. It is no doubt for these reasons that the Commission of the European Communities has drawn up a draft Directive which seeks to translate such information and consultation arrangements into law. While it should be made clear that as far as trade unions are concerned laws and codes are no substitute for trade union organization or activity, the draft Directive is particularly welcome, as it points to the importance of restoring agreement on economic and social policy.

Social Progress

Recent Studies by the World Bank, the ILO and other bodies show that unless drastic measures are taken, there is little hope that existing levels of unemployment and poverty can be reduced by the year 2000. One recent study[2] even takes the gloomy view that the number of people living in 'absolute poverty' could rise to over 1,000 million in twenty years time; the same study also calculates that it will be necessary to create over 900 million productive jobs by the year 2000 if unemployment and underemployment are to be overcome.

Clearly the task facing the world community is an enormous one and cannot be resolved by reliance on market forces. Economic growth-rates will certainly need to be increased from their dismal 1971-80 averages, but in addition a conscious direction of growth to benefit the less privileged in society is essential. Such a policy entails greater attention to employment-creation, the eradication of poverty and what the World Bank in its 1980 World Development Report termed 'human development'. Such human development is not an alternative to economic growth, but a condition of economic growth. Thus, for example, it is known that the economic rate of return on investment in primary education averages around 20 per cent – considerably higher than the return on much physical investment.

The Brandt Report recognizes the importance of integrating social objectives in development strategy, in particular in its chapter on 'The Task of the South', which deals with the policies developing countries should themselves pursue. Trade unions naturally welcome this emphasis and the recognition given to the pursuit of policies to satisfy elementary or basic needs and to achieve a redistribution of productive resources and incomes. The Report is also valuable in the recognition it gives to the role of the informal sector and of trade unions in development, stating that 'workers and peasants, women and youth – organized in trade unions, co-operatives and other groups – will often be the guarantee of implementing reforms in many social and economic areas' and 'such organizations can help in decentralising development activities, in mobilizing resources, particularly through self-help and public works projects, and in providing social services, extension services, credit, training and inputs on a group basis'.

Conclusion

In the view of the trade union movement the world community must agree and act upon Brandt's 'Programme for Survival' and in particular the 'emergency programme' proposed for 1980-85. If this is not done, the alternative will not be a preservation of the status quo, but solutions of an increasingly radical and indeed revolutionary nature. The potential for chaos and for global conflict of such a development and the consequent threat to all mankind should be apparent.

Bold and statesmanlike initiatives are therefore called for. Imagination and commitment should guide the actions of those in positions of responsibility, for the task facing them is not an easy one. Above all, however, public opinion, especially in the developed countries, must be made aware of the reforms which are necessary and be informed of the short-term adjustments this may entail. The trade unions will certainly play their part in this educational process and will inform their members about the need for new economic and social structures in the world. The Brandt Report has already made a significant contribution towards a better understanding of global problems and this awareness now needs to be consolidated and built-upon. Willy Brandt's own insistence that 'the shaping of our common future is much too important to be left to governments and experts alone' is therefore a call which should be heeded.

References

1. e.g. the International Confederation of Free Trade Unions, the Organization of African Trade Union Unity, the Commonwealth Trade Union Council.

2. M.J.A. Hopkins, 'A global forecast of absolute poverty and employment', *International Labour Review*, Vol. 119, No. 5, 1980.

ORVILLE L. FREEMAN*

(Multinational) Companies will play a key role in the mammoth economic advance I foresee in the last half of the 1980s.

There is an old saying that 'crisis spells opportunity'. As can be seen from the findings of the Brandt Commission, the

*USA. President, Business International Corporation

world is indeed in crisis but, as also highlighted by that Report, a combination of forces exists that can respond to the current world malaise and create a brighter and better way for mankind. I believe mutual needs and common dangers will prompt countries to take action in line with the reality of global economic interdependence. When this happens – and I believe it will and know it must if we are to survive on this planet – the enormous potential for growth and expansion that the world needs will be realized.

There are three principal actors in a non-gloomy scenario I see possible for the 1980s and beyond. First is the industrial world, the OECD countries that comprise the North. If present trends continue the developed world will be in deep trouble. Economic growth is lagging. Inflation is running at intolerable levels. The self-correcting forces usually associated with free market economies are being stymied by barriers created by the high degree of trade union power and of business concentration seen in most OECD countries. The resulting stagflation defies solution and is not made any easier by the tendency of countries not to coordinate their economic policies and instead to opt for nationalistic, narrow remedies.

The situation does not look encouraging. Over the next few years serious labour shortages threaten the North. Demography will work against sustained growth. During the decade there will be an increasing shortage of young people as populations in the North age; also the highly – educated people of the OECD nations simply refuse to do the traditional work necessary in an industrial economy. Other factors do not bode well. The cost of raw materials will certainly move up, since the oil most easily pumped, the trees most easily cut, and the ores closest to the surface have all been reached and used. Rising raw material costs will increase inflationary pressures. Finally, the energy crunch and chaos will only grow worse; at least 10 years are needed to develop the alternative energy supplies necessary to support a reasonable growth rate.

The same picture emerges for the developing world, the second actor in my scenario. The South, too, will be in crisis unless present trends are reversed. Population continues to boom in economically and socially unmanageable dimensions. Massive migration of people to the metropolitan areas creates acres of explosive slums. Unemployment and underemployment are at staggering levels, in many countries exceeding 50 per cent.

The demographic picture in the South is the exact opposite of that in the North. The South has heavy concentrations of population under 20 years of age; this creates job pressures with dangerous social and political implications. Hunger, malnutrition and, in some cases, starvation are the lot of almost a billion people on our planet. The demand for goods and services to meet even the simplest, most basic needs is enormous. Even in most of the advanced developing countries or NICs, in which striking progress has been made in economic growth and, in some cases, equitable distribution, costs of energy and supplies hamper faster progress.

Possession of oil is no panacea even for the nations that have it. Increasingly, the OPEC countries, the third set of cast members of my scenario, will find themselves in a vicious circle. Caught up in competition among themselves, both economic and ideological, unable to work out a rational pricing system, they will continue to escalate energy prices at a pace that will only succeed in raising world prices in general, eroding the value of their earnings and threatening the entire world's economy. They will accumulate dollars faster than they can spend or invest them. OPEC's leadership is beginning to realize the dangers that the course of action they are following holds, and yet they seem unable to get off the price escalator.

What we have, therefore, is a triple crisis: in the industrial world, in the developing world and in the OPEC world. However, it is a crisis which spells opportunity. When the parts are placed side by side, it is clear that the problems faced by each are complementary and can be solved through a new and promising global initiative. To state it in the simplest and most direct terms:

OPEC countries have massive funds;
The industrial world has technology and managerial knowhow; and
Developing countries have the need.

If health, education, skills, and local resources are nurtured in the developing countries the resulting economic stimulus will generate voracious markets for the developed world that will help stimulate global sustained growth and development. This is not an abstract theory. It is a fact drawn from historical experience. The economic breakdown of 1929 was, above all, caused by the sharp, spreading decline of demand among primary producers, including US farmers, after the boom of 1920's that in the end produced Wall Street's first signal of collapsing confidence. Unfortunately, it was met then not by restoring markets and encouraging investments, but by a fatal retreat into protectionism.

Another historic example of the kind of solution that is possible now can be seen by looking at the Marshall Plan that was devised to deal with the problems facing the Western world immediately following World War II. To be sure, the challenge the world faces now is infinitely more complex than the one in 1947. Then, in Europe and Japan, a skilled workforce and an experienced management cadre capable of putting to productive use material and financial resources were available. Further, the plan was conceived and implemented by a single nation that, in enlightened self-interest, recognized that a revitalized Europe and Japan were in its own best political and economic interests. It will be much more complicated, and require great patience and political skill, to put together a Global Marshall Plan, matching and merging needs and opportunities in a new global initiative.

Obviously, much more is needed than merely a massive transfer of wealth. A Global Marshall Plan must be geared to the self-interest of all concerned parties. And it must include a working relationship between governments and private sector to take advantage of the strength, ingenuity and inventiveness of the market economy.

One person who has put some flesh on the bones of the Global Marshall Plan concept envisioned in the Brandt Report is Dr. Ronald Muller. In his recent book, *Revitalizing America: politics for prosperity*, which deals with both US rebuilding needs and the importance of global cooperation, Dr Müller describes in some detail how such a Global

Marshall Plan might be carried out under the auspices of the World Bank and the Regional Development banks. The advantage of using these international institutions would be to advance the start-up of operations, because systems, methods, channels of communication and personnel would already be in place. Overall, what might be described as a Global Growth Pool equally funded by OPEC and OECD countries would provide the capital for bankable projects certified and supervised by the Development Banks. Such a "pool" or "investing centre" would set basic policy, including areas for investment and profitability targets that would be used in selecting projects. The investors and the receiving countries in the developing world would each have a representative voice in setting policy and direction as was the case in the original Marshall Plan.

Fortunately, the key elements that will make up the working parts of the Global Marshall Plan, or marshalling plan as I like to think of it, are, as the Brandt Report makes clear, in a position to deal effectively with each other. I refer to international companies and the developing countries. These entities are moving from an earlier period of confrontation to one of negotiation and recognition of mutual benefits that can be gained by working with each other. The multinational corporation (MNC) has already established itself as the primary instrument in the internationalization of production, and undoubtedly is the most significant economic development since World War II. Direct investment by international companies, based in countries all over the world, including now the advanced developing countries, totals at this point close to $500 billion. These companies produce some $1,500 billion per year, and their growth rate has been close to 10 per cent for over two decades.

These companies will play a key role in a mammoth economic advance I foresee in the last half of the 1980's. Most of the technology that is desperately needed in the developing world, if the Global Marshall Plan is to work, has been developed by these companies. Not only have they developed the technology, but also along with it, a special delivery capacity. What they have goes beyond technology per se and includes management capacity and marketing knowhow. International companies, far more effectively than governments, can move resources, including capital, technology or management skills, as a package of productive factors tailored to the needs of a given opportunity or project. This is what distinguishes them from what private and public experts and technicians usually do through technical assistance programs.

The efficient utilization that comes with a complete package of productive factors is crucial because it includes the backstopping service of head office staffs and research facilities, with access to procurement channels and marketing outlets, and the ability to mobilize and deploy all of those capabilities around the world, and is another important contribution made to the world economy by international companies - and only by international companies. These companies make it possible for home countries, host country and third country nationals to learn by doing in the crucible of the competitive marketplace.

Developing countries, too, seem primed for the quantum jump that mankind will now be able to make toward achieving working, functioning interdependence on the basis of mutual respect and interests. A number of developing countries such as Korea, Brazil, India and Mexico are economically ready to take on a bigger role in providing needed goods and services for both industrialized and other developing countries. Most developing countries have in place leadership and development officials who can formulate goals and methods of reaching them so that the masses of the citizenry of their countries are able to participate equitably in the fruits of their future accomplishments.

Equally important, most developing countries are coming to recognize the importance of international companies in achieving national goals. They stand ready to include them in their plans. Given the vast numbers of viable projects that are emerging in the Third and, even Fourth Worlds, in agribusiness, infrastructure, machine tools, transportation equipment and other basic sectors, the situation holds exciting possibilities.

What I see coming in the decade of 1980's is not a super economy spanning the globe, planned and controlled by a group of wise men sitting in some mysterious centre of economic activity. I think our world is much too complex to be planned. What will emerge is cooperation among the North, the south and the OPEC countries that will make available technological, managerial and financial resources for national or regional plans. It will be done through *bankable* projects in those areas of the world where the needs and opportunities are literally gigantic. The actual movement of knowhow, technology, management, and marketing skills will be carried out by international companies competing in a world market economy:

This process is not new or untried. It has been at work at an accelerating pace for a quarter of a century. There have been both failures and abuses, but the overall record of international companies as the originators and developers of the internationalization of production must be rated an unqualified success. I am further encouraged by the fact that developing countries, which in many cases were suspicious and antagonistic toward international companies, now not only welcome, but actively seek such investment, subject to national goals and needs.

This embryonic trend is the new face of nationalism, that enables developing countries to pinpoint quite specifically how international companies can contribute to national economic plans and goals, and makes possible negotiations between international companies and countries on a mutually beneficial basis. The same process, I suggest, will come into play as international companies bid for, and execute, the plans and programmes that are developed by a Global Marshall Plan.

JAN TINBERGEN*

> The all-important event about the Brandt Report is that a group of politically experienced persons finally agree that for the world to survive other policies are vital.

The Brandt Report constitutes an important step forward in

*Netherlands. Economics Nobel Prize winner. Chairman of the R.I.O. Report group the otherwise very disappointing evolution of West-South relations. I don't say North-South relations, since the concept of the 'North' for the time being is wishful thinking as long as the two parts of the North–West and communist-ruled East – don't trust each other. We must hope that one day some better, and not militarily determined, relationship between West and East will emerge.

But even when East-West relations are demilitarized, not much should be expected from contributions by the East to the programme of the Brandt Report. Let's leave this subject outside our comment.

The most important feature of the Report was eloquently set out in the address by the British conservative statesman Edward Heath in The Hague on May 17, 1980, where he explained to his Dutch audience that after considerable initial divergence of opinions the members of the 'Independent Commission on International Development Issues' (ICIDI) had reached consensus on the main conclusions set out in their Report. If we remind ourselves of the membership list, this means that politicians of recognized prestige had taken over the torch from the technicians who previously had come to similar conclusions. I am referring to the Pearson Report to the World Bank published more than a decade ago and the 'Columbia Declaration' adopted after a discussion of that report at Columbia University [1].

To be sure, the Brandt Report also added some new ideas and arguments – we are going to discuss them a bit later. But the main ideas had been expressed already in the Pearson Report, and many of them still earlier, in the 1961 Resolution 1710 (XVI) of the United Nations General Assembly on the Development Decade (1961-1970; later rebaptized the First Development Decade) whose main architect was Hans W. Singer. That resolution, as well as the Pearson Report and the Columbia Declaration, reflected the ideas of technical experts and representatives at the United Nations General Assembly, but these ideas were not supported by the most powerful Western politicians. In their policies the latter flatly negated their own countries' experts, such as Sir Edward Boyle of the United Kingdom, C. Douglas Dillon of the United States, Wilfried Guth of the

Federal Republic of Germany, Robert E. Marjolin of France, or Saburo Okita of Japan.

This is illustrated by the fact that official development assistance (ODA), recommended to amount to the famous 0·7 per cent of GNP, did not attain half of that figure for the West's two largest industrial nations (USA and Japan), was still not reached in 1980 by the medium-sized industrial countries (France, Germany, the U.K.) but only by four small Western nations, Denmark, the Netherlands, Norway, and Sweden. The latter, now also designated as the likeminded countries, are tending increasingly to co-operate, with a few more countries, in order to defend the interests of the Third World as well as their own, often also neglected by the large and the so-called large nations.

The all-important fact about the Brandt Report is that a group of politically experienced persons finally agreed that for the world to survive other policies are vital; and that in the medium and long run the interests of the industrialized and the less developed countries are parallel. One of these parallel interests – perhaps somewhat overlooked – is the creation of considerably more employment in developing countries, in order to offer to the so-called 'illegal migrant' workers better chances at home. This implies a need for better understanding of what the Group of 77 – through UNCTAD, UNIDO and the UN General Assembly – have been claiming. It also implies that the present German Chancellor was not at his best when he formulated his judgement about the UNCTAD Commodity Fund.

As observed, the Report not only supports some of the long-standing proposals by Third World representatives, but also sheds some new light on the issues. Thus, in his Introduction, Chairman Brandt, among many other valuable remarks, observes that Henry Ford's argument for higher wages applies to the case for higher incomes of the Third World: with higher incomes they will be better markets for those of our products which we are able to supply at competitive prices.

The Report also launches the laudable idea that the financing capacity of the World Bank be extended by increasing its own borrowing and that the raising of international taxes should become one of the world's normal institutions. Indeed if any lesson can be drawn from the last decade's experience it is that voluntary financing of development hasn't worked. It is important to act in line with that experience.

In addition, the Report proposes a new Development Fund, side by side with the World Bank, in order to attract money from sources not so easily accessible to the Bank, for instance OPEC money. Whereas I see the crux, I have an amendment to propose, which brings us back to the idea of world taxes. In financial jargon I want to state that we need a current budget for development financing. Among the arguments in favour of such a form of financing three stand out: (i) inside well organized countries the current budget is far more important than capital-market financing; (ii) current financing makes superfluous all negotiations on a repayment scheme and interest rate – and certainly renegotiations are needed if the debt load becomes too heavy; (iii) some important types of projects are not bankable for technical reasons.[2]

As the co-ordinator of a report to the Club of Rome known as the RIO report, I am pleased to find that there are several similarities between the latter and the Brandt Report. Not the least important is the idea, common to both, that a medium-term and a longer-term programme be specified.

Thus, in my opinion, the Brandt Report is innovative in several respects. As a consequence it has brought a new spark of hope; it may have opened some eyes. But even if it had not, those of us who have studied the problems of world development and are conscious of the immense responsibilities we have, should go on trying to persuade politicians and public opinion that a question of survival is indeed at stake. We should be inspired by the words reflecting the spirit in which William of Orange acted: 'Point n'est besoin d'espérer pour entreprendre, ni de réussir pour persévérer' (Hope is not needed to enterprise; nor is success a precondition to persevere).

As already pointed out, the most important goal of development policies must be the creation of far more employment. Among the poorest and the most miserable those without employment are worst off: their income is nil, since in developing countries no unemployment benefits are paid. They must live at the expense of relatives. Many of them are villagers, not needed since there is no land left or since the necessary investments would be beyond their capacity. They are trying to find employment in the already overcrowded cities, where their chances to find work are slim and decreasing and the quality of life is horrible. So the most enterprizing among them try to migrate to the developed world, about which they have heard from friends or relatives. The industrialized countries some time ago did exert a strong demand for their services, since the developed world's own workers saw fit – with the better education most of them had gradually obtained – to fill the better jobs, and no longer wanted to do the dirtiest and heaviest work at the rates of pay prevailing. As a matter of fact for quite some time the 'guest workers' (a strange misnomer – their treatment is not exactly what 'guests' is usually offered!) were only too happy to accept these jobs with a pay much higher than in their own countries.

After the stagflation period had set in many migrant workers were dismissed. Some countries, such as Switzerland, sent them right back: they were 'guests', no more. Other countries behaved in a more civilized way. But, especially in workers' quarters of our large cities the problems are cropping up: competition between migrants and our own people for jobs, dwellings, and transportation, to mention some examples. This is the most immediate way to explain to our public why we have common interests. Accordingly, a common recovery policy is, in my opinion, priority number one. In this respect we might even think of proposals I set out elsewhere that are complementary to those of the ICIDI[3]. The main idea is that a better division of labour between developing and developed countries might add to employment in the Third World, especially in the labour-intensive and mature-technology activities. The instrument of economic policy to use here would be reduction – and finally elimination – of protectionism, which is practised more widely than our own principles warrant. This is one of the points dealt with by the Dutch Minister for Development Co-operation, Mr J. de Koning, in his remarkable set of proposals offered in The Hague on May 17, 1980.[4]

A recovery in the Third World would raise their demand for equipment, which can be produced, in many instances, better in the developed world. The recovery should be supported by the execution of a large-scale research programme. Such a programme would match with Jean Fourastié's forecast of a since clearly apparent shift in the Western world towards service activities.[5] It would also match with the educational composition of our labour force. I tried to show that there is, at the same time, an enormous need for more research. Both the environmentalists and the experts mobilized by the Club of Rome have provided us with a number of very urgent problems whose solution is waiting for more research. The problem to be solved first is how to transform this 'need' into 'demand': i.e. to find the financial means to organize, say, a doubling of research activities. Here the idea of the Brandt Commission to double the World Bank's foreign (as distinct from its own) capital and so increase the Bank's lending capacity may help. It is certainly in the interest of the Bank's other activities that our knowledge of a number of vital issues is more rapidly increased. The examples are to be found in the fields of maintaining a sufficient area of forests, of finding and transforming into practical use safer energy supplies, of reducing undernourishment, of reorganizing western societies in several respects and last, but not least, of doing all this without new inflation.

This constitutes another high priority, although for me the second and not the first priority. Not only is it an important priority for our own economies which are disfigured by inflation, but also for the OPEC countries, whose newly obtained assets are threatened by it. There is, again, a common interest to eliminate inflation. The problem, in its present form, is different enough from older forms we knew to search for means to eliminate it which are better geared to the present structure of society. Whereas, in some of the proposals already discussed, anti-inflationary forces are built in, an integrated discussion of how inflation can be avoided is desirable and even necessary. As a starting point, a distinction may be made between two types of policies: on the one hand a policy of government intervention and on the other hand an automatic policy.

Recent trends have been more of the former type, where government (or central bank) intervention is intended to counter the increased organization of society in interest groups which, in an endless succession, try to expand their share of national income. Intervention, in principle, should counterbalance the powerful groups' claims, in order to protect the weak groups. A distinction may be made between overtly organized groups and non-organized groups commanding scarce resources or capabilities. Examples of the two types are trade unions, whose claims may be declared illegal (the 1980 situation in the Netherlands, where a wage stop has been imposed by government) and the free professions and high salary earners, not so explicitly organized, but characterized by scarce capabilities (also subject, from July 1980 on, to government intervention in Holland).

An interesting proposal, meant to introduce an automatic avoidance of inflationary income payments, has been launched by A.P. Lerner[6] and seems worth wide publicity and discussion with hopes of its introduction.

The need for an anti-inflationary policy is emphasized also by the proposals to the Brandt Commission formulated by Mr de Koning, the Dutch Minister for Development Cooperation, mentioned before. As part of an agreement with OPEC he underlines the necessity of (a) a reduction of energy consumption by the developed countries, (b) a pledge by OPEC to make available a negotiated quantity of oil, (c) a price agreement, and (d) a guarantee by the developed consumer countries to stabilize their prices. Mr de Koning does not enter into details of how to stabilize the Western price level.

The Minister is quite explicit, however, on a number of financial measures he recommends and which I think have been well chosen. In order to prevent a catastrophical increase in the debt of oil importing developing countries the Minister proposes two new policies. First, the IMF should be given the competence to attract new capital in order to help financing further balance of payments deficits of the countries just mentioned. This financing should take the form of loans at very low interest rates – e.g. one-third of market rates – and the conditions attached should be different from the usual conditions. They should consist of a two-goal policy: (i) to restore balance of payments equilibrium (the usual condition), and (ii), a new element, under the side condition that satisfaction of the basic needs of the poorest part of the country's population be guaranteed.

The second proposal sounds very radical but in fact is a matter of common sense. It calls for the complete remission, over a period of ten years, of the existing debts: ten per cent each year of the eighties.

In conclusion and summarizing my evaluation of the report of the Brandt Commission let me repeat that it constitutes a milestone in the development dialogue, especially because of the consensus reached by a group of experienced politicians, representing a wide spectrum of non-extremist and undoctrinaire opinions. It is constructive in the best sense of that word. This is what is needed; the large majority of mankind is against extremism. Yet, this 'programme for survival' will only work if the West's politicians keep in mind Goethe's words in *Faust*[7]:

> *Der Worte sind genug gewechselt.*
> *Lasst mich auch endlich Thaten sehn!*

or, in a free translation: discussions we have had enough; let us finally have something done.

This policy of doing something (by the Western world) will be furthered by a policy of self-reliance by the Third World. Again there is a parallel with our own labour movement: there was little improvement in the workers' situation until the latter organized themselves in trade unions and socialist parties. So we should understand such self-reliance and in our own interests join the Third World in its endeavour to create a better world.

References

1. Ward, Barbara, *et al*. (eds) *The widening gap,*, New York, Columbia University Press, 1971.

2. Tinbergen, J. 'International Taxes as an Alternative Means to Finance International Development', International Financing of Economic Development, Second

World Scientific Banking Meeting, Dubrovnik; Beograd (1980)

3. Tinbergen, J., lecture at the City University of London, *Lloyds Bank Review* July 1980

4. de Koning, J. 'Recht op bestaan en ontwikkeling. Concrete voorstellen op basis van het rapport van de Commissie-Brandt', *Aspecten van internationale samenwerking* 13, 1980. pp.226-233, Ministerie van Buitenlandse Zaken, Den Haag

5. Fourastié, J. *Le grand espoir du XXe siècle,* Paris, Presses universitaries de France, 1949.

6. Lerner, A.P. *et al.* MAP: *A market anti-inflation plan,* New York, Harcourt Brace Jovanovich, Inc., 1980

7. Goethe, W.A., Faust. *Goethe's Werke* Fünfter und Sechster Band. Berlin, G. Grothe'sche Verlagsbuchhandlung, 1881, S. 10

MICHAEL LIPTON*

It is the twin areas of debt and trade that most strongly support the Commissioners' case.

Brandt and his colleagues advocate the use of OPEC's reinvested surpluses to secure massive reflation of Third World demand for exports from rich countries. The Commission has, on the whole, got it right; on the other hand, the extreme monetarists, internationally as in Britain, offer only assertions and hopes. They *assert* that monetary reflation can raise only prices or imports, not production. They *hope* that monetary squeezes in IMF's client countries (whether Britain in 1976 or Turkey in 1980) may kill inflation rather than production. But, behind these alleged alternatives to Keynesian methods, there lies little more than a rhetorical readiness to dismiss opponents as

* United Kingdom. Professor of Economics, Institute of Development Studies in Sussex University. Consultant of World Bank, E.C., and several U.N. organisations. This article is a revised version of one which was originally published in *International Affairs* (Vol 56, No.2. Spring 1980). Reprinted here by permission of the Royal Institute of International Affairs.

'not real economists', and a track record of almost unrelieved failure.

But is it enough that Brandt is right about the shared North-South interest in planned reflation? Today there is no framework through which to *implement* even such a simple approach, let alone Brandt's complex, interventionist package. To this package the North and the South – each many-headed – would have to offer negotiated and free assent.

However, there is no formal schedule for follow-up or implementation. A 'summit' alone will not help much unless it at least proposes such a schedule.

Most of the package – massive cash transfers, international demand reflation, a retreat from protectionism – is courageous even if sometimes vulnerably-reasoned in detail. But how, in a squabbling world dominated by muddled monetarist contractionism, is it to be made real? Two necessary conditions are:

to satisfy powerful interest-groups that could block alleged 'general interest' deals – e.g. Western firms and trade unions with good reason to fear Third World textile sales, even if these do raise GNP in the buying and selling country alike;

to select priority or emergency areas for progress, and to be satisfied (in the first instance at least) with much less than universal participation.

Even these conditions are not sufficient to ensure success, as Western governments look increasingly inward. But they could guide 'loyal opposition', of neo-Keynesian internationalists, to build upon this Report a set of policies that is implementable and not merely right. They will be needed when the intellectual bankruptcy of current nostalgias (for monetarism, combined with non-interventionist free-marketry at home, but with protectionist gadgets abroad) becomes obvious to all. Whether neo-Keynesian alternatives can satisfy the 'radical opposition', outraged by mass poverty and by exploitation across race and 'First-Third World' lines, is more doubtful. But can any 'summit' be offered a reflationist option that the Northern powers, too, will see as being in their own interest?

Scope for common interest

(A) HUNGER. On this core question of poverty, there is limited scope for the 'common interest' approach. The central point is not self-interest but that – since the abolition of hunger by the year 2000 is well within the scope of known technology, and since extra food can be more cheaply produced by small farmers in the developing world than by large and subsidised farmers in the North – it is *morally* intolerable to deny the world's poor the means towards self-reliant food production. It is true, but incidentally so, that sudden massive harvest failure in developing countries imperils price stability in the North; and that food production uses much more fossil-fuel energy (directly and via fertilisers) in developed countries and on big farms than on poor people's farms in the Third World. But the case for massive Northern support to a genuine world food programme – not just an exercise in extended emergency protection – rests mainly on common humanity, not on common interests.

(B) DEBT AND REFLATION: THE PROBLEM. It is the twin areas of debt and trade that most strongly support the Commissioners' case. On trade, the Commission makes a powerful case against neo-protectionism, arguing that high levels of exports and imports by the South have measurably and substantially sustained Northern employment since 1973. However, expanded or even maintained North-South trade depends on a recycling of OPEC surpluses, to allow the South to cope with dearer oil. Hence North and South share an interest in Northern and OPEC transfers to, plus imports from, the Third World to redress the balance between OPEC and the North. In these matters, Brandt's talk of 'crisis' and of the need for a global solution – both at times overdone and counter-productive – is justified.

'Of the total flows to the developing countries in 1960, 60 per cent came from . . . aid. By 1977, more than two-thirds was commercial, mainly from private bank loans, direct investment and export credits' (Ch.14, p.222).

The supposed need for the banks to intermediate, between almost limitless OPEC surplus and severely limited investment opportunities,[1] has provoked an ever-riskier expansion of the role of private lending. In a frightening pyramid of musical chairs, each bank expects repayments out of the borrowing countries' capacity to borrow yet more, rather than out of the yield of the purchases financed by itself. Serious and *timely* discussion of default risks, and their pre-emptive management, is a sober necessity, not a 'scare scenario'.

It would be unhelpful simply to reduce the volume of private lending. Much of this, in effect, refinances old debts; some is genuinely developmental. Certainly the *quality* of private lending must improve; 'musical banking', financing imports, whether tractors or television sets, that does little or nothing for development or the capacity to repay, must give way to 'development banking', which lends for genuinely productive investments or current producer inputs.

However, while the Third World waits for such improvement, the North should not ask it to refinance debts mainly by reliance on the IMF, either for direct loans or for a 'certificate of good behaviour' to the commercial banks. Such procedures produce ever tighter deflationist 'conditionality' upon the borrower, to the virtual neglect of poverty, income-distribution, development, and therefore ultimately of political stability and long-run debt security. What, then, can be done?

If deflationism continues to reduce, at once, the West's capacities to buy from and to lend to the Third World, while oil prices rise in real terms, *a major default is odds-on before the end of 1983*.

In the likely crisis scenario, two or three large private debtors among LDCs – faced by dearer oil, depressed export markets, and poor harvests necessitating food imports – cannot repay, say, three to five major Western banks. Some $10 billion, which these banks expected to be repaid, is instead formally defaulted, or must be 'rescheduled'. What does a bank, faced with a big cut in its cash base, do? It is easiest to answer the question if we look at it the other way round. By law or by custom, a bank keeps a prudential 'cash ratio', typically 10 per cent, between cash-in-hand and liabilities to depositors. If cash-in-hand *rises* by $10 million due to extra deposits, such a bank will raise advances by (100-10) per cent of $10 million, i.e. by $9 million, and keep the extra $1 million as cash. Most of the extra $9 million – in a developing country (DC) typically about 80 per cent – finds its way as cash deposits into the banks, permitting a second round of extra advances: (100-10) per cent of the 80 per cent or $9 million or about $6·5 million. This permits a third round . . . and so on; in this quite realistic example, a $10 million cash expansion, for a bank, produces an ultimate credit expansion of $33·3 million from the banking system. But a 'cash outflow', such as a default on a loan due for repayment, 'puts the credit multiplier into reverse, when it becomes the credit contraction multiplier . . . Loans are called, investments are liquidated, and deposits contract by a multiple'.[2] The multiplier of only 3·3, in the event of a series of defaults of $10 billion concentrated on loans due to a few banks, is too optimistic, because the affected banks would have to call in even more cash: partly to anticipate panic withdrawals by raising the prudential cash reserve ratio; partly to make good the cash actually lost through such withdrawals; and partly to attract funds by raising interest paid to depositors. A $10 billion cash contraction due to default could lead to reduction in lending by the banking system of up to $50 billion. Not only LDCs, but even prime industrial borrowers who had been relying on renewed accommodations, would be at risk. Defaults and bankruptcies would echo, not mainly around banks, but around DC and LDC firms.

It would not in practice be quite that bad. The banks could restore part of the depleted cash ratio by selling securities, rather than by cutting advances. Swap arrangements among banks could achieve something. OPEC funds could help a little, though they are unlikely to go to banks over-exposed in defaulting (or 'rescheduling') LDCs; oil producers, if they lost trust in Western banks, will be tempted to leave their oil in the ground. Finally, developed-country governments might replace the defaulting LDCs by baling out the 'unlucky' banks; but current monetarist doctrine would render governments very reluctant to do much here, or to permit IMF to issue extra Special Drawing Rights (SDRs) with – if there were time! – analogous effects. All in all, general cures after defaults would do little to restore the lending capacity of the particular affected banks.

What is 'around the corner' in a non-Brandtian world is not catastrophe for all. It is a steady series of deflationary shocks, starting from non-repayments or rescheduling, and multiplied by the effect of eroded cash upon bank lending. The worst sufferers will probably be the LDCs, who borrow little from commercial banks, but partly depend for their precarious standard of living upon exports and concessional capital, which recession erodes.

(C) DEBT AND REFLATION: A COMMON-INTEREST APPROACH. Brandt's approach to avoid world-wide deflation is fourfold: to raise the share of Third World debt consisting of relatively safe – because long-term, concessional and renegotiable – aid; to stimulate *appropriate forms* of recycling of OPEC surpluses; massively to improve Third World export conditions in rich countries, both via stabler (and higher?) commodity prices and via a turning back of the protectionist tide; and to reduce assorted uncertainties in the world system. The central assumption is that extra Third World demand for Northern exports can reflate Northern output, bringing spare capacity and unemployed workers into use, without seriously bidding up price-levels. This should work, because Third World demand is primarily for investment-goods and other producer-goods, which tend to be much more depressed than the rest of the Northern economy in times of slump; so extra Third World demand will affect not only those sectors of the economy, but also geographic regions within North-West Europe and North America in which demand is particularly slack, and price-inflation particularly little of a threat.

This is, of course, international neo-Keynesianism. Is this not 'dead'? Well, imperfect Keynesian management and Bretton Woods gave the world economy 1945-73; imperfect monetarist management and Milton Friedman have so far supplied 1920-32 and (admittedly with unwelcome outside help) 1974-80. Reports of the death of neo-Keynesianism are, therefore, grossly exaggerated. However, Brandt's fourfold path to neo-Keynesian reflation must be judged by four criteria. Is it 'right', i.e. (in conjunction with appropriate plans for food and energy) can it induce resumed expansion of world output and employment, while reducing poverty, and without unacceptable inflation? Does it *potentially* mobilize a wide spectrum of supporting interest-groups? Is it argued in a way that will command maximum support, as regards both intellectual content and presentation? Has the follow-up for proper implementation been clearly specified? In my book, Brandt scores A on the first and most important issue, A on the second, B on the third – but Z on the fourth. To some extent, this is because the Commission has turned this final issue over to a rather loosely specified 'audience'. How can we, the audience, now respond? Below, I consider the four main issues raised by Brandt: aid; debt and recycling; trade in manufactures; and commodity policy and the reduction of risk.

The role of aid

Aid comprises only 12 to 15 per cent of recipients' investment, and pays for a similar proportion of their imports. There has been a major shift of emphasis, during the 1970's, away from aid towards other development issues. UNCTAD's search for 'massive transfers', now backed by Brandt, seeks to place aid in the broader context of total development finance, public and private. Yet, for all this fashionable downgrading, old-fashioned aid – concessional flows – will have to increase substantially, in absolute terms and relatively to private capital movements, both to mount a successful attack on world hunger and to stave off the risk of a debt crash. Just like its predecessor, the 1969 'Pearson Report', to the World Bank which centred chiefly on aid, the Brandt Commission tends to substitute rhetoric for evidence when linking aid to growth, to the reduction of poverty, and to the capacity to meet foreign debts. This is a pity, for such evidence is readily available. As for aid and growth, Papanek has shown that, of the variation among developing countries in growth rates, about 10 per cent is associated with variation in previous aid receipts. [3] As for aid and poverty, high-yielding cereal varieties, due in the first instance to aid-financed research in Mexico and the Philippines, were adding at least 6 per cent to foodgrain output in India alone by 1970-1[4] (and perhaps 10-12 per cent by 1977-8); and it was precisely in those parts of India with rapid agricultural growth (due in part to this aid-funded research) that the proportion of poverty had been reduced. [5] As for aid and the capacity to repay debts, private bank loans to developing countries – on hard terms and with maturities often crowded into the very short term – contrast sharply with the increasing concessionality, and with the geographical spread of risks, of most aid. (Of course aid could assist repayment even better than it does, and more lastingly, if it were directed towards improved savings capacity, and/or high social returns.)

The Commission rightly stresses the role of aid in ending hunger for the poorest people in the poorest developing countries. [6] 'Rural development' can feature high returns; indeed, agriculturual output gains in the Third World since 1960 have typically required barely half the investment needed for non-agricultural growth. [7] However, the Commission has not fully appreciated that aid projects in this area are menaced by a wave of groundnut-scheme-type failures, and consequent disillusion. Massive improvements in monitoring and evaluation, *which must be based on independent institutions in the developing countries themselves,* are essential to meet this menace. The building of an aid-financed Indian steel mill can perhaps be overviewed from Delhi, or even (with 'visiting experts') from Washington; but it is dangerous folly to seek to monitor widely-spread, software-intensive projects aimed at the rural poor without a continuing, trusted and competent presence in the field.

Four brute facts remain. First, the USA is increasingly contracting out of bilateral aid. Second, several other donors, notably the UK, are also increasingly reluctant. Third, there is a major switch to multilateral aid; this is endorsed by the Commission, but in the case of EDF (and perhaps parts of the United Nations Development Programme (UNDP) and the World Bank too) it means higher personnel costs, slower disbursement, and at least as much uncertainty about funds as prevail with bilateral funding. Fourth, the deficit donors (USA, UK) are likely to place even more emphasis on the tying of aid to the uncompetitive exports of their 'lame duck' companies. The Commission's plans to shift aid towards automaticity, untying, and programme lending, to finance it by taxes on foreign trade, arms sales, and energy consumption – while all perfectly reasonable – clash against these crude realities.

On aid, the Commission scores high on logic and imagination; high too, on picking an approach (sound debt structures, and adequately-fed and growing economies that can help to expand world trade) likely to mobilize support; but less well on presenting evidence that aid will do what is hoped. Too often, rhetoric and Unctalk are preferred. Moreover, it is not at all clear who is to monitor the global approach to these aid targets, and to apply effective pressure to the laggards.

Oil surpluses: tri-cycling or recycling?

The main task for international capital markets, as the Commission sees it, is to ensure that Third World countries retain the capacity to underpin world growth by imports from the industrial world. This capacity has two sources: Third World export incomes (threatened by instability of commodities and by Western protection of manufactures) and capital flows. The latter must come, not only from aid, but also from the reinvestment in the South of trade surpluses, above all those of OPEC. That is why, of two ways in which capital flows can adjust to oil price rises, [8] the Commission prefers 'tri-cycling' to plain recycling.

In 'tri-cycling', (i) OPEC lends to the Third World, (ii) thus enabling the Third World to expand imports of manufactures from the North, (iii) hence providing the North with the capacity to buy OPEC exports. [9] On the other hand, in recycling, (i) OPEC reinvests its surpluses in the North, and (ii) the North uses this foreign exchange to buy more oil. In this latter sequence, OPEC surpluses are not re-lent to Third World borrowers. Indeed, such borrowers compete for OPEC surpluses with Northern spendthrifts such as the USA and the UK, not usually with much success.

Apart from the moral evil of allowing the worst damage from dearer and scarcer oil to be inflicted on the poorest – as the Commissioners put it, on farmers' pumpsets in India, rather than on private cars in the North – 'tri-cycling' is better than recycling because of the impact on world trade and hence on income and employment in *North and South alike*. The major contribution of Third World imports to Northern employment is most effectively documented in the Report.

But the present maturity structure of Third World debt – and, in general, the fact that 'tri-cycling' has taken place through intermediaries that have often been rapacious, short-sighted and incompetent – threatens that contribution. Bankrupts cannot import; and their bankrupters will not export to them.

New institutions, supporting (and greatly widening the geographical scope of) OPEC's own, are required to steer the new round of OPEC surpluses into Third World activities *direct*, i.e. without excessive intermediation by 'musical banks'. Of course, Western financial institutions – insurers, merchant bankers, shipping brokers, consultants, even some banks – have an expert, and profitable, part to play in ensuring that 'tri-cycling' is reasonably safe and rewarding for all parties, including OPEC lenders. There is a new chapter of the history of international finance here, waiting to be written.[10] But the empty chair, at the post-Brandt discussions, has been that of, not DCs or LDCs, but OPEC. If OPEC is absent, so is the ultimate creditor in a tri-cycling process, and the party to whom most risky debts are *ultimately* due.

The need to build the institutions for improved tri-cycling – if the Scylla of echoing default, and the Charybdis of inadequate cash for Third World imports from the North, are both to be avoided – is therefore urgent. If private flows are still to comprise around half the South's external resource inflow in the mid-1980's, they must be publicly supported or intermediated to avoid a Kreditanstalt-Herstatt-Zaire scenario. This surely implies public, and joint North-South, overview of the *quality* of activities supported by such private lending.

Once again, the Commission has gone to the heart of the problem. Almost nobody (not even the bankers, who are badly frightened) would vehemently oppose action, once initiated. However, the argument is rather muffled, and scattered around the Report, perhaps in part because none of the interests represented by the Commissioners could be too openly attacked. No follow-up is specified, except perhaps at the proposed 'summit'.

Protection causes inflation and unemployment

It is above all through trade that North and South either expand or contract together. The Report (Ch.11, p.174) cites abundant evidence that Third World exports have done negligible harm to Western jobs – but have helped *create* many more Western jobs, by enabling the South to import, maintain and use vastly greater volumes of Western manufactures. Moreover, 'a 1978 survey of all US consumer goods, except food and automobiles, found that Asian and Latin American imports averaged 16 per cent cheaper than domestic products of the same quality' (Ch.11, p.178). Third World exports thus reduce not only Northern inflation, but thereby also the Governmental response to it: the contraction of demand and the consequent destruction of jobs.

Again, the Commissioners are not only right but rather original. They defend North-South trade, and attack the new protectionism, not just with familiar liberal arguments that *consumers* gain from freer trade,[11] but by arguing that the *volume of employment* in the importing North also benefits indirectly. Since there is such clear net gain, why the new protectionism? The Commissioners seek (where the GATT's Tokyo Round miserably failed) to persuade the North to accept 'safeguards against safeguards'. These are restraints on its capacity unilaterally to restrict Third World imports on the pretext of material injury to a vocal sector. But why are 'safeguards against safeguards' resisted if there is a clear, overriding loss to the Northern economy from such restrictions? The main reason is that 'loss of jobs [due to Third World imports] has tended to emphasize existing difficulties for economically weaker [Northern] regions', and that 'movement of labour out of declining industries is not always easy' (Ch.11, p.176). Unemployment, and inadequate adjustment assistance to retrain workers, worsens these problems; and both will suffer from Governmental non-interventionism, in the North's 'real world' of private monopolies and cartels. The OECD States, by moving domestic policies back towards non-intervention, paradoxically *reduce* the prospects of freer international trade. Conversely, at international level, freer trade must be planned; left to itself, private enterprise tends to restrict. not to enhance, competition.[12]

It has always been the case that powerful groups, even small ones, try to insist on a specific quid pro quo for reductions in protection. The general contribution of such reductions to GNP interests them little. But show a potentially jobless EEC producer of textiles, shoes or cutlery a rewarding and reasonably *secure* chance to make equipment, with which India or Korea can then produce what he produced before; and his assent to freer trade is likelier, as is the assent of his trade union or employers' organization. However, this requires:

international *bilateral* negotiations seeking, more or less, *bilaterally balanced trade expansion*, via monitored sectoral targets; and

representation of 'potential loser' and 'potential gainer' *interest groups*, from (say) both EEC and India, at such negotiations.

The Commission has spelt out the arguments, and the goals. Can multilateralism get us towards them? Or is there a better approach via group negotiations, with direct representation of potential 'loser groups' so that they can press for compensation beforehand, instead of exercising protectionist vetoes afterwards? As in 1974-6, an Indo-EEC 'package deal' may well be the most promising way forward.

Commodities and risks

Trade in manufactures exemplifies one central theme, and one rather hidden implication, of the Report. The theme is that Northern and Southern *nations* share common but complex interests. The implication is that, to make use of these overlaps, powerful *sub-national* interests must be taken into account in good time, and hence that – to make the complexity manageable – progress is likelier to involve two nations than 117. Trade in commodities raises another central theme: that reduction of risks, fluctuations, unanticipated events, can benefit even those involved in an apparently zero-sum conflict, such as a single buyer and a single seller of a commodity. The two themes combine in the Commission's case for increased commodity *processing* in the South – raising at once its capacity to import sophisticated Northern exports, and (because value added in processing is more stable than in the raw commodity) the predictability of the South's export receipts.

What of 'raw commodities'? The Commission appreciates that commodity price stabilization may destabilize earnings if it is supply, rather than demand, that fluctuates,[13] that receipts from stabilization funds should often be used to diversify production out of Third World commodities, not to increase their supplies and thus cut their prices; and that many important commodities are produced mainly in rich countries. Nevertheless, Brandt blesses both international commodity agreements for price stabilization (mainly under the auspices of UNCTAD's new Commodity Fund) and expanded compensatory financing by IMF. This complex mixture [14] involves effects – on stability and output, in North and South – that cry out for systematic economic analysis.

Clearly, however, the Commission is right to stress that the reduction of risk can benefit North and South alike. This implies longer-term automatic programming of trade, of aid, and of private investors' obligations and rights. It is noteworthy that radically risk-reducing policies on private investment in developing countries drew the united support of Commissioners ranging from Mr Peterson (a distinguished Republican banker and businessman, ex-Secretary of Commerce and aid expert) and Mr Heath, to socialists such as Mr Jamal (Tanzania's Minister of Finance and Planning) and Mr Yaker (Algeria's Ambassador to the USSR and ex-Minister of Commerce). One might disagree about whether particular proposals, such as more stable exchange-rates, would in fact reduce uncertainty; but nobody can doubt the massive, trans-ideological interest in such reduction revealed in this Report. What follow-up action will there be?

Arms, food, energy

The Pearson Report was rightly criticized for excessive concentration on aid. The Brandt Report will be criticized for scattering its fire all over an (admittedly vast) target. I have considered a few major issues around its central theme of joint North-South planning for joint interest. But in three other areas the Report's sub-title, 'A Programme for Survival', has special force: arms, food and energy.

The stress on ambitious but generalized *disarmament* proposals, or rather appeals, is in itself fully justified but in context probably mistaken. North-South relations are hard enough to turn to joint advantage, without saddling them with East-West issues also. Instead, a systematic analysis of how arms-control proposals – for example affecting India and Pakistan; or Algeria, Morocco and Mauretania – might reduce both death and waste in particular Third World arenas, and of how developed country actions would have to change in such a context, would have been useful.

Adequate *food* for the world's poorest people is *the* survival issue. It depends mainly on their command over income from, and rights in, land; and on technologies to enable them to exploit it. Aid can help, in conjunction with redirected domestic development efforts, if it is made available (a) to compensate losers from drastic, redistributive land reform; and (b) for massive 'research and development' on improved water management for users at the tail-end of irrigation canals, and on crop improvement and water control in unirrigated areas. The Commission hints at such proposals, but does not develop them. They do not depend mainly on common interest. They are needed because near-starvation, cheaply preventable, in a rich world is wicked.

Present trends in *energy* use and discovery, if continued for 25-40 years, will impose upon the West's present life-style adjustments so drastic as to carry risks of disastrous responses, economic or military. The Commission points out that 'drilling density in prospective oil areas in industrialized countries is about forty times that in those of the oil-importing developing countries' (Ch.10, p.164). It strongly argues, in the common interest, for much greater stress on prospecting in the South. Who could quarrel? Who will act?

And then what happened?

Academics can, and will, pick endless nits out of the Brandt Report.[15] However, Brandt has got the essentials right. The probable alternative is dwindling North-South flows of trade and capital, leading to chronic slumpflation in the world economy. This will not be cured by chanting the monetarist mantras, whether at poor countries stricken by bad harvests and oil price explosions, or nearer home.

What is now essential is sustained follow-up on implementation, and in some cases analytical deepening, of the major, linked proposals on aid, tri-cycling, trade, reduction of uncertainty, food and energy. Will the essential happen? Already the West's treasuries murmur about simplistic proposals, about realism; and they return to reinforcing one another in OPEC-assisted cost-inflation and IMF-assisted demand-deflation alike. The South could indeed be the catalyst that changes the reaction, among Northern and OPEC countries, for the better. If Brandt is unimaginatively shelved, it is more likely that major defaults, starting in the South, will catalyse the Northern OPEC 'world system' in a different way entirely. And monetarist Tweedledum, protectionist Tweedledee, and 'realist' Scrooge will all be eaten by the Monstrous Crow; and serve them right. But us? And the wretched of the earth?

References

1.   S. Griffith Jones. 'The Growth of Multinational Banking, the Euro currency Market, and the Effect on Developing Countries', *Journal of Development Studies*, 16(2), Jan. 1980.

2.   D. Geldenhuys, *Money and Banking*, McGraw Hill, 1975, pp. 10-11; see also A.C.L. Day, *Outline of Monetary Economics*, Oxford, 1957, pp. 130-1.

3.   G. Papanek, Aid, Foreign Private Investment, Savings and Growth in LDCs', *Journal of Political Economy*, 81(1), 1973; see also Lipton, *op cit.*, pp. 159-68. This '10 per cent' figure compares with the 15 per cent of developing countries investment that was financed externally in the 1960s: L. Pearson *et al.*, *Partners in Development* (London: Pall Mall, 1969), p. 30.

4.   C. H. Hanumantha Rao, *Technological Change and Distribution of Gains in Indian Agriculture (Delbi: Macmillan, 1975), esp. p.8.*

5.   M. Ahluwahlia, 'Rural poverty and agriculture performance in India', *Development Studies*, 14 (3), April 1976.

6.   This is the main remit of the International Fund for Agricultural Development, rightly praised by the Commission; it is, however, essential for this Fund to develop field representation. Its present Charter compels it to rely for project preparation and evaluation on the services of other

agencies—chiefly the World Bank and regional banks—for which its priority will inevitably be low.

7.   M. Lipton, *Why Poor People Stay Poor* (London: Temple Smith, 1977), Ch. 8.

8.   Note that both comprise ways for the non-oil developed North to convert an unmanageable financial (current-account balance) problem, into a perfectly manageable real problem: a 1·3 per cent GNP reduction spread over a period of years.

9.   Even at new and more realistic prices, at least if the North conserves energy.

10.   Such a chapter would have four sections: loans from private sector to private sector, from private to public; from public to private; and from public to public. The first section will not be the longest. Intermediation by 'the banking system' ought to be a footnote only—either because it is smooth and sensible, or else because it is replaced by direct transactions.

11.   As usual, these familiar arguments lose force, for want of clear proposals as to how the gainers are to compensate those particular workers who do lose their jobs when imports increase. This is where 'taxes on foreign trade', skimming off some of the consumers' benefits from cheap Third World imports to re-employ or compensate, e.g. the Western shoe producers, make most sense.

12.   'People of the same trade seldom meet together, even for merriment and diversion, but the conversation ends in a conspiracy against the public, or in some contrivance to raise prices.' Adam Smith, *An Inquiry into the Nature and Causes of of the Wealth of Nations* (Oxford University Press, 1976 edn., edited by R. H. Campbell, A. S. Skinner and W. B. Tobb), Vol. 1, p. 145.

13.   Without stabilisation falls in supply (e.g. for climatic reasons) can be compensated by rises in price, and *vice versa*: M. Lipton, 'Farm Price Stabilisation in Underdeveloped Agricultures: some effects on income stability and income distribution', in P. P. Streeten, ed., *Unfashionable Economics: Essays in Honour of Lord Balogh* (London: Weidenfield and Nicolson, 1970).

14.   It is especially complex alongside STABEX, which is confined to some African, Caribbean and Pacific exports to the EEC.

15.   For example, its presentation is often unfortunate, as with Herr Brandt's own "I" intensive and sentimental introduction; the gaps in the evidence on such matters as the effect of aid; and the frequent lapses into Unctalk.

TWO

MUTUAL INTERESTS:
THE 'PRAGMATIC' APPROACH

MARGARET THATCHER*

The greatest contribution which the industrialized countries can make is to restore a buoyant rate of growth in their economies, and then to enlarge the markets which they offer to developing countries.

The Report of the Commission chaired by Herr Brandt has highlighted one of the critical challenges facing us in the last two decades of the century – the need for joint action with developing countries to overcome the massive economic problems they face, and to try to end worldwide poverty.

At the time of writing, the world faces immediate and unpredictable dangers to its oil supplies as a result of the conflict between Iran and Iraq. This conflict, which we earnestly hope will soon be over, has underlined the fragility of the world's oil supplies and the degree of interdependence that has developed over the years. It strengthens the case for paying the most serious attention to the long-term issues addressed in the Report.

The great disparities in wealth between the nations at the top and bottom ends of the spectrum of national prosperity are contrary to the concepts of human dignity which underlie our own European civilization. It is morally right that those who can should help the poorer countries to help themselves. The Report is a valuable contribution to the debate, especially in its scope and vision. The unanimous findings of the eighteen distinguished persons who made up the Commission must command the attention of governments and public opinion alike.

The Report rightly stresses that vast numbers of people still live in poverty, are exposed to hunger, disease and homelessness and are almost helpless in the face of natural disasters. According to the World Bank, 800 million people still live in absolute poverty – one in five of the inhabitants of the world. The problems at the roots of this appalling

* Prime Minister of the United Kingdom

situation must be tackled urgently and effectively.

The economic outlook for the world is disquieting and it is the poorest who are likely to suffer most. Their problems are compounded by increased oil prices and rising debts. These difficulties threaten to mullify the advances which have been achieved over the last 30 years. I agree with the Report that this is not acceptable. We must find a way through the impending problems and difficulties. If, in the words of the World Bank's latest Report, we do not achieve renewed growth 'hundreds of millions of very poor people will live and die with little or no improvement in their lot'.

Success in tackling these problems would benefit all. The problems of the poor are not solved at the expense of the rich. Every country, whatever its level of development, will benefit from a stronger world economy and from a successful fight against poverty.

The British Government believe that the action necessary to resume progress towards prosperity must be based on a careful assessment of the realities. It is no longer realistic to speak of rich industrial countries and poor Third World countries; there are marked degrees of poverty and of prosperity within both Worlds, and they are not determined by geography. The term 'North-South', implying as it does a simple division of needs and interests, is an inadequate and often misleading description of the complex inter-relationship that now exists between countries in a wide variety of economic circumstances.

The world is already closely bound together by a network of economic and commercial links. The developed countries of the OECD have long relied on developing countries for supplies of raw materials and are increasingly absorbing their exports of manufactured goods. We in turn need markets in the developing world to sell our own products. The oil-producing countries depend on us for their markets and for supplies of capital goods. The developing countries without oil depend on oil producers and on industrialized countries for their oil supplies, for aid and other financial flows, for markets for their exports and for capital goods and other imports to support their development programmes.

This interdependence also requires political stability. Poverty may seldom be the direct cause of war. But economic difficulties can lead to restlessness and mistrust between and within countries. Moreover the poor are extremely vulnerable to the effects of political upheaval. We have seen this in the famine in Africa and in the plight of refugees in several countries in Asia.

As we enter the 1980's, we need to be clear about the contribution which each country can make to achieving a more prosperous world and to averting the difficulties which the Brandt Commission foresee. We also need to ensure that the economic system can adapt and operate efficiently for the benefit of all.

The greatest contribution which the industrialized countries can make is to restore a buoyant rate of growth in their economies, and then to enlarge the markets which they offer to developing countries. Growth cannot resume until inflation has been brought under control; otherwise government measures to stimulate growth will be dissipated in higher prices instead of going to increase production and expand markets. Persistent inflation in developed countries may hurt the developing world if it shifts the terms of trade against the latter; and if, by unsettling exchange rates, it discourages investment and trade. The fight against inflation must therefore be the first priority for industrialized countries. But while we thus prepare our economies for renewed growth, we must continue to resist pressures for protectionist measures. We must keep our markets as open as we can to the products of the developing world.

The industrialized world must also encourage private investment in development. Private financial flows already provide the bulk of the financing needs of middle-income developing countries. The financial markets will continue to be of major importance in recycling the oil producer surpluses. Private investment, as the Report itself recognizes, brings great benefits to developing countries in terms of technology, training and management expertise. Britain, like the Federal Republic of Germany, believes in the open economy. We have eliminated exchange controls, freeing the flow of investment to developing countries. Our tax structure does not obstruct companies investing abroad and our double taxation arrangements are generous and helpful to private capital flows. Of course developing countries themselves must play their part by creating conditions, political and economic, that encourage such investment.

The governments of the industrialized world must of course continue to provide official aid, especially to the poorest countries, which are particularly vulnerable to world trading conditions and generally lack credit-worthiness. For 17 of the poorest countries, Britain has already converted aid loans to grants or provided equivalent help providing relief worth more than $2 billion over the next 20 years. Our aid programme is the fifth largest among industrialized countries and the seventh largest on the basis of percentage of GNP. We hope that, when the British economy is restored to health, our aid will increase again. Meanwhile, it is essential that aid receipts are used in as effective a way as possible and in this context the domestic policies of recipient countries are of special importance.

A fourth contribution must lie in the field of energy policy. Our countries must do more to conserve energy, to develop new sources. Our aim must be to use less energy to achieve a given rate of economic growth. Progress in this field is critical to the medium-term prospects for growth in the industrialized world.

The oil-producing developing countries have acquired new opportunities and new responsibilities. Not only have there been substantial price increases, but there is an expectation that the oil price will remain high and may rise further. The price increases have been damaging to all countries, and especially to the poorer countries. The oil-producing countries have a heavy responsibility to avoid sudden changes in the oil price; this is as much in their longer term interest as it is the interest of the rest of the world.

A number of countries now enjoy massive financial surpluses. Those surpluses are likely to persist. The countries with surpluses have the ability to help oil-importing developing countries which cannot adequately meet their needs from other sources. Such assistance would contribute to easing the strains on the financial system that could arise from the continuation of these massive surpluses. I hope that the oil producers, recognizing their own interest in financial stability, will give the most serious consideration to these matters.

Among a third group of countries – the developing countries which do not export oil – circumstances vary widely. Many middle-income countries, notably in South-East Asia and South and Central America, made impressive advances during the 1970's. But their success may be put at risk by the slow-down in world growth. There is a need to ensure that, where they pursue appropriate domestic policies, they are able to obtain sufficient financial support, whether from the capital markets or from international institutions as well as from the growing markets for their manufactures.

Within this same group, however, many countries remain at very low levels of income. Their progress in the 1970's has been slow and the future outlook is uncertain. They need the assistance of all members of the international community, particularly as regards support for their agricultural development; the building up of their domestic energy resources; and external finance in the form of official aid – three areas rightly singled out in the Report.

If each country is to contribute effectively to world development, the economic system must work efficiently. Some would argue that the existing system needs to undergo wholesale reform. I would rather rely on continuing the constant adaptation of the existing system. Under it the developing countries have probably made in the last 30 years greater advances than in all the years that went before. Even in the last five years we have seen a major liberalization of world trade through the GATT; the extension of the European Community's Lomé Convention to 58 countries, including many of the poorest; new and expanded facilities in the IMF to benefit developing countries; agreement to double the capital of the World Bank to $80 billion and to provide an extra $12 billion to the IDA (to which Britain will contribute 10 per cent); and agreement on the creation of a Common Fund for commodities.

I do not believe that wholesale changes in the system would help it to cope better with the demands of present economic circumstances. Indeed, there is a danger that this kind of approach could leave the world without effective institutions at a time when it will particularly need them to work well.

Much international debate lies before us, in the United Nations and elsewhere. We in Britain were disappointed at the outcome of the recent Special Session of the General Assembly. In common with the United States and the Federal Republic of Germany, we were unable to accept certain proposals about procedures for the Global Negotiations. We considered that there was inadequate recognition in these proposals of the integrity and independence of the specialized agencies, such as the IMF and World Bank. However, discussions will continue during the current General Assembly. We will be working for the successful launch of the Global Negotiations.

The Brandt Commission themselves expressed doubts about the effectiveness of some recent multilateral discussions. They proposed a limited world summit to provide a new focus and a new impetus for future negotiations. This is an interesting and potentially worthwhile proposal. With careful preparation, such a conference could help to chart the way forward. But we must not underestimate the scale of the tasks before us. Attitudes and interests differ very widely; the problems are inter-related and extremely complex.

There is a great deal in the Brandt Commission's Report with which the British Government agree. The Report has performed a valuable service in bringing together so many vital problems. It has had a major impact on public opinion. We are all agreed that the world has become increasingly interdependent. I have outlined ways in which the industrialized countries can contribute to the solution of present difficulties – through the restoration of health to their economies; through trade, aid and private investment; and through measures to conserve energy. Others too can reasonably be expected to play their part – the poorer developing countries in their own domestic policies, and the oil-exporting developing countries by working for assured supplies of oil at reasonable prices and by allowing some of their financial surpluses to be used for the benefit of those in need. Action on these lines will allow the world economy to make real advances. Such progress is both essential and urgent if we are to avoid the dire prospects described in the Brandt Commission's Report.

HELMUT SCHMIDT*

... we must ... make it clear that ... it would be a mistake to assume that the Western industrial countries alone, whether by their development aid measures or even by fundamental changes in the world economic order, might be able to decisively change the developing countries' economic destiny.

The Independent Commission on International Development Issues under the chairmanship of Willy Brandt has made the general public all over the world aware of the fact that the development of North-South relations is one of the key issues determining the future of us all.

The Commission's Report was timely in that it was published at the beginning of the Third Development Decade and prior to the global negotiations on North-South relations. Moreover, the Report was published at the beginning of a problematic decade at a time when worldwide political and economic tensions and crises are shaking the foundations of international cooperation. As recognized in the Franco-German declaration of February 1981, the solution to fundamental and worldwide problems such as poverty, hunger, underdevelopment, and economic and monetary instability is anchored in the principle of equality of responsibility. All countries of the world must assume a share of the responsibility for working towards stable and effective international

* Chancellor, Federal Republic of Germany

cooperation, the independence and autonomy of nations and states, and an improvement of the international order, one whereby all peoples are guaranteed security, prospects of progress and recognition of their dignity and liberty.

International security and stability do not depend alone on a military equilibrium which, although necessary, is by no means their one and only criterion. Security and stability also call for control over ever more acute global problems such as the population explosion, economic and social disparities, mass poverty, balance of payments problems, and the disruption of the ecosystem. The economic and social development of the Third World countries is a safeguard for the long-term maintenance of peace. It is with good reason that the Commission makes mutual interest in mankind's survival the central element of its Report. No substantial convergence of the standards of living will be achieved in the near future, and there is no sense in closing one's eyes to this reality. What is possible, however, is to make some advances in development. A number of developing countries already find themselves on the threshold of industrialization; yet in most of the developing countries, the economic and social situation has worsened. The still virtually inexorable population explosion, together with the twofold explosion of oil prices and the subsequent burden which this inflicted on the world economy, have destroyed many hopes for economic development and a standard of living which is commensurate with human dignity. The sense of solidarity among all those who might be able to help is now challenged to a greater extent than ever before.

The Federal Republic of Germany has responded to this challenge and accepted its responsibility. It has considerably increased its efforts during the past years: in terms of the volume of its assistance, the Federal Republic now ranks with France as the second largest donor of development aid in the world.

However, we must also make it clear that, taking the world as it is today, it would be a mistake to assume that the western industrial countries alone, whether by their development aid measures or even by fundamental changes in the world economic order, might be able decisively to change the developing countries' economic destiny. No country on earth, that is to say, neither the developing countries themselves nor the state-trading countries of Eastern Europe, nor, in particular, the oil-producing countries can disavow their joint responsibility in this respect. All countries should join together in furthering economic cooperation at worldwide level in its manifold forms, in a spirit of pragmatism, without incurring any system breaks, and in such a way that the procedures and institutions which have proved their worth are left intact.

From the experience gained in the past we know that the governmental transfer of resources from the industrialized to the developing countries can render nothing more than a comparatively modest contribution towards the development of the poorer countries. Private investment, representing at the same time the most effective instrument for the transfer of technology, is also a factor of importance in this connection. It presupposes the creation of a good investment climate, supplemented by the increasing integration of the developing countries into international trade relations. Decisive, however, in this respect are the efforts made by the developing countries themselves. In their hands rests the principal responsibility as to whether efficient use is made of the external aid and whether reinforcement and support is forthcoming for the forces which ultimately allow the countries to become economically self-reliant. Development aid can never be more than help towards self-help.

I therefore fully endorse the Commission's demand that economic and social reforms be undertaken by the developing countries themselves. They must create the preconditions for the maximal integration of their populations into the development process and for the exhaustive use of their societies' productive forces. We, for our part, should refrain from considering national reforms to be merely a complementary factor and recognize that the establishment of development-promoting structures and the removal of the obstacles to development in these countries are imperative if the contribution rendered by the international community is to be optimal in its impact and of benefit to those whose need is greatest.

Such internal obstacles to development often include the national economic policy, the distribution of income and wealth, the tax and land tenure systems, the public administration, extensive expenditure for military purposes and, in nearly all cases, excessive population growth.

However, nobody is able to relieve the developing countries of their responsibility for their population policy. According to World Bank estimates, by the year 2000 the populations of the developing countries alone will have increased to nearly five billions and that of the world as a whole to six billions. This we must consider to be the greatest challenge of our times and the most acute problem for the developing countries themselves. The population explosion, in addition to endangering the reliability of food supplies and employment, entails an urbanization process with its own unsolvable problems. Experience has shown that an efficient family planning policy can result in a decline in the birth rates, and although family planning is certainly not intended to replace the development effort, in the long term it can contribute towards the latter's success.

Initiative and self-reliance also assume a special function as regards food supplies in the developing countries. The Commission quite rightly stresses that more extensive investment, better cultivation methods, and increased help from outside alone cannot bring about any decisive improvement in the food supply situation in these countries, where in many cases structural factors represent a decisive barrier to progress in this direction. Many governments do not yet give adequate consideration to rural and agricultural development in their countries. National price and subsidy policies operate to the benefit of the urban consumer only. Producer prices are often held so low that they fail to offer any incentive for the producer to increase his production above subsistence level. The postponement of agro-structural reforms, particularly those relating to the land tenure system, must be counted among the essential causes of the unremitting rural exodus and the inadequacies of the food supply situation.

Here, too, nobody can relieve the developing countries of their responsibility. Countries undertaking serious efforts to overcome internal obstacles by way of structural reforms should be able to count on our assistance in their work.

A large part of the Commission's Report is devoted to the problems of the world economy. It suggests a multitude of concrete solutions to often extremely complex problems which have been the subject of international discussion for many years. In this context I wish to mention just one area in which events have spiralled dramatically and which has assumed a vital importance for the economic development of the Third World countries, namely, the problem of energy supply. Its importance is vital in the very sense of the word: the developing countries are forced to spend an ever larger part of their foreign currency reserves on financing their oil imports. The funds thus deployed are then lacking for the procurement of other imports essential to these countries' efforts to improve their economic efficiency, satisfy basic needs, and combat hunger, thirst, and disease.

Estimates compiled by the International Monetary Fund reveal that the trade balance deficit of the oil-importing developing countries will increase from $US 62 billions in 1980 to approximately $US 69 billions in 1981. The development aid rendered by the industrial countries in 1980 was not sufficient to cover even the current increase in the developing countries' oil import bills: whereas the 1979-1980 increase amounted to $US 23.7 billions the aggregate sum of the development aid of the western industrial countries in 1980 amounted to only $US 23.5 billions. That development aid contributions are unable to cope with problems of such dimensions is self-evident.

It is here that the OPEC countries with their annual trade

balance surplus of from $US 100 to 120 billions should be asked to step in. It is up to them, by the way of more credit and larger subsidies, to support the oil-importing developing countries, 80 per cent of whose commercial energy consumption is accounted for by oil and whose economies depend on a continual inflow of oil. And they should also step in with oil delivered on special terms. I welcome the decision of Mexico and Venezuela to grant the oil-importing developing countries of South and Central America favourable terms of payment for their purchases of oil. This is a step in the right direction. However, a still outstanding yet essential step is that of investing the oil revenue surpluses in the developing countries, thereby benefiting the development of the world as a whole.

There is an urgent need for the oil-exporting and oil-importing countries to reach agreement on the vital problems of energy supply. Abrupt and drastic increases in oil prices asphyxiate the growth of the world economy to the detriment of all. The focal point of the negotiations preceding such agreement should be forecasts on the future development of energy supply and energy demand, this in the interest of achieving the stability of price development and energy supply which the Commission quite rightly called for.

At the same time, however, industrial and developing countries alike should seek steadily to reduce their high dependence on oil and initiate a smooth transition to relying on other energy resources to cover an increasing part of their energy requirements. In their efforts to overcome the problem of adaptation which this transition will entail, the developing countries will have to rely not only on extensive bilateral help from the industrial countries but also on aid from multilateral finance institutions, in particular the World Bank. In this connection we Germans have repeatedly declared our readiness to cooperate. But here, too, it is essential that the developing countries are ready to undertake efforts of their own.

A further decisive aspect is the integration of the developing countries into the framework of the international division of labour. However, such integration confronts the industrial countries with structural adaptation problems which cannot be solved overnight. This fact has to be taken into consideration by the developing countries as well. The Federal Republic of Germany has persistently objected to a policy of protectionism. We are aware that unimpaired world trade is one of the most essential factors for economic growth and that it is advantageous to all countries. Our objective should be to enable the developing countries ultimately to procure for themselves the required foreign currency reserves via the export of their goods and services.

These problems reveal that all countries and groups of countries should take an interest in bringing about a well-functioning world economy, since, in the last analysis, no country is able to succeed in procuring massive advantages to the detriment of others without endangering the overall system. The merit of the North-South Commission is that it set up a new yardstick for the discussion of these problems in terms of commitment, detail, and constructiveness. The future international debate on development problems cannot fail to take the Commission's Report into consideration. Indeed, the German Federal Government adopted a great number of the Commission's recommendations in its new Development Policy Guidelines approved on 9 July 1980. And the heads of state and government of the major western industrial states deliberated on the conclusions of the Report on the occasion of their summit convened in Venice in 1980.

I share the Commission's conviction that the various peoples and their governments – irrespective of the divergence evident in their respective points of departure and interests – are well able to solve the problems ahead by contructively planning their common future. The Report of the Commission is an impressive political appeal to the world community's ability to learn and readiness to reach agreement.

C. FRED BERGSTEN

. . . the present international economic system is so flexible, and demonstrably responsive to the legitimate needs of the developing countries, that they as well as the industrialized countries have a critical stake in preserving many of its fundamental tenets while giving it the time needed to adopt some of the features encompassed in their concept of a 'New International Economic Order'.

The Objectives of the Exercise

The basic strategy of the developing countries is to maintain maximum pressure on the industrialized countries to increase the transfer of resources and power from North to South.[1] This strategy, although it has not achieved everything sought by the developing countries, has been increasingly successful over the past five years.[2] Indeed, the cumulative effects of the reforms negotiated over that period at least begin to institute the 'New International Economic Order' sought by the developing countries: a dramatic increase in IMF lending to the poorer nations and major changes in the terms thereof, a substantial liberalization of imports by industrialized from developing countries, institution of a set of international commodity agreements and a Common Fund, and a major expansion in public transfers – primarily through the multilateral development banks, in which the developing countries share management responsibility with the donor nations.

The basic strategy of the industrialized countries in this policy area is to extend as much help to the poorer nations as will promote real development and is compatible with their own economic and political interests – which is a substantial amount of help, in view of the importance of the developing countries to both world economic growth and world peace. However, domestic political constraints in most industrialized countries, particularly the United States, place limits on what can be achieved in practical

* USA. Senior associate of the Carnegie Endowment for International Peace in Washington. Assistant Secretary of the U.S. Treasury under the Carter Administration. Former Assistant for international economic affairs in the U.S. National Security Council. Author of several books on U.S. international economic relations.

terms. Part of this constraint stems from scepticism that many of the proposals for resource and power transfers will make much contribution to real development, particularly of those within the developing countries who need it most. Sustained progress can result only from steps which are politically 'saleable' to the public, and their parliamentary representatives, in those nations. Such steps must clearly promote development and offer understandable benefits to the donor countries as well.

The Report of the Brandt Commission should thus be judged primarily by whether it provides a basis for increased political support in the industrialized countries for transfers to the developing countries, by persuasively advocating measures which provide real support for development – whether via old methods or new – and demonstrating their worth for all countries participating in the process. The Report should be viewed largely as a political document which seeks to advance the needs of the developing countries in ways which are at least potentially acceptable to the industrialized countries.

Seen in this light, the Report makes a number of false starts. Some of its efforts at intellectual innovation, such as the creation of a new World Development Fund to make unconditional balance-of-payment loans under greater control of the recipient countries, are unrealistic and thus unhelpful; in fact, it proposes the creation of at least four new international institutions whereas the immediate task is to assure needed funding for existing institutions. For the sake of its own credibility, the Report contains far too many intellectual contradictions: the alleged necessity of resource transfers to the South to boost demand for production in the North, whereas domestic stimulus within the industrialized countries themselves would of course be at least as effective (and no more inflationary); enhancing the international monetary role of Special Drawing Rights but distributing them (to developing countries) on non-monetary criteria; creating 'international fair labor standards' which would almost certainly push LDC wages to a level incompatible with the increased share of world output advocated for those countries. The Report also falls victim to major political contradictions, such as calling for both increased resource transfers from the North and further sharp increases in political control for the South.

The Report, however, makes one major positive contribution to the North-South effort. Its focus on the concept of joint gains, for both industrialized and developing countries, builds in an evolutionary way on the record of the past five years and helps lay an encouraging base for further progress in the future.[3] By applying that concept to the energy issue, which is by far the most important barrier of at least the current decade both to development prospects in the poorer countries and to the ability of the richer countries to respond constructively, it proposes a critically important focal point for North-South relations in the years ahead.

The Recent Record

It is necessary to review the results of the past decade of negotiations between industrialized and developing nations to explain this viewpoint. It seems to me that three basic lessons emerge from that period:

pragmatic progress in improving economic relations between industrialized and developing countries is eminently possible wherever the principle of joint gains is clearly present, whereas only stalemate can result from efforts which ignore that principle;

such progress can best – perhaps only – be achieved through functionally specific economic institutions (such as the IMF, World Bank, GATT and occasionally UNCTAD) rather than overarching political institutions (such as the United Nations, the Conference on International Economic Cooperation of 1976-77, or the 'North-South Summit' proposed in the Report); and

the present international economic system is so flexible, and demonstrably responsive to the legitimate needs of the developing countries, that they as well as the industrialized countries have a critical stake in preserving many of its fundamental tenets while giving it the time needed to adopt some of the features encompassed in their concept of a 'New International Economic Order.'

I believe that such conclusions flow from an analysis of recent events in the areas of trade, energy, food, the monetary system, aid and commodities.

Trade is probably the most important aspect of international economic relations for most developing countries, particularly those at a more advanced stage of development. Their greatest need is assured market access, and their record in taking advantage of the relatively open markets in the industrialized world is truly impressive. The volume of manufactured exports of the LDCs as a group has been growing at an average annual rate of over 10 per cent since 1963, and the rate has been far higher for many of the more advanced nations in the group.

As a result of the Multilateral Trade Negotiations (MTN) completed in 1979, the market access of the developing countries will expand further. The major industrialized countries will reduce their industrial tariffs by 33 per cent on a weighted average basis. A 25 per cent cut in developed country tariffs will be made on items of traditional export interest to LDCs. U.S. tariff cuts on LDC products, excluding textiles and apparel, average about 35 per cent.

New non-tariff codes on subsidies, government procurement, standards, import licensing and customs valuation will provide a more open and stable environment for future trade growth for all nations. The procurement code alone will open over $30 billions of trade to eligible countries. The agreements also provide a permanent legal basis for special and more favourable treatment of developing countries, accompanied by more liberal rules on trade measures taken by LDCs for development purposes.

The MTN agreements did not achieve everything that the developing countries sought – or that the United States sought, for that matter. However, they represent a major trade liberalization within a difficult world economic environment and thus a major step forward in North-South relations. They were also of great importance in helping participating countries resist protectionist pressures which might otherwise have actually retarded opportunities for LDC exports.

As pointed out by the Brandt Commission, trade

provides a clear example of mutual benefits for industrialized and developing countries alike. Exports to developing countries are an important generator of investment, production, employment and income in industrialized countries. For the United States, for example, the LDCs are by far the fastest growing export market – in the non-oil LDCs alone, U.S. sales tripled from $16 billions in 1973 to $48 billions in 1979. At the same time, expanded imports from developing (and other) countries help dampen inflation and encourage competition and, hence, productivity in the United States. The overstatement by the Commission of the impact of LDC economic development on the industrialized countries should not be permitted to obscure the very real importance thereof.

Despite the fact that the United States accounts for less than 35 per cent of the combined GNP of the industrial countries, it took more than 52 per cent of developing country manufactured exports to all industrial countries in 1978. Nearly 22 per cent of all U.S. manufactures imports in 1978 came from developing countries; the corresponding figure for the other industrial countries was less than 5 per cent. U.S. economic growth after the global recession of 1975 was particularly beneficial to the non-oil LDCs, whose exports grew much faster to the U.S. market than to either Japan or the European Community. The results of the MTN will substantially accelerate these trends.

As already noted, the costs and insecure supply of **energy** will probably remain the single most important constraint on development in the poorer countries for the foreseeable future. To help expand their indigenous sources of energy supply, the World Bank now plans to support oil and gas projects which, combined with private and government financing, will total more than $33 billions over the next five years. The Bank hopes to double this amount if sufficient financing can be arranged, in effect implementing the Brandt Commission proposal for a new energy exploration facility (and more). The present programme alone should ultimately provide an additional 2·5 million barrels of oil equivalent a day to the world market. Within the United States, the Overseas Private

Investment Corporation (OPIC) has established political risk insurance for oil exploration, production and development in developing countries, with significant results already.

These multilateral and bilateral efforts will help reduce the dependence of developing countries on expensive oil imports. At the same time, they can significantly improve the world energy balance. This is another clear example of mutual benefit to industrialized and developing countries alike. However, as the Commission rightly points out, much more can and should be done – a topic to which I will return.

Food production is another critical development target where much progress has been made. A $1 billion International Fund for Agricultural Development (IFAD) was created in 1976 and is currently in the process of being replenished. The United States alone has pledged 4·5 million tons of food aid annually under the international Food Aid Convention, nearly half of the Convention's 10 million ton target. U.S. farmers, acting on government incentives, placed 35 million tons of grain in reserve during 1977-78; the value of this reserve was demonstrated in 1979 when 14 million tons were released into the market in response to rising world demand. By ending the set-aside programme in agriculture, the United States has also helped provide more food for the world and more markets for its farmers – another manifestation of the concept of joint gains.

The multilateral development banks have developed effective food production strategies. Over the past five years, the World Bank's total lending commitments for food production equalled $11.6 billions – one-third of its total lending. The Bank expects to finance projects in the 1980's which will contribute approximately one-fifth of the increase in total food production in its developing member countries.

In the wake of the oil price increases of 1979-80, the **International Monetary Fund** has expanded its financing activities enormously – particularly for developing countries. In 1980, it committed more than $6 billions to LDCs compared with under $3 billions in 1979, which was in turn far more than had ever been extended in a previous year; the 1980 figure will probably double again in 1981. The Fund has greatly expanded the resources it can devote to this effort through creating the Supplementary Financing Facility ($10 billions), two recent quota increases ($10 billions and $20 billions) and the current plans to borrow $8-10 billions annually from governments and/or the private markets.

On the qualitative side, member countries can now in some cases obtain financing which exceeds 600 per cent of their greatly augmented quotas. Moreover, economic adjustment programs can now be implemented over a three-year period compared with the one-year programs normally required in the past – and frequently include supply-side considerations as well as the more traditional demand restraints. The maturity dates on some IMF loans have been extended to 7-10 years, compared with the traditional 3-5 year repayment periods. The IMF will also subsidize the interest cost on Supplementary Financing drawings for low income countries. As far as decision-making is concerned, developing countries now hold more than one-half the Executive Director seats and almost 40 per cent of the weighted votes.

During the past four years, the member countries of the **Multilateral Development Banks (MDBs)** agreed to replenish the funds of these institutions by over $80 billions. This includes $40 billions for the World Bank, about $20 billions for IDA and $10 billions for the Inter-American Development Bank. When these figures are added to the increased funding just cited for the IMF, virtually all of which is now being channeled to developing countries, it becomes clear that the industrialized countries have agreed to provide over $100 billions in additional finance through these institutions alone during the past three years.

Qualitatively, as already noted, the MDBs are making a major contribution to solving the world food problem and have begun a major effort to expand energy production in the developing countries. The World Bank has also instituted a program of structural adjustment lending, the provision of non-project loans linked to recipient countries' adjustment to the new world economic/energy environment. Active discussion has also commenced on altering the so-called gearing ratio, as proposed by the Brandt Commission, which could double again (or more) the lending capacity of the World Bank.

Commodity policy is the area which perhaps exhibits most dramatically the opportunity for North-South programs based on similar perceptions of joint gain, as well as for hostility over opposing sets of principles.

Prior to 1975, the industrialized countries – led by the United States – were unwilling even to discuss commodity issues, regarding all governmental intervention to these markets as anathema. For their part, the developing countries sought to transfer resources from importing to exporting countries (for products which *they* exported) via artificial price-propping and a multi-billion dollar common fund which would finance such activities. This dialogue of the deaf was one of the major sources of North-South tension at the time.

Beginning in late 1975, however, both sides began to change their attitudes. They decided there would be merit in trying to stabilize some primary product markets via the negotiation of individual commodity agreements, to reduce inflation and enhance reliability of markets for all countries.[4] As a result, a wide ranging set of international commodity arrangements was put into place or substantially expanded in just five years:

The United States joined the International Tin Agreement in 1976, and began to contribute to its buffer stock financing in 1978.

An International Sugar Agreement was instituted in 1979.

The United States joined the International Coffee Agreement in 1976, and the Agreement was renegotiated in 1979.

Active discussions were held on a possible international copper agreement.

The International Cocoa Agreement was renewed in 1980, though without U.S. participation because of disagreement over several of its provisions.

The World Bank commenced a major program of lending for non-fuel minerals production.

A Common Fund to enhance the financial capability of individual commodity arrangements was agreed in 1980.

These results suggest that constructive progress is possible even in areas where past differences have been acute, once the principle of joint gains is adopted by all major participants.

In all of the areas cited, the actual results were negotiated in the specific institutional forum responsible for the particular issue – the GATT, the World Bank or a regional development bank, the World Food Conference, the IMF or UNCTAD. Beyond the specific elements of negotiated progress, the basic resilience of the international economic system in the face of unprecedented shocks – two energy crises, the deepest recession since the 1930's, widespread double-digit inflation, huge payments imbalances – has been of inestimable importance for the developing countries. They would have been devastated by relapses into protectionism or competitive exchange-rate realignments or a drying up of private international capital flows, all of which occurred in earlier periods and were threatened in the 1970's. Systemic preservation has thus been of cardinal importance to the developing nations; its achievement has been of major benefit to them in the recent past, and must remain a major goal in the future.

Guidelines for the Future

The key issue for the future is how best to maintain the momentum of progress across all of these areas, which has been achieved during the recent past. This in turn raises the question of how to maintain domestic political support for such a process in the industrialized countries, and how to achieve sufficient patience on the part of the developing countries to accept steps which do not immediately fulfil all their aspirations.

Some of the proposals and rhetoric in the Brandt Commission Report are distinctly unhelpful in these regards. For example, reiteration of the tired (and intellectually barren) exhortation for the industrialized countries to allocate an arbitrary percentage of their economic products to concessional foreign assistance, and even to increase that ratio further by the end of the century, will stimulate only exasperation in most donor nations.[5] Proposals to create still more international lending institutions, such as a World Development Fund lending without conditions and controlled largely by the recipients, are even more counterproductive. The Report's failure to chastise the OPEC countries for the devastation they have wreaked on the poor, or the Communist countries for their callous disregard thereof, or the developing countries themselves for their many inadequate internal policies, badly taints any claim to moral (let alone intellectual) authority for the whole project.

The propagation of such views is not always costless. If they were to inflate expectations significantly, the developing countries might seriously seek to achieve them. When such efforts failed, as they inevitably would, one result might be increasingly strident rhetoric and a return to the harsh condemnation of the industrialized countries which characterized the early 1970's. This stridency, in turn, could actually *reduce* political support in the industrialized countries for sensible policies in support of LDC goals – such as those actually put into place over the past few years. In addition, the industrialized countries might actually give the developing countries the linkage they have always sought – perhaps conditioning such steps as World Bank capital increases and IDA replenishments on LDC compliance with specific DC demands. At worst, retrogression and deadlock in North-South affairs – as actually occurred in the early 1970's – could replace the sustained progress of the recent past. If it produced this chain of events, the Brandt Commission Report could thus set back North-South relations.

Fortunately, the Report does not seem to have had such an impact. To their credit, the developing countries have not dramatized the failure (at this writing) to launch a new set of so-called Global Negotiations in the United Nations – whose results could only be a great disappointment to them anyway, since pragmatic results are most unlikely to emerge from that forum. It seems most unlikely that the Report has had much effect on that or other recent North-South exercises, one way or the other.

What remains of the Report in practical terms, therefore, is an additional manifesto espousing the cause of the developing nations. It probably represents a marginal plus, in this sense, for two reasons: it adds to the general pressure for positive. response by the industrialized countries by enhancing recognition of their real problems, and it makes the major contribution of emphasizing joint gains with particular application in the energy area.

It is in the energy area, in fact, where the Report may provide some lasting benefit to North-South relations by suggesting a path for fundamental improvement in the world economic outlook.

The greatest external threat to development is prolonged world stagflation, in which markets for LDC exports (and capital inflows) do not grow sufficiently and which sours the climate in the industrialized countries for all varieties of help to the poor.[6] The greatest single cause of world stagflation, in turn, is the prolonged energy crisis. It is difficult to foresee a return to global economic stability and satisfactory growth, which are central to the prospects for development, without some meaningful stabilization of the world energy market.

It is difficult to envisage such stabilization in the immediate future, primarily because the oil-producing countries see no reason to commit themselves to supply and/or price stability. If business proceeds as usual, several more years may have to pass before the energy programmes of the oil-importing countries yield sufficient results to bring greater balance to the energy market itself – and thus to the bargaining positions of the exporting and importing groups of countries.

There is one basis, however, on which to proceed more quickly. As suggested by the Brandt Commission, it is the critical need of the developing countries for a return to stability in both the energy market and, through such a step, in the overall world economy. Indeed, energy is not a 'North-South' issue *per se*. It is a consummate question of global economic management. Its outcome will go far to determine the future of economic stability – and perhaps peace – of the world, particularly for the developing countries.

The Commission's 'emergency programme' for energy is thus truly an emergency issue. Moreover, it faithfully adheres to the principle of joint gains and makes eminent sense: assured levels of production by the exporters, stringent commitments on consumption by the importers, avoidance of 'sudden major increases in prices' set at levels which encourage both new production and conservation, major investment in LDC energy production. There can be no hiding the fact that the OPEC countries have savaged the developing countries with their massive price increases, and that the industrialized countries have contributed to the carnage with their excessive energy use. The Report slides too quickly over these key causes of the world's major development problem, but still points to the only viable solution – a producer-consumer accord to stabilize the world energy market.

Adoption of such a programme would do far more than any other single step imaginable to enhance the prospects for development in the poorer countries. At the same time, it would bring major benefits to the industrialized countries and to the oil-exporting countries themselves. There is no need to complicate matters hopelessly by adding financial and other considerations to the package, which will take some time to work out under the best of circumstances. There are huge gains available to all three sets of participants – oil exporters, industrialized countries, developing countries – from the energy accord itself. If it helps to launch such an effort, the Brandt Commission will leave an historic legacy for which all mankind will be eternally grateful.

References

1. The terms 'North' and 'South', as used in this context, are both factually inaccurate and badly misleading. They are inaccurate because some countries in the geographical North are poor (e.g., Turkey, Korea) and more countries in the geographical South are rich (e.g., the Persian Gulf,

Australia and New Zealand). They are misleading because they imply monolithic viewpoints in the two groups, particularly vis-a-vis each other, whereas the differences within the groups are often greater than the differences between them. I shall therefore generally use the more accurate terms 'industrialized' and 'developing' countries.

2. See below for details. For a comprehensive list of the results, see C. Fred Bergsten, 'North-South relations: a candid appraisal' in *The world economy in the 1980s: selected papers of C. Fred Bergsten, 1980*. (Lexington, Mass.: D.C. Heath and Co., 1981).

3. For an early discussion of joint gains as a guiding concept for international economic management see Lawrence B. Krause and Joseph S. Nye, Jr, 'Reflections on the economics and politics of international economic organization,' in C. Fred Bergsten and Lawrence B. Krause, eds, *World politics and international economics*, (Washington, D.C.: Brookings Institution, 1975), esp. pp.332-33.

4. The U.S. view is articulated in C. Fred Bergsten, 'The policy of the United States towards international commodity agreements,' in *The international economic policy of the United States: selected papers of C. Fred Bergsten 1977-1979* (Lexington, Mass.: D.C. Heath and Co., 1980) pp.265-72.

5. There can be no rational basis for relating an optimal level of aid flows to the GNP of *donor* countries. Taken literally, this calls for ever-increasing levels of aid whatever the needs of the recipients. In fact, no arbitrary formula yet devised can be defended intellectually.

A less objectionable *formula*, if one is needed, is to relate aid flows to the GNP of *recipient* countries – which at least suggests what part of their 'need', in some sense, is best met from outside. On this measure, incidentally, concessional aid to the least developed countries has risen substantially: from 4·6 per cent of their GNP in 1969-71 to 8·9 per cent in 1976-78. Similarly, all aid to all LDCs has risen significantly.

It should also be noted that the original international target of transferring 1 per cent of donor-country GNP through all means, including private investment and loans, was promptly met – and just as promptly forgotten, even as a target, by the developing countries.

6. The Report seeks to reverse this line of reasoning, by arguing that enhanced demand growth in LDCs – fuelled by help from the industrialized world itself – can rescue the latter from its own economic ills. The reasoning of the Report is badly flawed, however. It is excessive inflation and energy constraints which are limiting world economic growth, not some sudden inability to generate demand for output of the industrialized countries. Clearly, the adverse effects of world stagflation on support for development outweigh any possible resulting appeal to global Keynesianism in the United States and, I suspect, in most other industrialized countries as well.

KARL-HEINZ SOHN*

.... for their part, the developing countries should display a readiness for compromise in those instances where the future international economic order is at stake.

1. *The Contemporary Situation*

The Report of the North-South Commission raises the question as to whether our present relations with the Third World should not be reconceptualized and a policy of active cooperation with Third World countries initiated.

The facts favouring such an approach – the rapidly increasing indebtedness of the developing countries, their inability to catch up with the level of the industrialized countries, gaps in the supply of vital goods which evidently cannot be closed, increasing birth rates and decreasing life expectation, a low level of education and, last but not least, an unrestrainable increase in unemployment – although these facts were already evident when the Pearson Report was published in 1969, it is only in recent years that they

* Federal Republic of Germany. President, the German Development Company. Held several leading positions in the German Trade Union Federation. Former secretary of state in the Federal Ministry for Economic Cooperation.

have become part of general awareness. At times in the past one had the impression that the industrial countries were closing their minds to these problems, considering it sufficient to continue contributing the same amountg of official development assistance as previously. The difficulties facing the majority of the industrial countries in both East and West since the events of October 1974 have even tended to strengthen this impression. Galloping energy costs and their implications for trade balances and balances of payments have focused attention on solving national problems. Such difficulties also reduced the industrial nations' readiness to support those countries and regions which were suffering considerably greater hardship as a consequence of increases in the price of energy.

It is true that it was not alone the policies pursued by the oil-producing countries which caused international solidarity to weaken and the leading industrial countries to focus their attention primarily on alleviating their own difficulties; yet, on the other hand, it cannot be denied that these policies did favour these developments. A number of figures by way of illustration: whereas official development assistance payments increased between 1977 and 1979 by only $US 7·6 billions to reach a total of $US 22·3 billions, the oil revenues of the OPEC states alone increased during the same period by not less than US$ 67 billions. And if, in 1973, the official development assistance payments made by the industrial countries sufficed to finance in full the developing countries' oil imports, by 1979 they financed only 45 per cent. This year, the official development aid payments of the OECD countries will barely pay one third of the developing countries' oil import bills. On the other hand, the industrial countries are no longer able to dispose freely of – or distribute to the developing countries – those resources which they today need for financing their own energy imports. In view of this situation, it is imperative that an attempt be made to solve this problem, or at least to alleviate the hardship of those most afflicted by it.

Parallel to this development the Third World countries developed visions of a new international economic order which was to end their present state of powerlessness and render them the equal partners of the industrial countries. Power to dispose of their own resources, control over foreign concerns operating within their territories, greater independence from fluctuations in the price of commodities, increased imports of modern technologies and a larger share of the world's manufacturing industries (an increase from the present 7 per cent to 25 per cent by the year 2000) were to be the principal factors in realizing this vision. The industrial countries again responded to the demands of the developing countries in a primarily defensive manner. For regulatory reasons, but partly also in the interest of merely consolidating their own position, the industrial countries were not willing to negotiate with Third World countries specifically on such a catalogue of demands. Compromise solutions have since been arrived at for a number of subsectors. It would certainly be too much to expect the industrial countries to meet all the demands of the Group of 77 and at the same time declare themselves willing unilaterally to relieve the most disadvantaged developing countries of the consequences of the energy policy pursued by the OPEC cartel. Even if this expectation is fostered by at least some of the OPEC countries and COMECON states, it should not be allowed to influence the ultimate decision of the industrial countries. On the other hand, the situation cannot continue as it has done. Catastrophe is too close.

Under these circumstances, what might be the shape of any new policy of cooperation with the Third World?

2. Which Paths of Action Remain?

I. Now, as in the past, the developing countries need technical and capital aid from the industrial countries. They need it however in a different form from that of the past. It should be transferred less bureaucratically, on a long-term basis, and with greater reference to the specific needs of the recipient developing country. Too much time has been wasted in the past in a two-sided bureaucratic struggle. In order to remedy this problem, once a long-term financing commitment is forthcoming, the decision-making process on financing any given project should be transferred to the developing country itself, perhaps to the competent regional representatives of the donor country.

More importance should be attached in future by both industrial and developing countries to the entire complex of project operation, including maintenance and repair, in the projects based on capital or technical aid programmes. Roads and bridges fall into disrepair, hospitals and power stations are declared redundant, and universities stagnate simply because the running costs increase beyond the reach of the developing countries. A relatively low input of funds allocated within the framework of repair and maintenance contracts could make considerably better use of industry, transport, and service capacities.

Developing countries which, even when exercising the greatest austerity, cannot balance their budgets and cannot even pay for their vital commodity imports should be granted more capital aid from the industrial countries in the form of controlled budgetary grants.

II. On the occasion of the conference on economic issues conducted by the Friedrich Ebert Foundation in Hamburg in 1977, the President of the central issuing bank of Brazil proposed helping the more developed LDC's to leap over the final development hurdle by concluding a type of 'Marshall Plan' which would afford countries like Brazil, Mexico, Andean Group countries, Nigeria, Zaire, Indonesia, the Philippines, and Malaysia the opportunity to develop and commercialize their raw material deposits and use the revenue therefrom to repay loans. It is poor consolation to a potentially rich developing country to know that its population could have a higher standard of living while it is still unable to exploit its economic potential. Every type of development assistance is an investment in the future. The terms of reference applied to this investment should be oriented less towards the current credit rating of the client country than to its long-term possibilities.

III. In recent years, during the struggle for a new international economic order, the developing countries have done themselves a disservice by frightening off even those partners who would have been able to assist them in reaching more rapidly the take-off point for development by providing them with new industries and modern technologies. The relative decline in private investment in developing countries is to no small extent attributable to increasing misgivings of a political nature among entrepreneurs. If even prior to commencing operations abroad the potential investor learns that (no-compensation) expropriation is not impossible and that the government of the country in question intends to exert a dominating influence in his activities, his reluctance is not surprising. The political and economic climate of the host country is a factor of predominant importance to an investor. He wants to know whether he will be able – in principle and while respecting the laws of the country in question – to proceed and develop his undertaking in the same manner as his own government permits. In future relations between developing countries and private investors, the most important issue is the reestablishment of an atmosphere of confidence and mutual respect.

IV. A further prerequisite of decisive importance in the relations between industrial countries and developing countries is a reinforcement of two-way trade relations. It is not sufficient to establish industries in developing countries without guaranteeing them market outlets in high-purchasing-power industrial countries. An increase of only 1 per cent in the developing countries' share in international trade would bring these countries more foreign exchange in earnings than the total sum of the official development assistance which they receive from the industrial world. It will therefore be important to ensure that markets are opened to suitable products and other measures are adopted to improve the developing countries' balances of trade so that they are able to solve, at least partially, their balance of payments problems. One approach in this direction is an efficient commercialization of the tourism possibilities of Third World countries, even if these prospects are sometimes – and not always without some justification – regarded with considerable reservation.

V. The industrial countries will now have to assist the

developing countries much more than in the past in overcoming the balance of payments crisis provoked by the increasing price of energy. This should be made easier by the fact that in the majority of developing countries there are real opportunities for making changes in energy consumption and substituting for the major part of crude oil imports. The developing countries would not only be privileged locations for new solar technologies but could also use their own biomass energy to a much greater extent than hitherto. The use of charcoal, the production of methyl alcohol from vegetable matter in Brazil, and the increasing use of hydropower serve as examples to illustrate this point.

With regard to the crude oil which the developing countries will have to continue to import in future, before the bills are simply presented to the industrial countries consideration will have to be given to the role of the OPEC states. It is not right that the small group of countries which more or less fortuitously owns a commodity of such importance and in such short supply should unscrupulously exploit its position vis-à-vis developing countries with no or only scarce oil resources. At least between these two groups of developing countries it should be possible to arrive at a long-term arrangement which is of mutual interest.

3. Conclusion

Relations between the developing countries and the industrial countries will undoubtedly not remain without a certain degree of tension in the future. Now, as in the past, there are substantial differences as regards both the philosophy of our international economic order and the assumption of responsibility for the burdens imposed on the developing countries. The industrial countries have declared that they will honour their commitment to increase to some extent their official assistance payments to Third World countries. They should execute this commitment in the most unbureaucratic manner possible ánd with conscientious reference to the circumstances of each specific situation. For their part, the developing countries should display a readiness for compromise in those instances where the future international economic order is at stake and further open their borders to private investment. The industrial countries will in turn have to take the necessary steps to ensure that their markets are open to goods from Third World countries and to help the developing countries in solving the problem of their increasing energy costs. That this is not possible without a committed and substantial contribution from those countries which are responsible for the increase in the cost of energy is self-evident. Concerted action between the developing countries and the industrial countries on the one hand and between the former and the oil-producing countries on the other is an essential prerequisite to progress in this direction. Only then might it be possible to solve at least the most pressing problems of the coming decade.

HELMUT HESSE*

> . . . the Commission's thesis regarding a mutuality of interests is doomed to failure by the approach which the Commission adopts for its argumentation.

The appeal to eradicate hunger in the world and to prevent the inequality between North and South from becoming ever greater has become increasingly forceful over the past two decades. This is clearly reflected in the three best-known reports published during this period on North-South relations. The Pearson Report, which was published in 1969 and on which Sir Arthur Lewis, winner of the Nobel Prize for Economics, collaborated, opens with the still relatively mild statement that the widening gap between the developed and the developing countries has become a 'central issue of our time.' Seven years later, the Third Report to the Club of Rome, which was largely the

* Federal Republic of Germany. Chairman of the Economic Advisory Council to the Federal Government. Co-author of the RIO Report.

work of Jan Tinbergen, another Nobel Prize winner for Economics, and which is also known as the RIO Report, was more insistent in its tone. In its very first sentence the Report assesses the reduction of the inequality between North and South as a task of vital importance to both present and future generations; failure to reduce inequality would imply that mankind has 'no future.' And in 1980 the Independent Commission on International Development Issues under the chairmanship of Mr Willy Brandt, winner of the Nobel Peace Prize, adopts an almost imploring tone in its Report: referring even in the title to a Programme for Survival, the Commission predicts that humanity will meet with a precipitous end by way of self-destruction unless it succeeds in shaping a just and humane society.

The increasingly insistent demand addressed to the industrial countries for the elimination of international inequality is accompanied by arguments based in large measure on the contention that the industrial countries also, if not primarily, stand to gain from complying with this demand. The Pearson Report somewhat casually refers to this aspect of self-interest as being a respectable and valid basis for international action and policy. The RIO Report makes the point even more clearly by stating that the resolution of the poverty problem is in the mutual interest of all countries. The Brandt Report, finally, has upgraded the concept of 'mutuality of interest' between North and South to the point that it is taken as the guiding principle for the 'Programme for Survival.'

Nonetheless, the appeals made in the past for the elimination of hunger in the world have died away without any audible response. The number of the 'absolute poor' has increased continuously from 663 million in 1963 to 706 million in 1972 and 780 million in 1978.[1] The discrepancy in terms of per capita income between the industrial nations and the low-income countries has likewise increased substantially.[2] This prompts the question as to why the Pearson Report, the RIO Report, and similar works have failed to evoke any mentionable echo and whether the Brandt Report will not meet the same fate. Light can be shed on the answer to this question by a concept to which special emphasis was attached in the two most recent

Reports (RIO and Brandt), namely, that the North-South problem is not a matter to be left exclusively to politicians but one which concerns every member of the world's population without exception. This conviction concurs with the message proclaimed in the 1979 Report to the Club of Rome entitled 'Bridging the Human Gap,' according to which the precondition for mankind's survival is that every single human being develop a broader vision and an overall understanding of the ever more complex global interdependencies and reorient his lines of thought towards a scale which embraces the whole world. It is therefore of crucial importance that reports of this type, intended to provoke effective measures to ensure mankind's survival, should impress the totality of mankind and convince the majority. Does the Brandt Report meet this criterion?

In view of the great number of criticisms which have been voiced in connection with the Report[3], it is doubtful whether, given a worldwide context, this question can be answered in the affirmative. Yet we are concerned here merely with the question as to which response the report has found in the Federal Republic of Germany and whether it will succeed in transforming the majority of federal German citizens into committed fellow-combatants in the (imperative!) fight to remove worldwide inequality. Four selected aspects show that there is room for scepticism as to the likelihood of such an impact.

1. The first aspect is the comprehensiveness of the subject matter dealt with and the specific vocabulary employed for its presentation. The Brandt Commission decided to broach nearly all present-day problems of development and present and examine all the suggestions made to date for their solution. By so doing, the Commission endeavours to draw a global picture of North-South relations – this in fewer than 300 pages, a volume so restricted that much of its content necessarily turns out to be superficial. Indeed, in many instances that which is portrayed in these few words is merely the same ideal concept as has been expressed at each and every international conference organized in the recent past. This approach seems to be all the more dubious if the products of such ideal concepts are included without

any further analysis in the Programme of Priorities appended to the Report. This is what happened for example in the case of the proposal to reform the monetary system. The Brandt Commission's only comment in this connection was that we need a system 'which will establish more stable exchange rates, symmetry in the burden of adjustment to balance of payments deficits and surpluses, and an orderly expansion of international liquidity.'(p.272 F.) Despite the tremendous efforts undertaken, no passable road leading to this well-known objective of international monetary policy has as yet been opened up. Nor does the Commission disclose any indicators as to where such a road might lie. Yet by including this objective in its Programme of Priorities, the Commission gives us to understand that it could be achieved in the short term. Anyone to any extent familiar with the subject matter knows that this hope must necessarily be frustrated. The import of this example can be generalized: the comprehensiveness for which the Commission opted was realized at the expense of thoroughness and realism.

Connected herewith is another impression which the reader is bound to gain. The Commission refers to a number of requests made by the developing countries over the past fifteen years with respect to restructuring the world economic order. But the reasons which caused the governments of the industrial countries to reject these requests are not, or not sufficiently, discussed in the Report. This gives an impression of one-sidedness, an impression which grows even stronger when one reads that the governments and people of industrial countries were simply unaware of many facts or that specific facts were misinterpreted by the press in these countries. (Report p.66) Reading this, one cannot help but recall the fact that the governments which then rejected some of these requests were in fact headed by persons who are now members of the Brandt Commission.[4] Were these governments insufficiently informed at that time? The fact that the reader feels compelled to raise such a question reveals a new danger: is this not reason enough for the developing countries to gather fresh hope that the North will now be ready to comply with their old requests? Does this not necessarily place obstacles on the path towards increased realism in the discussion on the restructuring of the world economic order? Must not new frustration ensue? If a positive answer to any of these questions cannot be excluded a priori, there is reason not to view the Brandt Report exclusively as a progressive step towards the resolution of the North-South conflict.

Opting for comprehensiveness by the Brandt Commission is the cause of another shortcoming: the average citizen who is not particularly familiar with the host of specialized proposals to solve the North-South problem is more likely to be confused than converted to the cause. Substitution account at the International Monetary Fund, reduction of the escalation effects of the freight rates, expansion of the compensatory financing facility, opening of the second window of the Common Fund, the behavioural codex, fair labour standards, subregional economic integration of developing countries – these may all constitute partial solutions for the expert, but will this terminology be comprehensible to the average citizen and will it inspire the voter with the necessary 'new spirit'? Less substance would probably have made for greater effect.

2. The second aspect originates in the guiding principle proclaimed by the Brandt Commission, namely, the mutuality of the interest of both North and South in eradicating poverty and reducing inequality in the world. It cannot be denied that a solution to this problem is indeed in the interest of the Federal Republic of Germany. To be doubted, however, is whether this basic premiss has been convincingly substantiated by the Brandt Commission. The most striking example in this connection is the Commission's contention that world peace cannot be maintained without the elimination of international inequality. Yet the fact that not one of the armed conflicts which have shaken the world in the past decades has been attributed to this inequality suggests that this contention is unfounded. Just as unconvincing is the claim that the measures taken by the industrial countries to promote the economic development of the Third (or rather: the Fourth) World will lead to an increased demand for the products of the North which would remedy stagnation and

unemployment. This argument is based on the assumption that the problems of unemployment and decelerated growth, being essentially the result of decreasing demand, could be overcome by a policy of fostering demand (i.e. by a policy of 'worldwide Keynesianism').

Should Keynesianism, a concept from which national economic policy has become increasingly removed in recent years, in fact be able to achieve at international level that which it is no longer believed to be capable of achieving at national level? The reader indeed has difficulty in following the Commission's line of argument. Nor is he convinced by the ensuing contention that the dangers of inflation threatening the industrial countries could to some extent be removed by a policy fostering the economic development of Third World countries: low-price imports from developing countries would act as a brake to inflation. Yet since the North's imports from the South must necessarily fall short of its exports to the South in line with the volume of development assistance rendered, the braking effect within the overall system of inflationary forces would be relatively poor. Another point is that those who equate the developing countries' advance on the world market with a threat to their jobs do not find solace in the theory that economic growth in the Third World, besides reducing the upward trend in prices in the home country, operates in the interest of their export industries. The interest of a nation is not synonymous with the individual interest of each of its citizens. If this were so, all the measures called for by the Brandt Commission would undoubtedly long since have been implemented.

As has already been seen to be the case with the discussion on 'worldwide Keynesianism,' the Commission's thesis of a mutuality of interests is doomed to failure by the approach which the Commission adopts for its reasoning. By merely asking whether compliance with the developing countries' demands would also be in the interest of the industrial nations, the Commission restricts its examination to a unilateral approach. By electing to refrain from undertaking a comprehensive examination of the interests of the North and the multiplicity of its social problems, the Commission is unable to give due consideration to the standpoints of the North, standpoints which, incidentally, differ widely if one thinks in turn of the United States, Japan, and Europe. This approach is all the more unfortunate insofar as it does nothing to remedy the universal absence of any realistic and authoritative account of the interests currently fostered by the North. Such an account would in all probability have had an extremely stimulating impact on the North-South dialogue. Stimulation would have been forthcoming if the Commission, in an alternative report, had been able to prove that (and show why) the industrial countries are on the verge of losing control over the development of the world economy and that the North would be prepared to make this or that concession if it would thereby be able to regain a certain control over events and protect itself against even greater problems as regards unemployment, raw material supplies, and price developments.

This applies all the more to the Federal Republic of Germany as its economy depends in large measure on the supply of raw materials from abroad and almost every fourth employee earns his livelihood from the export sector.

3. The third aspect promoting scepticism is related to the Commission's recommendation that greater emphasis be placed on the social factor within the framework of a new world economic order. A market economy – the purchases and sales on our world markets are undeniably based largely on market economy principles – is always bound to neglect the social aspect. It does provide, with certain restrictions, for the efficient deployment of scarce resources and for the increased well-being of the citizens; it does not, however, necessarily provide for equality in the distribution process. Thus if a state is to be qualified as a social state, its market economy must be complemented with an element of social policy. To the federal German citizen the lien between market economy and social policy has been a familiar concept since its inception during the joint struggle against the distress of the immediate post-war period. Nearly everyone would agree that the market economy system would no longer be acceptable in the Federal Republic of Germany if the social security of the

individual citizen were jeopardized and that, likewise, social policy would lose its material basis if the market economy were to be too severely restricted. For this reason, the Brandt Commission's proposal to complement the world market, characterized as it is by the law of competition, with an international redistribution system is very likely to meet with broad consensus in its favour.[5] Any world economic order which fails to incorporate social aspects cannot aspire to survive in the long term.

Yet much as, for the above reasons, one is inclined to approve of the 'New Approach to Development Finance' (as Chapter 15 is entitled), one is nevertheless bound to reject the individual proposals for the implementation of this new approach. This is particularly valid as regards the proposal to levy a tax on international trade. Such a tax would impede the international division of labour, and this to the detriment of the developing countries: it would be levied inter alia on the industrial goods imported by the industrial countries from the developing countries, thereby raising their price. That the competitiveness of the producers from Third World countries would be impaired is a result which is in direct contradiction to proposals made elsewhere in the Report by the Brandt Commission. Even the proposal to levy a special tax on multinational enterprises engaged in the exploitation of seabed resources gives rise to serious reservations of an economic nature. Since such a tax would imply that the necessary balance between risk and prospects would no longer be ensured, it would operate as a deterrent to enterprises which would otherwise be prepared to bear the risks connected with the exploitation of manganese nodules in deep waters. In view of the fears that the growth of the world economy will soon meet its limits on account of the increasing scarcity of commodities, such a deterrent effect is certainly undesirable.

The most significant single proposal made by the Brandt Commission with respect to distribution machinery, a tax-based automatic funding procedure, is most certainly attractive. This would serve as an autonomous mechanism operating alongside the market to take charge of the social aspect within a new world economic order. However, the proposal will not enjoy full support until it is clear how the funds are to be distributed and how the industrial countries can escape such automatism if, in principle, they no longer agree with the manner in which the funds are deployed. Another reason why many people will be disinclined to agree with these ideas of the Commission is that they provide for the funds to be allocated to governments of the developing countries to finance development programmes as opposed to projects (as has hitherto been the case). The experience gained with development aid over the past three decades has clearly proved that funds granted to governments have not always been disbursed in the interest of the poor. Evidently, other comparable experiences have likewise not been adequately taken into account by the Commission. If the facts were otherwise, the Commission would not (wrongly) claim that 'the South needs, above all, finance.' (p.43) To consider lack of finance as the ultimate obstacle to development was a view propounded only in the development literature of the fifties. Since then other obstacles have been advanced to the fore: lack of dynamic entrepreneurship, shortage of skilled labour, inefficient administrations, behavioural attitudes of those in favour of industrialization, etc.

4. The fourth aspect becomes evident when one examines the Commission's attitude towards the market economy as a decentralized decision-making mechanism responsible for the efficient deployment of scarce resources. Its attitude is contradictory and thus not convincing. One is struck by the vigour with which the Commission points out how fatal it would be to oppose market developments. This warning is addressed in the first instance to those who, directly or indirectly, support a policy of neo-protectionism, i.e. the protection of domestic industries which are threatened by foreign competition. Foreign competitors are kept away from the domestic market in the interest of protecting workplaces, while the structural changes made necessary by the developing countries and their industrialization efforts are delayed or even prevented – and this to the detriment not only of the Third World.

Yet though the Brandt Commission insists unequivocally

that market forces should be allowed to operate unhindered, it seems to view equally sceptically the process of decentralized decision-making on aspects of production, labour deployment, etc. It seems instead to be convinced of the desirability and effectiveness of administrative intervention in many markets. Even administrative mechanisms harmonized at international level are viewed as reasonable substitutes for the decentralized decision mechanism 'market.' This suggests that the prices and quotas of specific products would be negotiated by governments. It would further imply bureaucratic measures to determine the structural changes which would in any case have to be mastered in the Federal Republic of Germany in the 1980's and thereafter. Since any administrative provisions in this context would be oriented largely towards greater justice (as is evident from the term 'just price') experience indicates that they would probably often run counter to the objective of economizing on the scarce resources of the world and using them to the greatest possible benefit (cf. the European agricultural market!). Even if no attempt were made to promote social objectives by way of market regulation, it is difficult to imagine that in times of change and uncertainty politicians and bureaucrats convening in international bodies and authorities would be better able than market agents to find efficient problem solutions. Unlike the former the latter have daily contact with the processes on the individual markets; furthermore they themselves have to bear the consequences of any wrong decisions. One might conclude that the Brandt Report would have found a greater following in the Federal Republic of Germany if it had emphasized, instead of viewing with so much scepticism, the possibilities of decentralized decision-making mechanisms in overcoming the North-South problem.

Notes and References

1. The figures cited for the years 1962 and 1973 are taken from a study prepared by the International Labour Office: *Employment, growth, and basic needs: a worldwide problem*, Geneva 1976, p.23.
Those living in 'absolute poverty' in 1972 are deemed to be

all those who had an annual income of less than $US 250 in Europe, $US 90 in Latin America, $US 59 in Africa and $US 50 in Asia.

The figures relating to the year 1974 are published by The World Bank: *World Development Report 1980*, Washington 1980, p.33.

2. *The World Development Report 1980* (ibid., p.34) gives the following gross national product per capita figures (in 1980 prices) for the years 1950 and 1980 respectively: low-income countries: US$ 164 and 245; industrialized countries: US$ 3,841 and 9,684.

3. See, for example, *Entwicklungspolitik*, no. 15/80 (July 1980) published by the Informationsdienst der Zentralredaktion des Evangelischen Pressedienstes (epd). This issue prints a number of to some extent extremely critical comments under the title 'Die Wahrheit über die Katze erfährt man von den Mäusen'. For a detailed examination of the Brandt Report, see also P. D. Henderson: Survival, Development and the Report of the Brandt Commission, in: *The world economy*, vol. 3, no. 1 (June 1980), pp. 87-117.

Finally, reference should also be made to the fact that the internationally respected *Third World quarterly* devotes its entire October 1980 issue (vol. 2, no. 4) to the Brandt Report. The majority of the authors, especially Dudley Seers, judge the Report for the main part negatively.

4. The Federal Republic of Germany, under the chancellorship of Willy Brandt, opposed the introduction of the 'link,' i.e. a linkage between newly created world money in the form of special drawing rights and development aid. The arguments used at the time were sound and are no less valid today.

5. The assumption that the Brandt Report will meet with a broad consensus in its favour is based to some extent on the fact that in 1977 the Economic Advisory Council at the Federal Ministry of Economic advanced and published a similar proposal for distribution to federal German diplomatic representations throughout the world; the essence of this proposal had been approved by all parties represented in the Bundestag. See: *Problems of a New International Economic Order*, Berlin, Heidelberg, New York 1977.

PAUL STREETEN*

. . . while there is considerable scope for positive sum games in exploring areas of common and mutual interests, and of avoiding self-defeating, mutually destructive policies, there is also a 'higher' interest in a world order that both is, and is seen to be, equitable, that is acceptable and therefore accepted, and that reduces conflict and confrontation.

The Brandt Commission Report emphasizes mutuality of interests as the basis of North-South cooperation. I should like to examine this basis and delineate areas of action that can be derived from it as distinguished from other areas that ask for a different justification, such as a genuine sacrifice by the North.

First, a pedantic point: mutual interests should be distinguished from common interests. Mutuality exists where one party can offer benefits in exchange for different benefits offered by the other party. Trade is an example. Common interests exist where partners share an interest in common which can be pursued cooperatively. Avoiding pollution of the global environment is an example.

Mutual and common interests should be distinguished from interdependence. Interdependence refers to current transactions whereas mutual interests may also refer to change. Two countries may be completely self-sufficient and therefore not interdependent, but opening up trade and factor flows between them could be in their mutual interest.

It is my argument in this essay that for purposes of analysis (though not for purposes of negotiation) it is useful

* United Kingdom. Director of the Center for Asian Development Studies, Boston University. Former Adviser to the World Bank and Director of Studies at the Overseas Development Council. Author of several books on development economics.

to distinguish more clearly than the Brandt Report does, on the one hand between areas of common and mutual interest, which in turn can be subdivided into areas of mutual or common benefits and areas of avoiding inflicting damage, and, on the other hand, areas of genuine unilateral sacrifice. In the language of games theory, the distinction is between positive-sum games, avoiding negative-sum games, and zero-sum games. In the case of the latter, it is necessary to find a justification for such action.

Common and Mutual Interests: Positive-Sum Games

The one-way dependence of the South on the North has now become a two-way interdependence. International interdependence implies the existence of both common and mutual interests in such a way that the action of one country is capable of inflicting harm, and bestowing benefits, on other countries, and vice versa.

The most generally accepted area of mutual interest is trade liberalization, and liberalization of the flow of the factors of production, capital and labour. On trade, it could be argued that fairly rich developed countries should weigh the costs of adjustment, probably repeated and painful adjustments, against the gains from additions to income. Affluent countries, or at any rate their governments, might decide that it is in their national interest to forgo at the margin further income rises for the sake of a quieter life, and greater industrial peace.

The difficulty with this position is that security of employment is not necessarily guaranteed by protection, for jobs in export trades are endangered, and that the cost of such a form of a quiet life can be very high indeed, particularly for a country dependent on foreign trade. Moreover, if several countries adopted such a position, the mutual impoverishment could be substantial. Production, productivity and incomes rise as specialization proceeds. It is on the interaction between the division of labour and the extent of the market that economic progress depends. To widen the market, to raise incomes in the South, makes greater international specialization possible, which in turn course, been questioned whether this style of development, relying on large-scale production and increasing specialization, is consistent with human dignity, self-reliance, and respect for the environment.

On present evidence and theoretical considerations, there is not much in the argument that *general* flows of ODA to developing countries – what is sometimes called a Marshall Plan for the Third World – can regenerate growth in the developed countries. For the Third World to be an 'engine of growth' for the industrialized countries, the quantities are too small (though they can make a contribution), and domestic measures (tax reductions and public expenditure increases) can do the same with higher political and economic returns, if the national interest were the only guide and if fuller employment were really desired. The argument of the Commission that exports would be matched by imports is a fallacy, for massive transfers are possible only if the exports, until debts are serviced, are not requited. Exports matched by imports reduce to the argument of the benefits from international specialization.

The argument that *specific* exports can be supplied from under-utilized capacity at low, zero, or negative costs, and that *specific* imports can contribute to bottleneck bursting, and hence to the resumption of orderly growth without premature inflation, deserves closer examination. How does this argument run in the case of energy and food?

Energy

Energy is likely to be scarce for the next ten years. Its scarcity will hold back capacity utilization and industrial production, and retard growth in the OECD countries. If we allow its current scarcity to be fully reflected in a very much higher price of oil, cost-inflation will spread to other sectors, worsening the terms of trade of oil-importing developing countries. If the cost-inflationary impact is countered by standard monetary restrictions in OECD countries, additional unemployment, lost output and retarded growth will be suffered. Since consumers' elasticity of demand is low, the price of oil could be raised to quite high levels, without substantially reducing demand, in the short and medium run. While the oil surplus countries (and those with plenty of money) gain, all others lose. These losses are especially serious, since they deprive oil-importing countries' investors of the means to finance the transition to non-oil energy sources, so prolonging the crisis.

Investment in reducing energy scarcity is perhaps the most clear-cut manifestation of a global common interest. It is unambiguous between North and South. All but a few OPEC countries have the same interest, because their oil reserves will soon be exhausted, so that it does not concern only the oil-importing countries. But raising the supply of energy reduces poverty only coincidentally. A special effort therefore is needed to cushion the poor countries against the triple evils of (1) rising cost of oil imports, (2) other inflationary-priced imports requiring energy inputs, and (3) reduced demand for their exports as a result of the recession.

How is the transition to the post-oil economy to be brought about: by a gradual rise in the real price of oil in several small steps or by large changes up or down, causing unnecessary disruption, crunches alternating with surpluses? It would call for the following six responses:

1. An agreed gradual increase in the real price of oil.
2. Investment in oil exploration, energy substitutes and conservation.
3. Some form of guarantee for the invested OPEC surpluses against erosion of their assets through inflation and depreciation.
4. A mechanism to channel a part of the surpluses to developing countries (on commercial terms).
5. An interest subsidy to cushion the poorest countries against heavy damage.
6. An international trade regime that enables debtors to export so as to service their debts.

There is, however, a problem. If the oil-exporting foreign exchange surplus countries have unused monopoly power (negative marginal revenue, so that they can have both more oil in the ground and, by reducing production and exports, larger total revenues), they do not depend on OECD guarantees for their revenues and have no incentive to secure access to supplies. If they were permitted (or even encouraged) to invest in oil-using enterprises (transport, refining, auto industries) in the North, they would have an increasing stake in a smooth-functioning oil regime.

Food

The case for investment in food production in the developing countries is often put on the same basis as the case for energy. But the correct approach to *food* would be somewhat different from that to energy. In the USA and Europe, rising prices of food have been an important component of inflation. An increase in food production anywhere in the world would reduce global inflationary pressures and permit the resumption of less inflationary growth. It would also contribute to the elimination of hunger and malnutrition, if accompanied by other measures. These would comprise (a) adequate incentives to small farmers to produce more food, (b) raising the incomes of the poor so that they can afford to buy food, and (c) creating the organization that channels food efficiently from producers to consumers.

But the case for more food (and a lower price) is different from the case for more energy (and a lower price), because (a) some rich countries are food exporters, (b) low food prices discourage production by those whose productivity and supply have not increased, and (c) lower relative food prices may be matched by higher relative prices of other goods, so that there is no anti-inflationary impact. Therefore the case should be argued on the global interest in eradicating hunger and malnutrition. It should be shown that at a relatively very low cost for the developed countries a major evil can be eradicated. The basis of this argument is moral.

Transnational Corporations

An area of positive-sum games is policies toward transnational corporations and direct private foreign investment. In the past, fears of expropriation, restrictions on repatriation or remittances, price controls and other policies reducing profitability or leading to losses have caused uncertainty and have raised the required rate of return on foreign investment. This high rate of return has, however, often led to the very measures that the investor feared, for host governments felt that companies were taking out of the country more than they were putting in.

The dilemma between foreign exchange losses and alienation of assets has led some countries to expropriate foreign enterprises. A reduction in the uncertainty about such measures would reduce both the rates of return required by the companies and the incentives for host governments to take measures that raise risks for companies. Well-designed measures to reduce uncertainty can increase the flow of foreign investment, induce companies to take a longer-term view, alleviate fears of host governments, and thus benefit both firms and host countries.

Among such measures would be investment guarantees, agreements on arbitration procedures, sell-out and buy-out options after agreed periods at prices to be determined by agreed procedures, model contracts, investment codes, joint ventures, and new public-private hybrid institutions, combining the virtues of private initiative and enterprise with those of a commitment to development.

Another area of mutual interest for policies towards multinational firms is the application of anti-trust action to the international behaviour of these companies. It is just as much in any industrial country's interest that its companies should not act like cartels or monopolies internationally, as it is that foreign companies should not monopolize its domestic market.

Global Commons

Common interests can also be established in cooperative management of the global commons: ocean fisheries, air and sea pollution, radio frequencies, civil air and merchant shipping routes and world monetary conditions. The success of some international institutions devoted to technical aspects of international cooperation, like the International Postal Union or the International Telecommunication Union or the World Meteorological Organization bear witness to the possibility of successful international cooperation if strictly defined technical areas are at stake. As a by-product of this global management, revenues might be raised from some of these activities, ocean fisheries for example, or international travel.

Avoiding Negative-Sum Games

The essence of interdependence is that members of the world community are capable, by unilateral action, of inflicting harm on others. The fear that others may take such action can be a sufficient condition for defensive, detrimental action of this kind.

The prime example in this field is the arms race which absorbs scarce resources and, beyond a certain critical point, which we have long ago passed, breeds violence. Three per cent of the total annual expenditure of $450 billion now devoted to armaments would be doubling the annual resources devoted to official development assistance given by the OECD countries. But such arguments do not cut any ice until it can be established that expenditure at present levels is counterproductive and that we would get better security by reducing it.

In the economic area protectionism and deflation to protect the balance of payments are instances of negative sum games. In the area of private foreign investment, actions by both parent and host governments to tilt the advantages from private foreign investment in their direction have similarly destructive effects. Large incentives are offered to bid for these investments in 'investment wars,' like the trade wars of the Thirties. Overfishing, the pollution of the sea and the global atmosphere, and the exhaustion of non-renewable resources are other examples. Coordination of policies and international institutions for cooperation are needed to avoid such mutually destructive actions.

The institutional responses might be illustrated by internationally coordinated action. In order to avoid the self-defeating and mutually destructive actions arising from attempts to correct balance of payments deficits imposed by a few persistent surplus countries, an international central bank, with power to create liquid assets, is necessary. It has been argued that the system of flexible exchange rates has restored full autonomy for national monetary policies. But this is by no means as obvious as is often thought. Hardly any government would permit completely 'clean' floating; and 'dirty' floating may well require larger rather than smaller reserves to counter destabilizing speculative attacks.

A second institutional reform would be a mechanism for some form of coordination of investment decisions, so as to avoid the swings between overcapacity and shortage of capacity from which we have suffered in the past. Opponents of such coordination fear that this may lead to market-sharing agreements and cartels, but in many national plans coordination of investment decisions has proved entirely compatible with maintaining competition.

Zero-Sum Games

Exploration of areas of zero-sum games, that is to say actions where a sacrifice is required on the part of the developed countries in order to benefit the developing countries, comprise three fields. First, the correction of imperfections and biases in the existing world order which work against the developing countries. Second, transfers of resources from the rich to the poor. And third, more 'voice' for them in the councils of the world.

1. Existing Biases, Imperfections and Discriminations in the International System and How to Correct Them[1]

An international economic order that discriminates systematically against one group of countries can give rise to confrontations and conflicts and to negative-sum games in which all lose. But the appeal to correcting inequities need not be wholly to national self-interest. There is an independent moral case for a just world order.

Countries should be willing to cooperate in correcting biases in market structures and government policies that are damaging to the developing countries. Such corrections would contribute to a more equitable and therefore acceptable world order and, by reducing frictions and conflicts can be seen to be also in the long-term interest of the developed countries. A response along such lines would meet the demands of both efficiency and distributive justice. Not only are the specific proposals more in line with the canons of economic efficiency, but, by accommodating the developing countries' call for a fairer international order, they would prevent the recriminations and conflicts that are bound to cause international disorder, one of the greatest sources of inefficiency.

Whatever our motivation for correcting imperfections or biases in the present international economic order, such biases occur in various fields. The division of the gains from trade may be very unequal because a few large buying companies from rich countries confront many weak sellers from developing countries, and the demand for the final product is fairly inelastic. Or the bulk of the processing of raw materials from developing countries may be done in the developed countries, which reap the large value added, not because they enjoy a comparative advantage but because of market power and policies, such as cascading tariffs, or discrimination in shipping or credit. Or the distribution of the gains from productivity growth between exporters and importers may be uneven, so that improving commodity terms of trade are consistent with deteriorating double factoral terms of trade.

There are imperfections in the export markets of developing countries, and also in the supply of imports. Developing countries are often faced with import prices that are higher than those charged to industrial countries and often suffer from price discrimination, restrictive trade practices, export cartels, inter-firm arrangements for the allocation of markets, etc. There are imperfections in access to market information; there are imperfections in access to knowledge and technology; there is a bias in the developing countries' access to capital markets.

Imperfections in labour markets are reflected in the present bias in the admission and encouragement of certain types of professional manpower, often trained by the developing countries (Brain Drain), and the considerably less free movement of unskilled labour. Does the international monetary system discriminate against developing countries? Monetary restrictions have an important impact on unemployment.

Transnational corporations also introduce imperfections. How can we strengthen the bargaining position of developing countries in drawing up contracts with TNCs? How enlarge the scope for 'unbundling' the package of capital, management, know-how and marketing? What is the role of public sector enterprises in negotiating with private TNCs? There are biases in information on political news coverage. Are the media biased in the scope and content of their news coverage? Is there a need for additional press agencies representing the point of view of developing countries?

2. *Resource Transfer*

The Brandt Report calls for a substantial increase in the amount of resources to be transferred to the developing countries, with the primary objective of eliminating the worst aspects of poverty within the lifetime of a generation. The specific form this transfer takes is a secondary question. It has been proposed that developed countries should commit themselves to a total, but that each country should be free to decide in what form it wishes to make its stipulated contribution, whether through commodity agreements, preferences, debt relief, additional ODA, etc. Such an approach would prevent differences among developed countries over specific instruments blocking the achievement of an agreed objective.

The rational way proposed by the Commission would be an international, progressive income tax, with a lower exemption limit and a rising aid/GNP ratio as income per head rises. Other tax proposals have been made, such as a tax on over-fishing, on global pollution, on seabed resources, on international travel, on armaments, etc. But an international income tax would be the most rational way toward automaticity in contributions and fair sharing.

3. *'Voice'*

The demand of the developing countries for greater participation in the international decision-making process calls for a reform in the membership and voting system of international institutions. More 'voice' for the developing countries is likely to remove some of the frustrations that spring from the perception of powerlessness. But greater participation by the developing countries would be pointless if it were accompanied by reduced contributions from the industrial countries. The demand for 'more voice' is, of course, ultimately a demand for a different power distribution.

The Relation Between Narrow and 'Higher' National Self-Interest

We can build on areas of common national interests, emphasizing mutual benefits to be derived from, e.g. resumption of orderly and equitable growth in the world economy, forswearing self-defeating protectionism, exploring ways of increasing resources that are in globally scarce supply, etc. But while there is considerable scope for positive sum games in exploring areas of common and mutual interests, and of avoiding self-defeating, mutually destructive policies, there is also a 'higher' interest in a world order that both is, and is seen to be, equitable, that is acceptable and therefore accepted, and that reduces conflict and confrontation.

All societies need for their self-regulation and for social control a basis of moral principles. Individuals are ready to make sacrifices for the communities they live in. Can this principle stop at the nation state? A belief in the harmony between self-interest and altriusm is deep-seated in Anglo-Saxon thought and action. It is odd that a moral, disinterested concern by rich countries for the development of the poor is hardly ever conceded. As hypocrisy is the tribute vice pays to virtue, so professions of national self-interest in the development of poor countries may be the tribute that virtue has to pay to vice. Let us, in the present fashion for stressing common and mutual interests, not under-estimate the power of moral appeals. Holland, Sweden and Norway, which have put international cooperation squarely on a moral basis, have hit the 0·7 aid target. It is the countries in which aid has been sold to the public as in the national self-interest where the effort is sadly lagging.

Common interests must also be defined in terms of different time horizons: next year, the next five years, the next twenty years. There may be conflicts and trade-offs between these different time spans. For example, concessionary aid to the poorest may involve economic sacrifices in the near future but, by laying the foundations for a world in which all human beings born can fully develop their potential, it contributes to the long-term interest of mankind.

The 'higher' interest in an acceptable world order can be defined either in moral terms or in terms of the desire to avoid negative-sum games to avoid breakdown and chaos. Whatever the definition and justification, its aim is to transform adversary relationships into cooperation. When interests diverge or conflict, the task of statesmanship is to reconcile them. This is a task quite distinct from, and more important than, that of exploring areas of common or mutual interests. It is in this light that cooperative actions to eradicate world poverty and to restructure the international economic order have to be seen.

Reference

1. This subject is well treated in Gerald K. Helleiner *World market imperfections and the developing countries*. Overseas Development Council, Occasional Paper No.11, 1978.

THREE

HOW TO MAKE 'SURVIVAL' POLITICALLY FEASIBLE

NORMAN GIRVAN*

How to educate the short-term beneficiaries of the present system that their own long-term interests are better served by adapting more equitable arrangements – this is the challenge facing the North and South alike.

Developing countries need security of income, of economic growth, and of all-round economic and social development. These are needed in order to give their peoples security of material well-being, especially in terms of the basic necessities of life such as food, employment, shelter, medical care and education. Primary commodity exports, upon which their economies depend so heavily, are seen as means to the above ends. Arrangements for the security of supply for the developed countries importing such commodities must equally satisfy these objectives. Otherwise they will be inherently unstable.

It is true that some developing countries have considerably diversified their export economies, reaching the point where manufactured and semi-processed goods account for the majority of their export earnings. But it is still the case that 'Most of the Third World's export earnings come from primary commodities – 57 per cent in 1978, or 81 per cent if oil is included – and commodities contribute as much as 50 or 60 per cent to the gross national product of some countries.' (Brandt Report p.141). Moreover, the vast majority of the poorer developing countries – the so-called 'Fourth World' – are overwhelmingly dependent on the export of a few primary commodities. Income levels and dependence on primary product exports are inversely correlated: the poorer a country, the greater its concern with the problems of primary commodities.

These problems have for long been identified and

* Jamaica. Former Deputy Technical Director, National Planning Agency. Internationally known development economist.

thoroughly documented. They provide the rationale for the establishment of the United Nations Conference on Trade and Development – UNCTAD – which has gone through five international conferences and produced mountains of paper.

First, there is price instability. Second, and to some extent related to price instability, there is instability of demand. Third, there is the lack of participation of producing countries in the processing, marketing, transport and distribution of their raw materials. Fourth, there is the unequal distribution of the benefits from the exploitation of mineral commodities. The Brandt Report has formulated a number of sensible recommendations to deal with these problems. Many of them are not new but they are worth repeating:

1. Tariff and non-tariff barriers to processed raw materials should be removed and processing industries should be relocated nearer to their raw material sources in the developing countries. This would be facilitated by the adoption of effective adjustment measures in the North.

2. Freight rate escalation and restrictive business practices which also inhibit the export of processed primary commodities should be removed.

3. There should be more R & D into new uses for natural products.

4. Joint market promotion of natural products by developing country producers could make them more attractive compared with synthetics.

5. Funds should be provided (for example from the Second Window of the Common Fund) to finance commodity development activities such as storage, processing, marketing, productivity improvements and diversification, in order to improve the producers' share of the final price of commodities.

6. International Commodity Agreements (ICAs) should be actively pursued by both producing and consuming countries as a means of stabilizing the prices of primary commodities, controlling inflation, and discouraging cartelization and confrontation.

7. The Common Fund should be provided with adequate finance to allow it to play the role originally envisaged for it in supporting buffer stocks and other price stabilization measures.

8. Stabilization of export earnings should also be pursued; the IMF Compensatory Facility should be improved to assist this objective.

9. Substantial multilateral finance should be provided for mineral exploration and development in Third World countries. This should be handled by an international institution in which the developing countries have an equal share in decision-making and management.

10. Mineral development and exploitation agreements between governments and TNCs should be negotiated on the basis of assured and equally shared knowledge about the extent and potential value of deposits, so that they may have long-term stability.

Perhaps the Commission would have made a more useful contribution to this issue by investigating the reasons why these measures and others of the same kind have not been adopted. Certainly the reason cannot be that they were not previously proposed; for each of them has at one time or another been demanded/requested by representatives of the developing countries at a plethora of international conferences sponsored by United Nations organs: on Trade and Development, Industrialization, Science and Technology, Shipping, and so on. What is new about the Brandt Report is the support given to these ideas by a number of highly respected, prestigious 'establishment' personalities from the North.

There are perhaps three sets of reasons why the old market structures remain so resistant to change. First, there are powerful vested interests in the North which stand to lose from the kind of changes demanded. Second, the developed countries themselves often have strong positions on the supply or production ends of commodity markets, which are used to undermine the bargaining position of the developing countries. Third, there is frequently a lack of collective action on the part of developing countries in areas where changes are necessary.

The Report speaks of a growing mutual interest between the North and the South on many of the important issues of the international economic order. The overriding mutual interest is in human survival, for the present huge disparities in wealth and income between the North and South are ultimately incompatible with a secure and stable world. But to change market structures requires specific actions by governments and private entities, which act in accordance with their immediate objectives and their perceived interests. Reducing protectionism and relocating processing activities nearer to raw material sources is resisted by trade unions and workers' organizations and national enterprises. Increasing developing countries' participation in transport, marketing and distribution, and reducing restrictive business practices, will hurt the TNCs, as will the provision of multilateral finance for exploration and development in the mineral sector. Speculators like a world of wildly oscillating prices, for it is that which provides opportunities to make quick profits that are in no way related to production and efficiency.

Secondly, the developed countries themselves produce and export many of the primary commodities which are in need of the action indicated, or close substitutes for them. Sugar, rubber, bauxite, iron ore, nickel, are only some of the more important examples where the potential benefits from joint action by developing country exporters are considerably diluted by the impact of certain developed countries on the supply side of the market. In such cases these developed countries are able to compensate themselves for market instability through a variety of measures, such as national buffer stocks, vertical integration of producing activities, and price support schemes.

Finally, collective action by developing countries in the promotion of their joint interests has often been slow to materialise and tortuous to construct. Developing countries differ widely among themselves as regards levels of development, objective economic circumstances, and nature of political regimes. Great time, energy and resources have been devoted to the attempts to establish effective International Commodity Agreements and the

Common Fund, and to promote cooperative action on a number of other fronts, such as shipping and multinational industrial projects. At the same time the pressure of bilateral and multilateral relations with the North acts as a continuous distraction from and competitor with South-South relations. Those interests in the North which feel threatened by such cooperation also do little to assist, and sometimes actively discourage, such efforts.

At this time what is needed is not so much new proposals, ideas and schemes about how restructured international commodity markets would operate: what is needed are effective strategies of political action which improve the rate of agreement on and implementation of such proposals. Security of supply may be obtained through the exercise of power on the international plane – political, economic and military power deployed to coerce suppliers into accepting terms and conditions with which they are dissatisfied and which they consider to be fundamentally unjust. This has been the traditional method of obtaining such security in an imperialistic world. But history teaches us that sooner or later such arrangements are resisted, challenged and – whenever the opportunity arises – overthrown. The case of oil is the most dramatic example of this.

How to educate the short-term beneficiaries of the present system that their own long-term interests are better served by adopting more equitable arrangements – this is the challenge facing the North and South alike. At present the mood in the South appears to be one of growing cynicism, scepticism and despair, especially as the economic crisis in the North gives rise to more and more governments of a conservative outlook more inclined to fall back on traditional approaches to these problems rather than visionary enlightened self-interest. It is to be hoped that grounds for renewed optimism will soon be provided.

JOHN P. LEWIS*

Governments . . . while remaining unfailingly polite, put increasing distance between themselves and the report – as an action document.

The year 1980 has proved to be a much more difficult one for the cause of Third World development and North-South reconciliations than there was reason to expect at the outset. The economic outlooks of both the industrialised and the oil-importing countries worsened. The same changes that increased the latter's need for support diminished the former's ready capacity to respond. New tensions and strains in international relations pre-empted political energy that could otherwise have been funnelled into support of development. Within blocs it became more difficult to muster support for policy vectors with a potential for inter-bloc convergence. Inter-bloc bargaining, becoming more defensive, tended towards stalemate. At the end of the summer the accumulating frustrations of the year were dramatised in the failure of the Special Session of the U.N. General Assembly to reach agreement on the launching of a new round of Global (North-South) Negotiations.

Obviously, the Brandt Commission deserves inclusion in any telling of this 1980 North-South story. The Commission was far too eminent a group and the issue of its report too prominent an event to be left out. But also the potential role, still, of the report speaks to the need that all of us interested in development cooperation now face for finding strategies to revitalize our common efforts.

The distinction and diversity of the Commission's membership plus the signal fact that this highly varied team, half Northern, half Southern, was able, having argued its way through a very large and thorny set of issues, to write a unanimous report would, in any event, have commanded attention. But it is also clear that the Commissioners and their small staff did a formidably good job. Their span of attention is broad. Their tone of urgency about the ends towards which global affairs are headed

* USA. Chairman, Development Assistance Comittee of the O.E.C.D. This statement is adapted from the DAC Chairman's annual report, 1980, Chapter I.

lacking major policy changes is convincing. Their programme is bold and yet (for the most part, and in the longer run) not unrealistic. Their specific emphasis on phasing – on the need to press an emergency programme without delaying the beginnings of urgently needed longer-term reforms is especially valuable.

Any reviewer can fault the product. It can be argued, for example, that, in the U.N.-ese, the report is more an NIEO than an IDS document, that it talks more about helping poor countries than poor people, that, with its balanced North-South membership and despite its chapter on the responsibilities of the developing countries (which the Southern Commissioners were at pains to include) the Commission evidently felt inhibited from addressing the needs for antipoverty and other intra-LDC reforms as much as the situation demands or as would have resonated well with Northern publics. Along the same lines, it may be objected that the Commission overplayed mutual interest and underplayed straight-forward global solidarity as its theme for North-South policy convergence – and, related to this, that it finally fell back on a too simplistic ('Keynesian') rendering of the mutual interest connection*. Moreover, as to political feasibility, there is a strange unevenness among different proposals made within the same time frame; some – those concerning international taxation are an example – almost sound as if the authors momentarily had forgotten the differences between decision-making in national and multilateral contexts.

But these all, compared with the span, thrust, and, above all, the unanimity of Brandt, were *comparatively* minor flaws. When it appeared in February, very quickly the private perception of the wide range of quite senior governmental actors in both North and South was that, not only was this about the best comprehensive programmatic piece of paper anyone had laid on the table for some time; it was one of the very few to arrive bearing neither a Group of 77 nor Group B label. Among those whose hopes for positive Global Negotiation outcomes were still high,

* See Chapter II of the 1979 DAC Chairman's Report.

therefore, there was an immediate sense that Brandt had come at just the right time to serve, very possibly, as a vehicle for positive convergence.

Thus far, in the doing, Brandt has served less as a vehicle to carry things forward than as a barometer – of declining expectations. There have been institutional efforts – in the World Bank, in OECD itself – to study its recommendations and sustain interest. In May the Dutch held a remarkable rally of the Queen, the whole Government, and thousands of citizens with the reassembled Brandt Commission to celebrate and analyse the report. But compared with their initial unofficial reactions, governments generally, as the spring and summer proceeded, while remaining unfailingly polite, put increasing distance between themselves and the report – as an action document. The Venice Summit was able to compress its comment into two sentences: 'We welcome the report of the Brandt Commission. We shall carefully consider its recommendations.'

Almost surely this reception so far has not mainly been a matter of failed logistics (e.g., delays in getting out the French, Arabic, and other editions) nor of such problems of content as those touched above. If the Holy Scriptures of any of our major religions had been freshly issued in February, 1980 – addressing Brandt's subjects – they would not have excited a different response. It has been a hard year.

However, it is reasonable to hope the barometric metaphor is a precise one. For barometers stay in place for some time, and their readings can rise as well as fall. There is a considerable determination building now – in various private quarters and sections of the press, as well as among some government leaders, in parts of governments and in some international agencies – to keep the Brandt Report in view. Broadly, its content is likely to remain fresh and relevant for several years. It may yet take on the vehicular properties that timing thus far has denied it.

AURELIO PECCEI*

> . . . without any question, the joint meeting of world leaders
> to consider how the current state of crisis can be ended and
> the human condition improved is not only the key to the
> success of all the programmes proposed but also the key to
> our common future.

The contributors to this book are so many and their talents so outstanding and diverse that I am at a loss to envision what my own contribution might be. Probably I can only repeat what some of them have already expressed, no doubt in more appropriate ways than I could ever do. And there have been so many meetings and comments about the Brandt Report that the reader of those pages would not find my piece of interest anyway.

I must therefore address myself to one point only, and be very brief. I will not consider any other facet of the Report, but merely focus on this single aspect. It is certainly an item which has its roots in the Report and clearly stems from it. However, it will soon acquire its own autonomous and forceful character, as was indeed expected. It is in fact destined to become the key to the whole enterprise launched by the Independent Commission on International Development Issues, and represents the Commission's unparalleled accomplishment and major claims to excellence.

Evidently what I am referring to is the summit of world leaders the Commission's Chairman Willy Brandt wrote must be convened in close cooperation with the United Nations, in order to elaborate new solutions to the global problems of our time. Rightly he says that the shaping of our common future is much too important to be left to governments and experts alone. And, without any question, the joint meeting of world leaders to consider how the current state of crisis can be ended and the human condition improved is not only the key to the success of all the programs proposed, but also the key to our common future. If the key works, mankind will be moving in the right direction; if it does not, today's world deadlock will just get worse.

* Italy. President of the Club of Rome

Such a precious key therefore is not in the hands of the worthy members of the Brandt Commission, who have rendered such an important public service in their time, or in the hands of Willy Brandt himself.

It is not in the hands of the personalities who contribute to this volume, however insightful and authoritative they may be. It is not in the hands of United Nations either, or any other international organization, much as they may be interested in the outcome. It is not even in the hands of parliaments or other legislative bodies, which will have to play a crucial role later on. It is certainly not in the hands of the citizens, or the press, or any community of humanists, economists or intellectuals, although all of them can exert moral and political pressure on the holders of the key.

This magic key that can start to open the door to a different, better, and more just and human future, or let it remain shut, is in the hands of, or controlled by, a few people – perhaps a few dozen, or a few hundred, or a few thousand. These are the national leaders who will participate in what will be called the North-South summit meeting, and their assistants, analysts and advisers. They will chose the point of entry from the realm of ideas, of hopes and of recommendations into the realm of political action. And they will indicate how to make these points effective – thus showing how to shape the future. Never was so much in the hands of so few.

Now, our attention should be centered on these national leaders. We must hope and pray that, at least for this occasion, they will become world leaders, too. For, if they go to their rendezvous as negotiators in the name of their respective nations, whatever legitimate interests they may advocate and whatever goodwill and understanding may motivate them, their deliberations will remain at too low a level to change world situations and reverse trends. Not only is the world's economy in bad shape; its demographic, social, ecological, military, psychological and – last and not least – moral and ethical aspects also give rise to serious concern.

Considerations of mutual interest short of global solidarity are therefore not sufficient to trigger off the long-overdue epocal change in world mood, relations and behaviour. The powerful and certainly enlightened leaders who will convene at the world summit have thus a mandate much vaster than was ever entrusted to them by their own national constituencies. They have to meet as partners who want jointly to establish what equitable contribution each of them should make for the common, global good. They do not need to go into details, to discuss technicalities. Others can do that and will do so later on.

What the world leaders, meeting at the beginning of this fateful decade of the 80s, have to do is to respond by an act of leadership commensurate with the dangers and opportunities of this age to what more than four billion people expect of them.

HELIO JAGUARIBE*

> The operational interests of (the rich) countries are . . . in favour of continuing for as long as possible, to take advantage of all the favourable asymmetries, leaving for the other actors and for the future the job of adopting a regulatory regime that will be more viable for the world system as a whole.

1. *The basis of the proposals*

A DUAL BASIS. The Brandt Report is an incisive and systematic diagnosis of the principal world imbalances; the basic problems are clearly identified, giving, as far as possible, a quantification of their general aspects as well as a succinct but comprehensive survey of the conditions or factors that generate these problems. On the basis of this diagnosis, the Report puts forward various solutions which, in extremely realistic and perfectly viable terms – quantified whenever possible – could produce, over varying lengths of time, an answer to these problems.

The Commission's diagnosis does not, on the whole, introduce any important new ideas into the already

* Brasil. Director of International Affairs of the Candido Mendes University at Rio de Janeiro. Taught political science at M.I.T., Stanford University and Harvard. Author of several books on politics in developing societies.

voluminous literature on the subject. Its analysis of world imbalances coincides with those undertaken by the technical secretariat of UNCTAD and by Third World countries, as well as Tinbergen's studies in his RIO Report. The major contribution of the Brandt Report lies in setting out the reasons why there should be an urgent and imperative world-wide attempt to correct the North-South asymmetry. These reasons are of two kinds. On the one hand, there are reasons of a pragmatic order, resulting from the existence between the North and the South of mutual interests of a structural, systemic nature and, therefore, of decisive importance for both poles. Then, there are reasons of an ethical kind, involving unimpeachable values proper to mankind and world society.

The principle of mutuality is less obvious, at first sight anyway. It would seem that the affluent societies of the North, endowed with resources incomparably superior to those of the Third World, would only have cause to concern themselves with the problems of the South for ethical reasons, acting out of human solidarity. One of the principal merits of the Brandt Report lies in clearly demonstrating the fallacies of the presumed self-sufficiency of the North, and in revealing the structural and systemic nature of the interdependence of the two hemispheres and the extent to which, in contemporary conditions, the prosperity of the North can no longer be maintained at the expense of the impoverishment of the South, nor is it compatible with the persistence of this poverty.

The Report is, moreover, a document that is realistic and at the same time imbued with a deep universal humanistic sense. The mere understanding shown by the central societies of their systemic links with the Third world would not in itself be sufficient to overcome all the different forms of misery and to universalize, for all men, the modest well-being and dignity that Brandt, like Tinbergen, considers to be the obligation of every man in relation to the rest and of every society in relation to the others. Here, of course, principles of an ethical nature are the decisive factor and it is only by acting in accordance with these moral imperatives that we will achieve the universalization of justice and modest material well-being.

THE PRINCIPLE OF MUTUALITY. According to the Report, the principle of mutuality becomes clear when we comprehend the basic fact that, in today's world, the excessive concentration of resources and opportunities in the central countries necessarily condemns their economies to the impasse of stagflation and that this can only be overcome by a deliberate policy of retransferring, on a large scale, resources and opportunities to the South.

Today it is a well-known fact that the North-South gap was produced and aggravated by the circumstance that the central countries initiated a mercantile revolution, accumulating surpluses by way of international trade, and then multiplied this accumulative capacity by also becoming the initiators of the industrial revolution and enjoying, for over a century, a virtual monopoly of the production of manufactured goods. In this way these countries were able, from the end of the Middle Ages to the middle of the present century, – viewing the world as a whole – to exchange their hours of work, on increasingly favourable terms, for an incomparably greater number of hours of work on the part of the peoples of the Third World, with the growing enrichment of the former and the impoverishment of the latter. At a certain moment in time, however, this system began to yield diminishing returns. The central countries had produced an immense productive capacity, in terms of equipment and human specialization, operating at high, non-reducible fixed costs that called for an increasing world demand. This demand, however, failed to keep pace with the needs of the productive system because the continued impoverishment of the Third World countries did not allow the demand for the products of the central countries to accompany the increase in the latter's supply capacity. If the industrialized states finance their own consumer sectors in order to keep up the demand for their products, they generate inflation. If they correct the inflation, they produce unemployment and have idle capacity in their productive system.

The only possible solution for the central countries is to create conditions that will lead to a substantial increase in the demand for their products on the part of the peripheral countries. This entails four principal types of measures: (1)

the large-scale transfer of financial and technological resources to the South; (2) a significant improvement in the terms of trade, especially with regard to better and more stable prices for raw materials coming from the South; (3) the continuous redistribution of opportunities and specializations, by giving the South a much greater share in the world supply of manufactured goods; and (4) the opening up of the central markets to manufactured goods coming from recently industrialized countries.

The large-scale transfer of financial and technological resources to the South will bring about an expansion of productive capacity and a reduction of production costs, leading to a decisive activation of world trade. Thanks to this, the North will be able to have full employment, due to the increase in exports, and will be able to control inflation through an increase in the supply of goods to its population, coming from the South. For the South, the increase in its productive capacity, generated by this large-scale transfer of resources, will enable it to incorporate the great masses into the productive process and raise their general standard of living.

The stabilization and improvement of the prices of raw materials, which will continue to be, for a long time, the major export products of the South, will correct the excessive asymmetry that exists in trade relations, enabling the South to start its own process of surplus accumulation and, with this, finance its own development.

The redistribution of industrial opportunities constitutes the other facet of the correction of the North-South asymmetry. This asymmetry could not, without world-wide inflationary effects, be corrected except by raising the prices of raw materials. A more equitable distribution of the world productive capacity and supply of manufactured goods would balance international trade without leading to inflation. It would also be a decisive stimulus to technological progress, which would become more and more important as the more conventional productive methods became widespread.

Finally, the opening up of the central markets to the manufactured goods of the Third World countries would complement the effects of the preceding measure, reducing the cost of living for the central countries and, at the same time, encouraging them to shift their productive effort into areas of greater technological sophistication.

Besides formulating the foregoing reasons in a very convincing way, the Report also provides persuasive quantitative illustrations of their positive aspects for the central countries. By showing, for example, the large number of jobs (900 thousand) generated each year, in the OECD countries, by the recycling of petrodollars. Also by pointing out that the negative impact, in the central countries, brought about by the dislocation of their industries of more simple technology as a result of imports from the newly industrializing countries (NICs), is more than compensated for by the expansion in high technology sectors and by exports to the South. In 1977, the EEC and Japan sold over one third of their total exports to the South. And EEC exports to the Third World were three times as great as those to the United States. And in the United States, at the moment, one out of every twenty jobs is connected with exports to the Third World.

THE ETHICAL PRINCIPLE. The principle of mutuality, however, is not enough, by itself, to lead to a correction of the world imbalances. 'As far as the poorest people and the poorest countries are concerned especially, the principal motives for our proposals are human solidarity and a commitment to international social justice. There must be an end to deprivation and suffering. It cannot be accepted that in one part of the world most people live relatively comfortably while in another they struggle for sheer survival. As we shall argue, there are material reasons for trying to end this state of affairs – international political stability, expanding export markets, the preservation of the biological environment, the limitation of population growth. We speak of solidarity as something that goes beyond mutual interests' (p.64).

The ethical aspect of the North-South question is a basic, fundamental dimension of this issue throughout the Report. In his Introduction, Willy Brandt stresses the decisive relevance of the moral dimension, emphasizing that 'the new generations of the world need not only economic solutions, but also ideas to inspire them, hopes to encourage them, and the first steps to implement them. They need faith in man, in human dignity, in basic human rights; a belief in the values of justice, freedom, peace, mutual respect, love and generosity, a belief in reason and not in force'(p.20).

Starting from an international social-humanist position, the Brandt Report proclaims, independent of any reciprocity of interests, the obligation of all in general, but particularly the rich countries and peoples, to put an end to hunger and misery in the world. It is necessary to act immediately, to reduce in the next few years the number of victims of an absolute lack of the bare essentials for survival and to abolish, by the end of the century, the conditions that generate and maintain the most serious forms of misery. To achieve this, it should be arranged that the poorer peoples and countries of the world receive aid equivalent to not less than 0·7% of the rich countries' national product, together with measures to increase local productive capacity, especially in the area of foodstuffs.

2. The political problem

FROM REGULATIONS TO OPERATIONS. The Brandt Report is the most conclusive document that has so far been drawn up with a view to promoting, both for practical and ethical reasons, a new North-South relationship. As we have already pointed out, it has the merit, on the one hand, of consistently systematizing the analyses that have been carried out into the causes and effects of the asymmetry in the relationship between the Central countries and the Third World, together with a clear indication of the appropriate measures needed to right the major imbalances. On the other hand, it formulates, in an extremely correct and persuasive way, the reasons both of a pragmatic and ethical nature that underlie the proposed measures.

There is, however, something missing in the Report and it is by no means certain that its pragmatic and theoretical excellence and the irrefutable nature of its ethical appeal will lead to the effective implementation of the measures proposed. The thoughtful reader of the Report is bound to feel that the actors at whom the paper is most directly aimed, that is to say, the governments of the central countries and, behind them, the sectors of greatest weight in decision-making and the formation of public opinion, will tend to agree, in principle, with the proposed measures and, above all, with the general foundation put forward for these measures, and yet they will not be effectively moved to put these measures into practice.

The interval between the acceptance, in principle, of a project and its effective implementation is something that is constantly to be found in human relationships. Such an interval is always indicative, on a broader plane, of a lack of articulation between the world of values and the world of interests. On the specific plane of the world of interests this interval marks the distance between the conveniences of a regulatory nature and those of an operational nature.

The moral appeal of the Brandt Commission to the rich countries to put an end to hunger in the world and adopt measures that would lead to the eradication of misery will certainly be heard by the statesmen of these countries and their most influential sectors. But the existence of other urgent matters, also ethically relevant but politically more pressing, tends to prevent their sympathy for the cause from turning it into continued action for real results. This is what tends to happen, for example, in relation to the granting of aid equivalent to 0·7% of the rich countries' GNP. As this aid has to come from budgetary funds coming from taxation, and as all the rich countries are facing, concomitantly, problems of reducing expenditure, in order to control inflation, and at the same time demands for supplementary funds for their welfare sectors, to pay unemployment benefits, it is almost impossible for the governments of these countries to resist the internal pressures that propose greater priority for anti-inflation measures, or for dealing with domestic unemployment, in exchange for postponing the granting of more aid to the Third World.

On the more utilitarian plane of the pragmatic motivations put forward by the Brandt Report in favour of the measures that it recommends, there arises the interval we have referred to between the regulatory and the operational conveniences. The statesmen and entrepreneurs of the central countries will tend to agree with the Report where it talks of the systemic dependence that exists between a better world sharing of wealth and productive capacity and a dynamic restructuring of international trade, to overcome the impasse of stagflation into which the industrial countries have fallen. The interest of the rich countries in this restructuring of world trade, however, is of a regulatory nature. The operational interests of these countries are, for each of them and for each specific transaction, in favour of continuing, for as long as possible, to take advantage of all the favourable asymmetries, leaving for other actors and for the future the job of adopting a regulatory regime that will be more viable for the world system as a whole.

SOCIAL ORDERING. The interdependence between the regulatory interests and the operational imperatives is quite clear. The deterioration of the regulatory conditions is reflected in the specific transactions of a society, affecting the respective operational interests. It is for this reason that societies, through their political subsystem, adopt appropriate regulatory conditions for the protection of the predominant operational interests. And it is here that there arises the question of social ordering and public service.

In contemporary industrial democracies, political power is representative of broad majorities, although certain privileged minorities – important entrepreneurs, trade union leaders and controllers of the press and broadcasting – have an influence that is disproportional to their representativeness. In the conditions of these countries, despite these distortions, the state tends to ensure regulatory conditions that are acceptable for the great majorities and to give them effective assistance, by way of the appropriate public service. The operational interests are therefore exercised under regulatory conditions that ensure the general equilibrium of the system and that are beneficial for all, or almost all.

In contemporary under-developed societies, and also at earlier periods in the history of today's industrial democracies, the dominant élites exercise, or exercised, power with low representativeness. In such circumstances, the regulating of society and the type of public service provided are, or were, designed to serve the convenience of the dominant élite, at the expense of the great majorities and the general interest of society.

Even in societies, nowadays or in the past, that were dominated by a restricted élite, the existing political relationships involve a minimum degree of representativeness. Sometimes a very small degree – as in Haiti today, and the absolute monarchies of the 17th century – and sometimes quite large: enlightened despotism. This is due to the pressure that is exerted, in a national society, by the national links of solidarity and, within them, to a minimum of reorientating feedback that the reactions of the masses impose on the conduct of the élites.

The domination – representation relationships become far more complex when we go from the internal framework of a national society to the international system, which is not governed by equivalent solidarities nor by corresponding forms of representativeness.

THE INTERNATIONAL ORDERING. In the international system, political domination tends to be exercised in an indirect form, through the limiting pressures of the options of another country or by way of satellite governments. On the other hand, international representation hardly exists, except in terms of war. One country does not represent others, except for the limited effects of certain international bodies. The exception connected with the risks of war, however, involves representation of a dominating nature. The United States represents its NATO allies in nuclear matters, and the Soviet Union similarly represents its Warsaw Pact allies. Both alliances are, however, extremely asymmetrical and represent a relationship of hegemony of each of the super-powers over their respective allies.

International organizations, of course, involve various different forms of representation. In many cases, international organizations have mandates by the countries concerned and they exercise them through an international bureaucracy, quite independent of these countries. In other cases, one delegate may represent several countries. Finally as in the case of the United Nations Security Council, some countries are permanent members of a super-state power, exercising an implicit delegation of the rest.

The representativeness of international organizations, however, is either limited to technical-secretarial areas that do not involve any modifications in the relationships of power – UNESCO, the World Health Organization, etc – or, in the form of the delegation of powers, it leads to international domination, as in the case of the powers that make up the Security Council, and inside this, the hegemonic position of the super-powers.

The lack of a true system of representation in the international system reduces the latter to a regime of indirect domination. This makes it impossible for international ordering to be achieved in a transcontractual form, as in national societies, even the least consensual. Nor does it allow, except within the restricted limits of a technical-secretarial delegation granted to certain international organizations, the setting up of any system of international public service. The minimum degree of representativeness that exists in all the national dominations makes it possible, although on terms that favour the dominant élites, for national societies to be regulated in a collective fashion and to enjoy a public service. In the case of international society, the United Nations Charter represents – regardless of the merits it may contain – the unilateral imposition of the winners of the Second World War and the regulatory system of the international order is either determined imperatively by the super-powers, within the limits of their reciprocal equilibrium, or it depends on the rarely-achieved unanimity of the member countries.

3. Prospects

The situation outlined above obviously does not present very favourable prospects in the short or medium term. Given the lack of a true international order, in which the competent international decisions would be of a compulsory nature for all countries, the recommendations of experts and the deliberations of the United Nations are mere exhortations that are only followed by a small number of countries with a highly developed sense of international responsibility, such as Holland and Sweden. On the other hand, the great differences that separate the three sectors of the Third World – the oil-producing countries, the semi-industrialized countries and the poor countries – and the consequent differences in their international behaviour decisively weaken the operational unity of these countries.

The most likely course of events, therefore, for the next few years is that the differences between the three types of Third World countries will become even greater. The oil-producing countries and, on a more modest scale, those countries producing raw materials for which there is a growing world demand, will accumulate extraordinary economic surpluses and large international monetary balances and will become the great sources of international financing and recycling. And, more dangerously, they will also become the target of world-wide greed and resentment. To the extent, however, that they administer their extraordinary surpluses competently, they will be in an exceptionally favourable position to modernize and develop, as long as the world is not plunged into a large-scale military conflagration.

The NICs (New Industrial Countries) that manage to compensate, in one way or another, for their oil deficits, maintaining a high level of exports, despite the probable worsening of international stagflation, will also be in a favourable position to achieve economic growth and national development, while not forgetting the reservation made above.

The weight of the deterioration of international conditions will, then, tend to fall on the other countries, which constitute the great majority. Among these other countries are the NICs that cannot compensate for their excessive oil deficits – as may happen to Brazil, if appropriate policies are not adopted. All the countries of the 'Fourth World', the majority of mankind, are here. And so too, although on comparatively much more favourable terms, are the industrial countries which, as a result of a fall in the import capacity of the Third World, within a general framework of recession, may be faced with a high level of idle capacity and a resulting tendency towards stagflation.

This irrational scenario of distortions and deterioration of world conditions is, however, inherently unstable. If such a situation is prolonged, it will lead to an extraordinary increase in international tensions, exponentially raising the likelihood of war. The unacceptable risks contained in the prospect of a large-scale military conflict would constitute a powerful incentive for the establishment of a more viable world order.

The two basic conditions for a minimum viable reordering of the world are a return to peaceful coexistence on the part of the super-powers, and the implementation of something like the minimum program for redressing the balance between the North and the South proposed by the Brandt Commission.

JOZSEF BOGNAR*

> If, under today's exacerbated and uncertain conditions, it were to prove impossible to arrive at a comprehensive agreement . . . , then a 'state of economic emergency and immediate danger' could be declared for this set of problems and all related issues withdrawn from the sphere of political-security rivalry between the leading powers.

The 1970's witnessed new initiatives, endeavours and approaches in science and research on issues relating to rational human action. The characteristic feature of these new approaches was globalism, in the sense that various research teams working under the guidance of eminent political and scientific personalities sought to understand better the problems likely to confront the world in the remaining decades of this century and to formulate, on the

* Hungary. Director, Institute for World Economics in Budapest. Chairman of the Commission for Planning and Budget of the Hungarian National Assembly. Former Hungarian Minister. One of the leading East-European experts in international economics. Author of several books on socialist economic policy and on world economics.

basis of anticipated developments, appropriate action strategies on a world-wide scale. These research groups were set up – and this itself is a novel phenomenon – on an international and interdisciplinary basis.

The ranks of these pioneering scientific initiatives and undertakings included the various publications of the Club of Rome[1], such as the RIO Report (Tinbergen) and the Report of the Commission headed by Leontief, on issues of development in the Third World. The objective of these ambitious works was to formulate a world-wide action strategy to enable mankind to survive and develop further in these extremely sensitive and conflict-ridden times. But the rationale of these action strategies should not be understood in the usual and everyday sense of the term. In reality, no rationale is imaginable which is independent of existing structures and interest relations since even optimal economic and social action is but a compromise accommodating structures, interest relations and the nexus of natural, social, and economic processes.

Yet in this case, we need to consider necessities of mankind and the world which have neither structures nor concrete interest systems in the economic, market or political sense.

The analyses and strategies referred to above represent very divergent concepts and activate such fundamental issues as the burden-bearing and self-renovative capacity of the existing economic and social structures, the nature of the economic system viewed from the constraints of scarce natural resources, or the short-term and long-term components of the present economic crisis. But a relative consensus has been attained which recognizes that the development of the Third World is the key condition for the survival and progress of our civilization, since it is impossible in an interdependent and extremely mobile world such as ours with impressive transport and admirable communications systems to maintain the present disparities or the fact that under the existing systems they are likely to increase. This statement does not lose its validity even when confronted with the fact that in the meantime variants of technical-technological development which open up sources of productivity formerly unknown and considered inconceivable have likewise been introduced in the developed capitalist world without the productive branches and demand capable of absorbing the resulting surplus labour having been established.[2]

Thus the Brandt Report has formidable antecedents, decades of brain-storming in which the most outstanding representatives of the natural and social sciences were engaged directly, either as members of the various commissions, or indirectly, by their works and discoveries. It is the findings of that brain-storming that the Commission seeks to synthesize and complement with new ideas. It is self-evident that I regard this as a merit of the Report, since the primary task of commissions is not to discover new facts and phenomena but rather to correlate the facts, phenomena and processes discovered by science and research into new combinations, to project them into the future, and to formulate, in the light of objective facts, a new action strategy. The Brandt Report, in aiming to synthesize and further develop scientific findings, therefore opens up a new epoch in the history of the North-South dialogue. The Report is more consistent in its content and more realistic in its approach than the pioneering works of the 1970's; it is also more mature and circumspect, mainly by virtue of the way the various problems are handled which bears the hallmark of a personality with great experience in statesmanship.

It is not my task, nor is it my aim, to compare the recommendations made by the Commission with the ideas put forward in various forms in the past. I consider it particularly important that the Report – unlike others before it – suggests the establishment of new international organizations and agencies (the ultimate aim of all technocratic solutions) only in exceptional and indispensable cases, since a bureaucracy which is detached from democratic mass movements and removed from control and pressure inevitably becomes alienated and expensive and is bound to lose much of its efficiency.

I most heartily welcome the suggestion made in the Report that heads of state and representatives of governments should meet to discuss international economic issues. Similar proposals, backed up by detailed arguments, were advanced by myself several years ago.[3]

I disagree with criticisms which find the Report of the Brandt Commission unrealistic[4] or untimely. These critics raise the problem: what is, or should be, considered as realistic or unrealistic and utopian; and what point in time should be regarded as suitable for the implementation of reforms – the 'favourable' point in time, when conditions are good but the interested parties are not convinced of the need for change and the old structure is still strong, or the 'unfavourable' point in time, when conditions have deteriorated and fewer resources are available, but the structure is shaken and, as a result, change is inevitable. We shall discuss these questions in more detail below.

It stands to reason that the relation of a rational action strategy to reality should be examined not only by the critic but also by any objective analyst. What does reality mean in this case? It means such established situations, institutions and interest structures as are the prime movers of rational action (in the market-economic sense) aimed at the short-term maximization of benefit. It is evident, however, that rational economic action also has objective components other than structures and interest relations, e.g. natural and social relations, long-term trends. No doubt – and this constitutes the greatest problem – the established situation is directed against a system of action like the action strategy suggested by the Brandt Commission, or encourages a different action system.

Accepting and following the logic of this line of thought, one has to find an answer to the question of what has to be done in the event that a confrontation/contradiction develops between rationality in its broader sense (the needs of humanity and its chance to survive and develop) and rationality in its narrower sense (the established structures and interest relations). In a national economy, the answer provided by change-promoting social or revolutionary forces is that the existing structures and interest relations have to be replaced by new ones. In that case, however, the problems assume an international/inter-state character, and accordingly, those states which are interested in maintaining the old structures and interest systems are likely to protect these by all means at their disposal, pursuing a policy which may in turn lead to conflicts and war or wars which mark the end of peaceful co-existence and imply mankind's encounter with the horrors of a nuclear war. Atomic war, indeed any war causing a massive destruction of material goods, not only questions the possibility of survival (at least as far as the species homo sapiens is concerned); it also makes it impossible for problems leading to confrontations and conflicts to be resolved. There is no doubt that strong and effectively operating economies are needed for the transfer of material and intellectual resources, since the wealth of mankind today lies not in the accumulation of treasures and rare values, but in the efficient operation and renewal of productive equipment.

Nor is it disputable that the world market – which, by the way, is beset with a great many imperfections and inequalities – cannot be replaced by something else or simply put out of operation. Such a step, undertaken in an interdependent world which badly needs more and improved mutual interaction and institutions acceptable to all, would push mankind back into a subsistence and barter economy.

As a response to this international dilemma of epochal significance (what should be done when one knows that while the established situation, structures and interest relations will plunge mankind into the risk of catastrophe or cataclysm, the forms of action which appear at international level to be the most radical are allowing humanity to drift towards a nuclear war?) the Brandt Commission, in accordance with the very spirit of its Report, states unambiguously that attempts must be made by way of conscious and mutual compromise to expand and change the existing structure in such a way that it is drawn closer to the objectively necessary action system.

Thus the answer of the Commission is as rational, while the action systems opposed to the programme (including inertia) obviously lead to catastrophe, i.e. are irrational. Yet, looking at the problem with scientific objectivity, one comes to the conclusion that there is a conflict between rational human action interpreted in its broader and the same interpreted in its narrower sense. Rationality, both economic and political, in its narrower sense cannot be separated from those structures and interest relations which exert a decisive influence on action; moreover, it is a short-term and not a long-term issue, for gains in the economic sphere and the maintenance or acquisition of power in the political sphere constitute a short-term, or at most a medium-term problem. The specialist in economic practice, and likewise the politician, cannot proceed in his action (not in his mentality!) independently of the structures and interest relations surrounding him, since he must also take account of his competitors (who are always present, in one way or another, in both economic and political life). Therefore, it may happen that the economic or political personality taking action is right in the long term but fails or even loses power in the short or immediate term.

One of the deficiencies I see in the programme and recommendations is that no attempt was made or research initiated in this framework to examine the prospects and methods of introducing long-term effects into economics and politics. The future of mankind depends in no small measure on a successful approach to this immense range of grave problems, since experience (including that of the socialist countries, with, or despite, the dominance of public ownership) provides evidence that the overwhelming majority of economic leaders are unwilling to take action which goes against structures and interest relations but is in favour of lofty and abstract interests and aims. Hence, the new and long-term factors have to be transposed into driving forces, which means that they have to be present in a concrete form in those structures and interest relations from which the rationality of action can be derived.

For it appears obvious that economic action geared to interests is not simply a 'contrivance' of philosophy or economics, but also an endowment consequent upon the nature of man as a biological being. Insofar as the action deriving from structures and interest relations is necessary or inevitable, the task facing us is to make the effective relations, taken in their dynamic sense, reflect in the relevant structures and interest relations.

I hold it to be imperative in the framework of world programmes to launch a research project designed to clarify these problems. The working groups whose task it would be to deal with this set of problems should be organized on an interdisciplinary basis, with primary emphasis being given to biologists and political scientists. That the latter have not been invited to cooperate in the elaboration of the various world programmes is absolutely incomprehensible to me, as the establishment of the international economic order intended to resolve the problems of the developing countries is no less an issue of political security than one of economics.

As regards the appropriate time for an action programme, the question has already been raised as to which point in time is suitable for the introduction of reforms or comprehensive changes. On that issue, two opposing views can be identified: the first places emphasis on the means, the second on the readiness for action of the structure and of public opinion. The supporters of the first view hold that the appropriate time for introducing reforms is determined by when the means of implementation are available. Following the logic of this line of thought, one would concede that the present time is really less favourable than was the past decade (the 'golden age'), because a world economic crisis has since emerged, economic growth in the developed capitalist countries has slowed down, unemployment is already rife and will be further aggravated by the advance of microelectronics[8], inflation is steadily intensifying (as if we had given up attempts to curb it), and substantial disequilibria have made themselves felt in the socialist countries of Europe. On the other hand, experience provides evidence, contend those who hold the opposite view, that in a favourable and stable situation (or, to be more precise, in a presumably stable situation), most people reject the idea of change and reform since changing the prevailing situation entails risks which people enjoying security are reluctant to take. Therefore, in a shock-like situation, when the structure is in a state of crisis, the people and their leaders are more inclined to take risks.

My personal experience supports the latter view. I therefore maintain that the present time is appropriate because the structures and interest relations established as a result of the world economic crisis have to be changed for reasons relating to the effects of other factors.

In conclusion, I should like to add a few ideas concerning the opportunities and problems of East-West cooperation in providing assistance to the Third World. I am induced to set out these ideas by the fact that the Brandt Commission repeatedly emphasizes in its Report the opportunity for the East to join in the efforts made by the West to implement the programme, and even formulates this in a straightforward appeal. Mr Brandt has not only correctly recognized that the vital issues of humanity and of the world economy today cannot be resolved on a partial basis, but he is also fully aware – and this we are entitled to assume from our knowledge of his political record and his personality as a statesman – that cooperation of this type might promote direct East-West cooperation, diminish the terrifying proportion of the present mutual distrust, and create a favourable climate for settling other issues as well. But I feel compelled to make a few critical comments on the political implications of his appeal for cooperation. I am doing this in the awareness that the Commission, with its concept, is not synonymous with the West, where very divergent positions and behaviour patterns have developed regarding Third World issues, ranging from those of the business community to those of politics and government.

From the appeal of the Report (and a variety of Western manifestations), one might conclude that the East is indifferent, engrossed in its own problems, and not interested in the fate of the South, and that it should therefore be urged to do its duty in this respect. Yet how is it possible, if it is possible at all, that the international working-class movement, which, even during the colonial period, with its modest resources had afforded so much help to the developing countries in training their leading cadres, raising their mass movements to consciousness, and often even in their liberation struggles, has become so indifferent to these countries just at a time when the issues of economic development have gained stature?

Statements on the alleged indifference of the European socialist countries are not in consonance with the facts. It is common knowledge not only that significant results have been achieved in establishing bilateral economic relations, but also that a substantial expansion has been attained in the past few years, especially since the socialist development models became more intensive. (It is in fact a characteristic of the intensive development period that external economic relations become a growth-promoting factor.) Substantial progress can also be registered in the establishment of technical-technological relations. It is also commonly known that in the socialist countries of Europe eminent scientific institutions are engaged in studying questions related to the socioeconomic development of Third World countries. Furthermore, political relations between the Third World and the socialist countries have likewise expanded appreciably.

There can be no doubt that a more rapid and more vigorous manifestation of these tendencies is aggravated by several factors. Of these, I should like to single out two. Firstly, in a divided world in which no comprehensive agreements between the leading powers exist regarding the non-European part thereof, the relations established and the assistance provided do not necessarily benefit those countries which most need them or are best able to make use of them, but those which are preferred on the strength of political and power considerations. This may be inevitable in a world in which menacing confrontations and serious international tensions prevail. When certain developing countries have approached a country of the socialist community, the USA and the Western capitalist countries have usually retaliated by imposing an embargo on economic relations or reducing them to a minimum in one or other form of discrimination. It was of course the unilateral discontinuance of historically established relations which obliged the socialist countries to compensate, in the dual system of assistance and exchange, for the deliveries not effected by the capitalist states. There is no doubt that the consequence was less aid and assistance for the other developing countries. In this way, the Western countries compelled the socialist countries to increase their assistance extended on the basis of political preference, while Western liberals and progressives protested against the uneven distribution of aid and assistance among the developing countries.

To turn to the second factor of aggravation, it is also true that for the past few years the socialist development model has been less outward-looking than the capitalist development model. This has several reasons, which relate to both internal and external circumstances. But it can hardly be denied that the economic blockade against the Soviet Union, the embargo policy pursued after the Second World War, and the COCOM lists have played a very important role in making the socialist development model inward-looking. An initially inward-looking economic policy implied that the socialist countries were rather late (the 1970's) in beginning to participate in the world economy with any degree of intensity and, even then, only on the export side. However, their continued progress along this path is now impaired by a new embargo imposed on the Soviet Union in 1980. A policy of embargo applied to any country is of course not a bilateral problem but a factor which heavily disturbs world economic relations and the international climate. As a result of these factors, when measured against the position which the socialist countries occupy in world production and world politics, their external economic activity has remained relatively modest.

The opinion has of course also been advanced in the socialist countries that an international system without bureaucracy would, in this respect too, be more efficient than the bilateral system. It is perhaps not immodest to point out in this connection that in a major work of mine published in 1964[9] I too suggested the 'internationalization' of assistance under certain conditions.

It is obvious that, in a tension-ridden world which is susceptible to confrontations and sensitive to shifts in the equilibrium of relations, the settlement of such comprehensive issues is possible only on the basis of an international consensus, in the achievement of which the leading powers play a decisive role. If, under today's exacerbated and uncertain conditions, it were to prove impossible to arrive at a comprehensive agreement embracing several substantial issues of the world economy and world politics, then a 'state of economic emergency and immediate danger' could be declared for this set of problems and all related issues withdrawn from the sphere of political-security rivalry between the leading powers. This kind of settlement would also call for an agreement between the leading powers. Such a solution would imply a certain 'depoliticization' of the economic problems relating to the developing countries,[10] since international politics today automatically requires action to be taken within the traditional value system of the nation state.

But the settlement of this problem on the basis of a relative international consensus is aggravated under present conditions by a few serious factors. Of these I wish to examine the following three. Firstly, the new embargo, imposed on grain and the technologically most developed commodities, which is the expression of one party's reluctance to trade in the spirit of mutual benefit and of that party's intention to do harm to the other party by breaking off relations; secondly, the fact that to date no comprehensive agreement regulating and safeguarding East-West economic and trade relations (between EEC and CMEA, between the USA and the Soviet Union) has been concluded; and thirdly, the arms race, which endangers the climate necessary for normal economic relations and implants the features of a defence economy into national economies in a period of serious economic crisis.

From a world economy standpoint – and the satisfactory operation of the world economy is today a decisive precondition for the survival of mankind – I therefore attribute very great importance to the recommendations made by the Commission to the effect that, in the interest of settling development issues in consensus, the heads of state (or, more precisely, the holders of power) should meet on a regular basis, not in the representative sense to approve agreements already concluded but in a negotiatory sense to seek to conclude agreements.

I regard this course of action to be both necessary and inevitable, (as affirmed in a study of mine published a few years ago[11]), because although the practical problems of the world economy today (OECD – CMEA) often call for meetings and negotiations among the holders of power, the discussion and solution of economic issues between countries with different social systems and at different development levels are handled by economic specialists with no decision-making power or authority in the political-security sphere. As a result, they can take decisions only on such economic issues as they can solve without having to transgress the limits set by political and other considerations.

I should like to emphasize again that the East is neither indifferent to, nor uninterested in, the issues of either the South or the world economy. On the contrary, over and above its motivations, which were examined above in connection with the developing countries, the East is becoming increasingly aware of the severity of the danger facing mankind as a whole in the present world economic crisis. Irrespective of which part of the world we live in, we must make every effort to ensure that the holders and managers of power recognize the dangers menacing the survival of mankind and, in awareness of these dangers, make the inevitably necessary changes in the existing structures and interest relations to formulate finally a policy which brings about the indispensable conditions for cooperation and joint action in solving the problems of the last decades of our century.

References

1. The limits to growth: report of the Club of Rome's Project on the Predicament of Mankind; Donella H. Meadows, Dennis L. Meadows, et al., New York, Universe Books, 1972, p.205.

Mesarovic, Mihajlo, Pestel, Eduard: *Mankind at the turning point: second report to the Club of Rome*, New York Dutton, 1974.

Laszlo, Ervin: *Goals for mankind: report to the Club of Rome on the new horizons of global community*. New York, Dutton, 1977. XXI, p.434.

Botkin, James W., Elmandjra, Mahdi; Malitza, Mircea: *No limits to learning: bridging the human gap. report to the Club of Rome*. Oxford, Pergamon Press, 1979. XVI, p.159.

2. Colin, Norman: *Microelectronics at work: productivity and jobs in the world economy.* Oct. 1980. Worldwatch papers, 39.

3. Bognár, József: 'Political and security factors in East-West economic relations.' *New Hungarian quarterly.* 1979, no.75, pp.41-68.

4. *Der Spiegel,* 11 February 1980, p.94.

5. *Wirtschaftswoche,* 15 February 1980, p.12.

6. Colin, Norman: op. cit.

7. Bognár, József: *Economic policy and planning in developing countries.* Bp. Akad. K. 1968, p.627 (In Hungarian 1967).

8. Bognár, József: 'Global economic security and growth.' *New Hungarian Quarterly.* 1980, no.79, pp.9-24.

9. Bognár, József: loc. cit., item 5.

CURT GASTEYGER*

. . . developing countries find themselves drawn into East-West-competition whether or not they like it.

The Brandt Report calls itself – not without ambition – a 'programme for survival'. It pleads – and rightly so – for more, and more evenly spread economic development, a greater awareness in North and South of their mutual interdependence, and new initiatives for implementing these two objectives on a global level. Nobody in his right mind would dispute the legitimacy of this appeal even though one may disagree with some of its practical recommendations.

But the basic problem we have with the Report lies elsewhere. It relates to the overall background against which its diagnosis was made and its therapy prescribed. Here we are left with the Report and its eminent authors, the crucial issues and perspectives of the North-South dialogue are discussed only within a predominantly economic-social framework. This conveys somehow the impression as if – to put it somewhat crudely – politics did

---

* Switzerland. Leading expert on problems of international security.

not really matter. By 'politics' I mean the overall international political environment which, in the final analysis, determines the scope and orientation of economic development and cooperation and their eventual success or failure.

To undertake anything like a comprehensive evaluation of the political dimension of North-South relations may not have been the task of the Brandt Commission, or was perhaps beyond its reach. Whatever the reasons, without it the Report with all its merits remains incomplete. It risks seeing things with only one eye – the 'economic eye'. In so doing it distorts or omits fundamental facts and currents of the international political scene that are likely to overshadow, slow down or render completely illusory many of the Report's valuable recommendations. Its all too simplistic chapter on 'Disarmament and Development' is probably the most striking case in point.

It may therefore be useful to look at some of those politico-strategic factors which, in one way or another, will influence the future course of North-South relations. More likely than not, they will further complicate the issues at stake, add new strains to the wear and tear of international negotiations, and thus make compromise still more difficult. In a brief exposition like this we cannot do more than outline some contours of the changing political framework within which the North-South dialogue will take place, ask a few questions that would seem relevant in this context, and put forward some modest suggestions as to what might – or should – be done to create the kind of political climate capable of promoting rather than hindering this dialogue.

The changing international framework

It is a commonplace to state that, in recent years, the international system has undergone profound changes. What is less clearly understood is their precise nature and far-reaching consequences. Their pace and scope have been – and still are – so rapid that our minds, and even more so our institutions, find it difficult to adjust to them.

International politics today are characterized by at least

three major contradictions*. The first has to do with the extension of the 'cold war' in general (and superpower rivalry in particular) beyond the traditional East-West context and the growing complexity of the international system. It creates, as Professor Hoffmann points out, a serious dilemma for the United States and the Soviet Union. They find themselves caught between, on the one hand, the wish or need to intervene in the 'Third World' for reasons of security or influence, and, on the other hand, a necessity for mutual restraint in order to avoid a potentially catastrophic confrontation. By opting for the first they may hope to stabilize an otherwise explosive situation or prevent an unacceptable shift of power in favour of the other; by choosing the second they would demonstrate respect for the independence of the region or country in question but forsake commitments or responsibilities that their local friends or allies expect from them.

The farther afield the Soviet Union is expanding by means of her growing naval forces and transport capabilities, the more difficult it will be to keep the Third World out of superpower competition and to deal with its conflicts on their own merits or demerits. But it is not just the growth of Soviet military power which lessens the chance of such dissociation and enhances that of association and reciprocal involvement. Other developments may produce similar effects: a potential spread of nuclear weapons beyond the present five or (including India) six nuclear powers is likely to provoke more rather than less superpower intervention; equally, the vital importance of many developing countries as suppliers of raw materials would suggest a mutual predilection for North-South 'association' rather than 'dissociation'. The way Middle East oil producers have acquired stakes in Western economies (and vice-versa) is the most obvious example.

All this is to say that the much praised 'interdependence' and a more equal spread of 'power' have their price. They

---

* For the following I have greatly profited from the stimulating paper Prof. Stanley Hoffmann submitted to the 22nd Annual Conference of the International Institute for Strategic Studies at Stresa (Italy), 11-14.9.1980, entitled 'Security in an age of turbulence: means of response'.

keep East and West politically more involved in the developing world than would seem desirable. Thus developing countries find themselves drawn into East-West competition whether they like it or not (hence remarkable attempts by some of them with previously pro-Western or pro-Soviet orientation to steer towards a more balanced position). Most importantly, conflicts among or within these countries acquire suddenly an importance which neither East nor West can afford to ignore. The war between Iran and Iraq, or Ethiopia and Somalia are cases in point: the West can remain no more indifferent to a break-down of Iran than the Soviet with regard to the future of her Ethiopian ally.

The conclusion from all this would be that any improvement of the economic relationship between North and South is unlikely to be attained without some parallel improvement in the politico-strategic field. The two are bound to interact upon each other. A transfer of East-West antagonisms to the South can be avoided or attenuated only if both East and West perceive the economic development and policial stability of the South to be in their own interests as well as in that of the latter.

The second contradiction is the one between a 'one world' view of global interdependence and 'common destiny' on the one hand, and a clearly discernible trend towards greater differentiation or diversification in regional groupings on the other. The first rightly recognizes that on a planet with shrinking resources, growing pollution and many other developments of 'transnational' consequences common action becomes mandatory.

If this is a correct assumption (and we think, like the 'Club of Rome' and the Brandt Commission, that it is) then the multiple signs of disintegration, of frictions and crises within universal organisations, multilateral alliances and regional communities are worrying indeed. Several postwar alliances have crumbled or simply faded away. The communist world which was supposed to have for ever eliminated armed conflicts has recently witnessed more of them than any other region. Regional associations like the European Community, the Latin American Free Zone or the Organisation of African States either stagnate or are inadequate for the tasks they are faced with. It is the inherent contradiction between desirable interdependence and actual diversification which makes any call for a substantial reform or improvement of institutions like the United Nations or regional organizations sound rather hollow: these bodies are as good or bad as their members will allow. First priority should therefore be given to stemming the trend of fragmentation by promoting regional cooperation and integration – among both industrialized and developing countries. Any strengthening, for instance, of the European Community or ASEAN would immeasurably improve the chances for more efficient development cooperation here, and greater political stability there.

The third contradiction can be found in the indisputable need for more and more rapid economic development in most Third World countries and the increasingly unstable political environment in which this development is expected to take place. Economic development requires first of all at least a minimum amount of political stability, both internal and external. It is the precondition for allocating a greater share of the GNP to such non-military sectors as welfare, agriculture, education or infrastructure.

Unfortunately, this is precisely what many developing countries cannot or dare not do. Rather, they seem to move in the opposite direction, i.e. towards more military spending. They see themselves, rightly or wrongly, in an increasingly insecure world, with more actors and sources of conflict and a concomitant diffusion of military power. All this makes for an environment that promises to become more, not less, volatile and uncertain, with more rather than less turbulence and a resurgence of the use of military force and intervention that many of us had hoped would not happen again. It is the revived and spreading belief in the utility of this force as a means of foreign policy that absorbs valuable resources which are so badly needed for other, non-military purposes.

To be sure, lack of economic progress is a source of conflict itself. But an overview of recent conflicts – from Ethiopia and Uganda via Indochina to Afghanistan – shows that it has rarely, if ever, been the immediate cause of armed conflict. Its real causes usually lie elsewhere – and so do those of the profound feelings of insecurity that pervade most parts of the globe. While therefore every effort should be made to promote economic development, even greater efforts are needed to create a more stable international framework for it. There is no doubt that such a framework provides less incentive, or justification, for the acquisition of ever more expensive armament, be it by way of arms imports or the build-up of indigenous arms industries. Again, both sides – suppliers and recipients of arms – will have to act: the former by limiting arms transfers or supporting regional efforts for stability; the latter by resisting the temptation to acquire weapons not absolutely essential for their security or, what is even more demanding, by soberly calculating the negative repercussions their arms purchases are bound to have on their neighbours.

All the three contradictions in the present international system – and there are probably more – deserve greater attention when new forms of better cooperation between North and South are being discussed. They show that 'economics' alone, however important, do not suffice for understanding, let alone solving, these problems the Commission wants us to act upon, so do those in the political and military field: they have to be seen and taken together if real progress and not mere patchwork is the objective.

The quest for stability

'Stability' is certainly a key objective for a world in need of peace and development. By 'stability' we do not mean either the absence of change or an immutable or rigid status quo. Rather we mean a political situation, both at home and abroad, that allows for *peaceful* change, without major disruptions or violence, and assures conditions of negotiations and cooperation instead of confrontation and conflict. This is no easy thing to achieve – not within a country and even less so on the international level. Two observations may illustrate my point. They are directly relevant to, but have unfortunately not been sufficiently discussed by the Report.

The first is meant to warn us against the too facile assumption that economic development – while necessary – is almost tantamount to a greater degree of stability. It may be so but we cannot be sure. Experience has shown that the danger of conflict and crisis is often greater once a certain level of economic development has been reached. It is at this point that expectations of ever greater parts of the population are awake and rising, that awareness of inequalities in the distribution of wealth is reaching a sensitive threshold, and that the wish for more political participation grows. It would seen that the Report has not sufficiently addressed itself to this kind of problem – either because it did not question the assumption that 'economic development' is something good *per se*, or because its authors shied away from a delicate but nonetheless real problem, namely the glaring discrepancies of wealth in many developing countries which separate the ruling élites and the rest of the population. This points to the existence of an internal North-South conflict that should bother us no less than the gap between North and South.

The second observation concerns the relationship between East- West détente and the North-South dialogue. There is no doubt in my mind that a stable relationship between the Western industrialized countries and the Communist world, particularly between the superpowers, is essential for their respective policies towards, and cooperation with the Third world. Any serious deterioration in this relationship, a break-up of the strategic dialogue or a return to the cold war would not only be harmful for the two sides but have profound repercussions on their relations with the rest of the world. In this sense the South has a direct interest in a stable North. It should therefore refrain from playing out the West against the East so as to get the maximum from both. These are almost bound to be short-term gains, hardly apt to promote mutual confidence.

Of course, the reverse is also true. One of the main obstacles to a gradual stabilization of the South is the fact that it is still considered to be open to all kinds of competition and rivalry – a 'free for all' with many 'grey areas' merely waiting to be aligned with one or the other side. It is in the very nature of the South that its various shades of non-alignment and shifting loyalties leave many areas of influence and responsibilities undefined, whereas détente precisely presupposese their clear circumscription. Such lack of clarity in the South stands in the way to commonly observed 'rules of the game'. It makes it difficult to distinguish between legitimate assistance and questionable interference, between honestly satisfying Southern needs or willfully imposing Western (or Communist) views and concepts. Arms sales to developing countries provide a good illustration of this ambivalence: are they an attempt of the North to gain greater influence in these countries, or are they the response to legitimate security requirements; a mere business transaction or a strategic ploy? Does a refusal of highly sophisticated nuclear technology reflect on the part of the North a genuine concern for the stability in the South – or is it a discriminatory denial of technological transfer?

None of these – or similar – questions can be answered in a general way. But they show how difficult it is to do justice to the legitimate claims of the South without neglecting the equally legitimate concerns and dilemmas of the North.

Some suggestions

There is evidently no once-and-for-all recipe and no overall strategy. Rather, we must brace ourselves for a long and tiresome search for answers to specific issues without losing sight of the global framework into which they must fit in order to attain the double aim of greater stability and more equal social and economic welfare. Some suggestions come to mind.

First, we should aim at a clearer and common understanding of what 'security' in its wider sense means and how it should be assured for all parties concerned. The attempt alone to find an acceptable definition will show how far apart our views on security still are. The Soviet Union, for instance, has certainly a different notion of security from Western countries – and as long as this is so we have still a long way to go in developing common responsibilities and policies towards the South.

Second, and in the same vein, it would be invaluable if the Soviet Union could be brought to accept the present international system not only in practice (which she basically does) but also in theory as something that surely ought to be reformed but not revolutionized.

Third, greater restraint with regard to military force should be observed by everybody. We must fear that many developing countries will follow the bad example of the North by over-estimating the utility of military power as a political instrument and yielding to the ever present temptation of having recourse to arms once diplomacy seems to have failed.

Fourth, some 'rules of the game' should be developed that could help to reduce the danger of misunderstandings or miscalculations in our actions vis-à-vis the South: Western investments in developing countries are not *a priori* a manifestation of 'neo-colonialism', as the Soviet Union has it, nor is Soviet support to a country like Syria necessarily a proof of Soviet expansionism. But developing countries in turn will have to show that 'non-alignment' has little substance if it shies away from assuming international responsibilities or exhausts itself in a more or less balanced condemnation of both Eastern and Western 'imperialism'.

Finally, while economic development is crucial and a central concern of both North and South it represents just one sector of the international order: its progress remains at best partial and conditional if this order does not progress as well. Whether we like it or not: the success of failure of reports like the one submitted by the Brandt Commission depends on whether they succeed in finding answers that help to reconcile the economics and politics. In other words: Politics *do* matter – and much still remains to be done in this field.

FOUR

MUTUAL INTERESTS:
AN ILLUSION?

RALF DAHRENDORF*

> The decades ahead are more likely to be decades of a widening gap between rich and poor than decades of cooperation.

The least that should be said about the Brandt Commission's North-South Report is that it has revitalized an essential discussion. Moreover, the Report incorporates a number of proposals which merit inclusion on the agenda of more than just a one-off summit conference. Nonetheless, there is reason enough to beware of fostering illusions. Virtually no subject is so beset with misnomers confusing the desirable with the probable as is development policy. The Report is no real exception in this respect. This attempt to unravel these confused issues is intended to further the serious debate on the subject.

The first myth frustrating the development discussion is also the least often contested; the Commission likewise fails to question its validity. It is the myth of the One World. Hardly any public speaker – whether politician, professor, or preacher – omits to allude to a world which has become an interdependent unit and in which events taking place in one corner likewise affect the most distant corner, and this sooner rather than later thanks to modern means of communication. There is probably some truth in this assumption, yet it is in essence erroneous. Despite all that television and transistor radio may like to imply, our world is not yet One World.

Arthur Lewis, the eminent development economist and Nobel prizewinner, observed in 1969 'If Africa, Asia, and Latin America were to sink into the ocean tomorrow, their submergence would not affect the present or future

* Federal Republic of Germany. Director of the London School of Economics. Former Commissioner of the European Community. Former Undersecretary of State of the Federal Republic of Germany. Known for his sociological work on modern society and democracy. This article first appeared in *Die Zeit* No.33, August 8, 1980

prosperity of Europe and North America to any appreciable extent.' The OECD countries could so economize on their assistance payments that the losses made by the few transnational tobacco companies and technical consultancy firms would be recompensed. The converse hypothesis is of course equally true. If Europe, North America, Japan and Oceania were simultaneously to disappear into the sea, this would similarly not greatly affect the contemporary or future prosperity of the Third World. It might even be to its advantage if the Third World were not constantly admonished by the example of the First World. Admittedly, there is a certain amount of economic interdependence, there are political ties and evidence of cultural exchange. Yet nothing has happened to date which could render these interrelations irreversible or even afford them any cardinal significance in the eyes of those affected. For hundreds of thousands it may be of fateful consequence, but the fact is that our world is not yet One World.

The Gap is Widening

It is for this reason that a second myth must be dispelled, namely that of the New International Economic Order. It may well be desirable that an international economic system be designed which guarantees the poor those rights as citizens of the world for which the populations of the OECD countries have fought so hard in the last two centuries. In reality, the rights of the individual throughout the world perhaps form the salient point of that which has hitherto erroneously been termed 'development.' However, it is at present illusory to presuppose the existence of any mutual and irrefutable interest in the creation of such an order. The majority of raw materials are either located in the developed countries or candidate countries for the Club of the Rich or they are resources for which substitutes are available.

Difficulties in sustaining economic growth in the developed world are far more likely to lead to an intensification of protectionism than to a genuine interest in cooperation. And as far as the developing countries are concerned in this respect, their ability to exert pressure will remain very limited for a considerable time to come. They have no closely allied partners in the developed world, regardless of what government speakers might find expedient to proclaim to the General Assembly of the United Nations. The decades ahead are more likely to be decades of a widening gap between rich and poor than decades of cooperation.

At the Gateway to the Club of the Rich

This bears a certain relation to the third myth to be dissipated, that of a solidarity within the Group of 77, to which far more than one hundred states now belong, or among the non-aligned community. The behaviour of nations, like that of social groups and individuals, is determined in the final analysis by interests and not by ideals. A gigantic nation which moreover disposes of nuclear technology is hardly the most suitable spokesman for the Third World; China is more a superpower than a mere member of the Group of 77. And when a nation approaches the gateway to the Club of the Rich or at least believes that it has proceeded thus far, although it may indeed follow the dictates of its conscience and continue to make payments to its former brothers in poverty, it nevertheless behaves as an 'arrivé' and no longer as a country in need. Brazil, Nigeria, and Singapore are hardly suited to serve as the spokesmen for Bolivia, the Central African Republic, and Bangladesh. It is possible that the OPEC countries, with the highest per capita income in the world and with pre-modern state and society structures, will provisionally assume an intermediate position. But they are the most improbable campaigners for the rights of the poor. The 'international class struggle' will not break out within the next two decades for lack of the One World which might otherwise create an inseparable bond between the classes, or for lack of any apparent interest in finding a common solution and the necessary solidarity among the have-nots of the world.

One must raise the question as to what kind of future awaits these have-nots. Here again, there are myths to be dispelled. The fourth myth is that the poor countries will develop to draw alongside the rich countries and that the injustices of the world will thereby gradually disappear. Although economists have long since abandoned their belief in this fairytale, it remains to a greater or lesser extent the fundamental premise in public opinion and the point of departure for political action.

Jan Tinbergen, in his informative report to the Club of Rome on this subject, showed that in 1970 per capita income in the developed and developing countries could be expressed as a ratio of approximately 13:1. He further contended that even on the basis of fairly optimistic hypotheses regarding economic growth and North-South relations, it is statistically impossible that even the slightest improvement over the ratio $13:1\cdot2$ could be attained by the year 2012.

Others may have formulated the same theses in different ways but all are unanimous in their opinion that the relative difference between the developed and the developing world will not change much in the future (unless a catastrophe catapults the developed world back into the Stone Age), and that even in absolute figures and values the majority of the population in the Third World will have no opportunity within the foreseeable future to arrive at the average standard of living already enjoyed by a middle-class German, Australian, or Japanese. The developing countries will not catch up with the developed countries.

No mention has yet been made of development aid. This, however, is often linked with a fifth myth, the so-called trickle-down theory. This incorporates the assumption that even if development aid benefits only a narrow stratum of privileged population groups in the Third World, their newly won standard of living will somehow trickle down to other population groups, either because it serves as a stimulus to emulation or because it awakens the interest of the nouveaux riches in creating the conditions which will permit their privileges to be upheld for their children, or for any one of a number of other reasons which have been put forward.

Raúl Prebisch is not the only development policy expert of renown who has elected to abandon this concept.

Prosperity has not filtered down in the developed countries of Europe and North America. Although motivation to improve living standards has characterized all these societies, examples abound in history of societies in which small upper strata groups accumulated untold riches while the poor and the beggars perished in misery on the streets outside their palaces. A generation of international officials has naively defended the trickle-down theory. Although some still uphold it the majority know that the theory is unfounded.

Unfortunately, a sixth assumption is likewise a myth, namely that stable development is an achievable reality. Even if the developing countries cannot catch up with the developed countries and even if they are taking the development process at very different rates, the more humane of the advocates of development aspire to a stable process whcih does not disrupt existing societies more than is absolutely necessary. However, there is little, if any, evidence that this is possible. Samuel Huntington has analyzed 52 countries throughout the world and concludes that 'it is not a lack of modernity but the attempt to induce modernity which provokes disorder . . . . Not only is political instability itself provoked by social and economic modernization, its extent is dependent on the pace of the modernization process.' Political instability is merely the visible expression of far-reaching dislocations of new and old. It cannot be denied that to date no Third World country has found a development path which was simultaneously effective and stable.

'Alternative Civilizations'

This leaves but the seventh myth to dispel. (It is at this point that the door is opened in some opinions to alternatives to the gloom described above.) The seventh myth is that of the universality of modernization. However strange this may sound, even Hegel's most committed opponents have implicitly or explicitly accepted the existence of something of a spirit of universality, a 'weltgeist' marching through time and imposing its will in the face of acceptance and resistance alike. Even today, only few consider it possible that modernization will not ultimately envelop the entire world.

However, one should perhaps examine more carefully the undertones of the analyses made by a number of the leading lights in the developing countries themselves, such as that of the Indian political scientist Rajni Kothari or the Indonesian expert Soedjatmoko. When the latter speaks of 'alternative civilizations' (and characteristically adds that 'only ten years ago it would have been unthinkable to postulate the desirability of alternative civilizations, much less their feasibility'), he gives us a foretaste of events such as the reaction of the Islamic world to the onrushing advance of modernization and at the same time illuminates in retrospect developments such as the Chinese before, during and after the Cultural Revolution. We should not accept unquestioningly that industrialization and modernization are necessary, and much less that any such processes should automatically follow the European/North American pattern.

So much for dispelling the myths which confound our understanding of development. What conclusions can be drawn? Does this imply that we can now shelve the problem of development and devote our energies to the problems of the OECD countries without 'wasting' much thought on the New International Economic Order? Of course not. It implies the very opposite. It implies that our world is beset with a big, unsolved problem which we do not even understand. Regardless of all the now exposed myths, we are still people who live together in this world. We are all threatened by common dangers and conflicts which may not be realities today but may become so tomorrow. But, above all, the fact that we are all people means that we all have certain basic rights. After the problem of safeguarding the world from nuclear war, the most important issue on the international agenda is that of the world's poor.

But only if we are honest, if we abandon our illusions and unmask our empty words for what they really are will we be able to deal with this problem. The issue at hand is not one of arriving at a world of industrial or 'developed' countries. It is for the time being nothing more than that of obtaining elementary civil rights for all. This alone will keep us occupied for a while. For many hundreds of thousands it will come too late. So, let us call the problem by its proper name: it is first and foremost a moral problem and it is as such that we should approach it.

ROBERT W. TUCKER*

Development and a greater measure of equality portend a competitive rather than cooperative future; they hold the promise of far more conflict than consensus.

The Brandt Commission Report is the latest in the lengthening series of manifestos on what many in the past decade have come to regard as the great issue of our time: the division of the world between the rich and poor. In its general outlook and assumptions, the Report does not break new ground. The lengthy analysis of the 'grave global issues arising from the economic and social disparities of the world community' faithfully reflects views now quite familiar by virtue of similar efforts in past years. Thus there is an air of *dejà vu* in the note of extreme urgency that pervades the Report. The two decades ahead, we are warned, 'may be fateful for mankind.' This is presumably so for the reason that the disparities between the world's rich and poor, if not substantially reduced in the near term, will lead either to war or to uncontrollable chaos. We can no longer put off a choice between destruction or development – between continuing along our present dangerous path or adopting new directions that reduce existing inequalities between rich and poor and particularly that promise the speedy alleviation of global poverty and hunger. In his introduction to the Report, the chairman notes: 'While hunger rules peace cannot prevail. He who wants to ban war must also ban mass poverty.' And in its 'programme of priorities' the Commission warns that: 'At

* USA. Professor of Political Science at the Johns Hopkins University. Author of *The Inequality of nations* as well as several books on U.S. Foreign Policy.

the beginning of the 1980s the world community faces much greater dangers than at any time since the Second World War.'

The dark night that all too likely awaits us if we do not address our efforts to the problems of the Southern states – and, above all, the problems of the poorest among them – appeals to our sense of self-interest. That sense is reinforced by the argument that the recommended measures to alleviate mass poverty and otherwise to reduce present disparities in income and wealth will operate to the benefit of the West as well as the South. The rich industrialized states of the West are exhorted to take measures to reform the international economic system not only to avoid catastrophe but to benefit themselves. The theme of mutual interest, the consequence of an ever growing interdependence, is central to the Report. Thus we read that if the 'South cannot grow adequately without the North,' it is also the case that the 'North cannot prosper or improve its situation unless there is greater progress in the South.' The large-scale transfers of resources to the South the Report calls for 'can make a major impact on growth in both the South and the North and help to revive the flagging world economy.' Properly seen, the South 'can be said to be an "engine of growth" for the North,' 'a new economic frontier' that, once fully opened, will contribute to growth and employment in the North.

Yet it is not only to interest that the Report makes its appeal. It does not do so because its authors apparently do not believe that interest alone can provide an adequate basis for all the changes that are needed. 'Especially as far as the poorest people and the poorest countries are concerned,' the authors declare, 'the principal motives for our proposals are human solidarity and a commitment to international social justice. There must be an end to deprivation and suffering. It cannot be accepted that in one part of the world most people live relatively comfortably, while in another they struggle for sheer survival.' These words echo earlier reports on international development. In the 1969 report of the Pearson Commission we read: 'The simplest answer to the question [why the rich should concern themselves with the plight of the poor] is the moral one: that it is only right for those who have to share with those who have not.'

It is, then, in the postulate of a shared humanity that the Brandt Report, in the manner of its predecessors, finds the duty to alleviate the suffering of the world's poverty stricken and, more generally, to reduce present global disparities of income and wealth. A collective responsibility – particularly, to ensure a minimal substance to all – that heretofore has applied only within the state and then largely only in the post World War II period is projected onto the greater society of states. What are the grounds for assuming so momentous a transformation as this implies? Previously the sense of obligation to sacrifice for the welfare of others has depended if not upon proximity then upon discrete and identifiable social grouping. The nation-state has been the largest social grouping able to command such sacrifice. Given this experience, it is clearly not enough to proclaim that 'the great moral imperatives that under-pinned [domestic] reforms are as valid internationally as they were and are nationally . . .' Even if accepted, the assertion does nothing to advance the prospect that the 'great moral imperatives' will not only be acknowledged as valid but will also be made effective.

The Report does not simply ignore the past and the lessons it conveys. The 'great moral imperatives' it proclaims will not be followed because men find their contents self-evident and, for this reason, compelling. If the sacrifices called for by the Report are considered quite possible, this is because in addition to the claims of human solidarity and a shared humanity 'experience confirms that there are other imperatives also, rooted in the hard-headed self-interest of all countries and people, that reinforce the claim of human solidarity. World society now recognizes more clearly than ever before its mutual needs; it must accept a shared responsibility for meeting them.'

Once again, we are brought back to the argument of mutual interests. In turn, the argument of mutual interests rests upon the fact of interdependence. If the case for a global distributive justice is considered apparent in the Brandt Report, as it is in many similar statements, it is because the authors consider such interdependence as exists in today's world as constitutes not only order but justice as well. And if one – indeed, *the* – essential ingredient of that justice is a greater measure of equality, it is presumably because an interdependence that cannot be avoided save at prohibitive cost also cannot be expected to function without substantial reduction in present disparities of global income and wealth. It is the commonality of fate imposed by a growing interdependence that creates the need for, while making possible, a greater measure of international equality. It is a mutuality and intensity of interest, manifested in the main by a variety of economic and social relationships, that transforms the concept of a shared humanity from a noble aspiration, though one without much practical consequence, into a positive duty to provide minimal subsistence to the world's peoples without regard for national boundaries.

This is, in brief, the outlook that informs the Brandt Report and that conditions many of its recommendations for global reform. Articulated on many earlier occasions, this outlook has not gained in persuasiveness through repetition. It is not true that the peace of the world is gravely threatened today by the persistence of global poverty and hunger. Today, as yesterday, the world's peace is placed in jeopardy by those who have the power to mount an effective challenge to the status quo. The poverty-stricken do not possess such power. The argument has been made that the destitute nevertheless may provide the occasion for war between the rich and strong. But though much has been made of the presumed power of the poor to transmit their misery in the form of chaos and war, there has yet to be drawn a scenario that plausibly demonstrates either this potential of the poor or how this potential might be effectively employed.

What can be and, indeed, is being plausibly demonstrated are the difficulties posed to the affluent by those who though far from poverty-stricken nevertheless remain far from satisfied with their lot. Resistant to and resentful of what they see as persisting inequality, these conditions are, for the most part, among the middle class, if not the *nouveaux riches*, of international society. Their power depends not only upon their possession of vital resources (most notably, of course, oil) but also upon the inability or the forbearance of the developed states to take, or even seriously to threaten, severe sanctions against them in the event of exorbitant demands on their part.

To a degree, the Brandt Report recognizes the above, despite its apparent emphasis on poverty and hunger as the great threat to world stability and peace. Although never quite clearly articulated, a major assumption of the report is that marked inequality must threaten an interdependent society and for the reason that interdependence is considered a synonym for vulnerability. A society made up of increasingly interdependent units is a society made up of increasingly vulnerable units. If the great moral imperative of the age is equality, an increasingly interdependent world that does not respond to this imperative is evidently a world with a very bleak future.

One might avoid this conclusion simply by rejecting, or seriously qualifying, the assumption on which it is based. In fact, if we make exception for the case of oil, the theme of interdependence has been greatly exaggerated. Certainly it has been exaggerated as applied to the West's presumed dependence on the South, a dependence that – even when we take oil into account – is markedly smaller than the South's dependence on the West. What is significant in this context, however, is that the Report though avidly accepting the theme of interdependence avoids the pessimistic conclusions suggested by the juxtaposition of marked disparities in income and wealth with an equally marked interdependence. It can do so because it largely accepts the liberal belief in a harmony (or mutuality) of interests, now greatly strengthened by an ever growing interdependence. Implicit in the Report is the assumption that interdependence itself is largely constitutive of order and even of justice as well.

Yet given the conditions that continue to define international society, the reverse is very nearly the case. Although such interdependence as we have in international society today creates the need for a greater measure of order, it provides no assurance that this need will be met. Indeed, if the state is being slowly drained of its former autonomy, as the believers in interdependence insist, then, in the absence of effective alternative political institutions, what order international society has hitherto enjoyed must be jeopardized. Interdependence cannot, as such, fill this need. As the oil crisis has demonstrated, it is as much a source of conflict as of consensus, if not more. It is a source of conflict not only because it promotes insecurity and competition while failing to provide the means for assuaging insecurity and setting bounds to competition. Even if interdependence is seen to result in benefits to all parties, these benefits may nevertheless vary considerably, particularly in a world made up of states at very different levels of development. In the absence of agreement on the distribution of benefits derived from interdependence, an absence so apparent today, a sensitivity to what are perceived as substantial disparities in benefits will provide at least as great a source of conflict as of consensus.

Nor can development provide what interdependence cannot provide. The issues that interdependence raises are also in large measure the issues development must raise, however widespread the approval development elicits in principle. For whatever else development may mean, it is evidently a commitment to a greater measure of equality. If the experience of domestic struggles over achieving greater equality has any relevance for the problem of global inequality, we can only expect that the development imperative – again, whatever consensus it elicits in principle – will provide an acute and continuing source of conflict. Given the notorious lack of cohesiveness and solidarity of international society, the demand to reduce present disparities of income and wealth would produce conflict even in quite favorable circumstances. For even in quite favorable circumstances, international economic relationships would still be relationships of equity with their clearly redistributive overtones. Moreover, the prime movers in the demand for equality will be states. It is through the existing frame-work of states, sovereign and independent, that disparities in income and wealth are to be reduced. Is there reason to expect that the claims of developing states to greater equality will be moderated with a steady improvement in their standards of living? Here again, if the experience of domestic society is relevant, the answer cannot prove comforting in its implications for international conflict. Several years ago one of the great champions of the world's poor, Gunnar Myrdal, warned against 'the glib assertion that the underdeveloped countries must be aided in order to preserve the peace of the world.' '[If] any generalization can be made,' he went on to say, 'it is rather that people become restless and rebellious when they are getting a little better off, but not enough so.'

This conclusion is all the more apparent when it is considered that the inequalities development is expected to redress are also inequalities of power and status. Indeed, they are probably above all inequalities of power and status. The authors of the Report do not appear sufficiently to appreciate this, though Southern élites have not sought to obscure the essential meaning equality has for them. The great objectives of development have been seen by these élites primarily in terms of the state, that is, of the state's power and status, and not in terms of individual consumption standards, or welfare, as the Report is wont to do. Yet it is this very emphasis of the Report that permits its authors to maintain their otherwise mystifying optimism over the consequences of development and to persist in the belief that development will prove, on balance, a source of consensus rather than of conflict. For consumption and welfare are not inherently exclusive goods, whereas power and status are very close to being so. Any consensus on developing would have to comprise, at some point, a consensus on power and status . Any redistribution of wealth would also have to comprise a redistribution of power and status. The former redistribution may occur without the rich and powerful paying a substantial price though this now appears increasingly doubtful, but the latter redistribution cannot but occur at the expense of the rich and powerful. Development and a greater measure of equality portend a competitive rather than cooperative future; they hold out the promise of far more conflict than consensus.

At least, they must do so in the absence of a preexistent measure of cohesiveness and solidarity sufficient to. safeguard against the conflict raised by demands for greater equality. The claims of the Report notwithstanding, such cohesiveness and solidarity do not exist in today's world. They cannot be deduced from the fact of interdependence. Nor can they be seen in the triumph of a conviction that the rich nations bear a collective responsibility for reducing international inequalities of income and wealth. Were this duty as self-evident and compelling as some assume – among them the authors of the Report – the exhortation to alleviate the plight of the poverty-stricken would not have to be attended by appeals to the self-interest of the rich.

If anything, such ties as once did exist between the West and the Third World, and that gave a modest measure of reality to the proposition of a collective responsibility, are now visibly eroding. One reason for this is the widening psychological and moral gulf between the West and the Third World. It is often forgotten that those who once rebelled against the West nevertheless identified in large measure with the ways of the West. The evidence of the abandonment of this identification is everywhere today. The West is no longer the model for the new states; it may even become the anti-model for much of the Third world. If so, this will scarcely contribute to the kind of cohesiveness and solidarity on which the Brandt Report, and similar efforts, must perforce rely.

Then, too, it is becoming increasingly apparent that there is a very great difference between the way in which Western élites have viewed the problem of international inequality and the way in which Southern élites have viewed it. From the prevailing Western perspective, the moral obligation or responsibility arising from the vast disparities in income and wealth is one that is owed to individuals. This obligation may have to be mediated by the state, but it is still one that has the individual and his welfare as the proper subject. This is why it can ignore questions of power and status and otherwise often appear so strikingly apolitical. From the prevailing Southern perspective, the moral obligation arising from disparities in income and wealth is one that is owed to collectives. It is the state that is the moral unit upon which claims for equality centre, just as it is the moral unit that is held to endow these claims with legitimacy. The primacy thus placed on collective (national) goals and the insistence upon subordinating individual to collective goals cannot but have a dampening effect upon even the more ardent Western advocates of a moral obligation to reduce international inequality. So long as it seemed plausible – and, to many in the West, even self-evident – that, in Robert McNamara's words, 'the improvement of the individual lives of the great masses of the people is, in the end, what development is all about,' the 'moral imperative' of development remained, as a moral imperative, virtually unchallenged. Once the realization progressively dawns that this is not what development is all about as far as the majority of Southern élites are concerned, this moral imperative can no longer pass unchallenged.

In sum, the outlook and assumptions that underlie the Brandt Report must be seriously qualified or, in some respects, simply rejected. The world that the Report describes is not the world that dispassionate inquiry reveals. The apocalyptic vision that is held out by the persistence of poverty and, more generally, of marked inequality fails to persuade. So too, the world of mutual interests, the realization of which is held back by lack of awareness of the dangers confronting us and by the absence of political will to face up to these dangers and take corrective action, also fails to persuade. The Report assumes that the essential conditions for the transformation of international society—and, indeed, of man—are already at hand and that there is only the need to remove the obstacles which impede this transformation from finding its natural expression. There is very little evidence in support of this view and a great deal of evidence that supports a quite different view. Our expectation must be that the many conflicts of interest between developed and developing states will be resolved in ways similar conflicts have been resolved in the past. Given the poor economic prospects of the states of the West today – prospects critically affected by measures one group of Southern states (OPEC) has taken – the outlook for compromise and moderation is not good.

CONSTANTINE V. VAITSOS*

The issue . . . is . . . whether higher economic growth rates in the world economy will so alter the relative power internationally (with respect to OPEC) and nationally (with respect to the trade unions) that 'Northern interests' will find themselves in considerable jeopardy.

The Sudpolitik of the Brandt Commission: visionary or wishful thinking?

In the midst of a major economic crisis and structural disequilibria in the world economy, the market for prophets of doom or, alternatively, of hope for new opportunities is booming. The problems now facing us though are so profound and complex that any serious attempt not only to describe what is taking place – an area which is increasingly flooded by masses of opinions and writings – but to propose specific and major international co-operative actions merits close and thorough evaluation. This is the case of the report drafted by the Independent Commission on International Development Issues under the chairmanship of Willy Brandt.

Admittedly, the Report includes no individually novel suggestion for improving economic relations between the haves and the have-nots in the world economy. It also lacks any plain speaking about the reasons for the present stalemate in and/or the absence of any meaningful negotiations between the North (both northwest as well as northeast) and the South. Yet it represents one of the most comprehensive and far reaching policy packages for needed changes in the relations between rich and poor countries. The prestige and international recognition of the

* Greece. Professor of political economy at Athens University. Consultant, UN Centre on Transnational Enterprises. Known for his studies on transnational corporations and technological development.

Commission's members add special weight to its recommendations. The latter, as the report states, 'are not revolutionary . . . .[but] part of a process of negotiated reform and restructuring' (p.66). Ideas and particularly Southern initiatives which in the past were received with scepticism and, in certain cases, with open hostility by spokesmen for traditional Northern orthodoxy or by related vested interests in the South, are made 'respectable' by their inclusion in the Report.

In the proposals presented by the Commission, a central element – in what the report refers to as 'a mutuality of interests' between North and South – concerns the massive transfer of financial resources from the rich to the poor countries. 'Above all, we believe [the Commission members wrote] that a large-scale transfer of resources to the South can make a major impact on growth in both the South and the North and help to revive the flagging world economy' (p. 36 of the Report). In the past, national deficit finance and related Keynesian policies helped smooth out the oscillations of business cycles in individual economies. In a similar manner, world-wide demand management – through international Keynesianism directed to selected and major purchasing needs of the South – is proposed by the Brandt Commission in order to help relieve the world from the hardships of stagflation facing us today.

In its specific contents, then, this proposal addresses itself not only to the concern for international co-operation to alleviate the inhuman conditions of mass poverty and suffering afflicting hundreds of millions of people in the developing countries (for whom repeated and compassionate references abound in the Report's contents); instead, it proposes measures which – with an eye on the political acceptability of its policy requirements – reflect an expression of enlightened self-interest by the North. In plain language, the market prospects from the needs of the 700–800 million people living in destitute conditions in the South and the consumption and investment requirements of their more fortunate neighbours also in the South, will provide a much needed stimulus for the sluggish economies of the North.

According to the Report's expectations, the resulting growth in economic activity will help alleviate unemployment in the North, which at present reaches a figure of about 18 million people in the OECD countries. It will also put into use some of the underutilized capacity also in the North. This redundant capacity has been estimated to represent at least $200 billion in terms of annual potential output.

The apparent economic sense of this argument borrows its credibility from the undeniable fact that the growth prospects of the markets of the South are far greater than the existing trends in the structures of the saturated Northern markets and in the faltering productivity growth in the industrialized economies. The Report presents some empirical evidence on these issues (e.g., p.p. 70, 178, 238). There is, though, a potentially significant exception to this dim long-term picture for macro-economic dynamism originating from within some of the economies of the north in the future. This might take place if a Schumpeterian wave of new investments and significant productivity increases are prompted by radically new technological developments. Such candidates include the massive industrial applications of micro-processors in the remaining years of this century and, extending to the post 2000 period, the evolutions in bio-engineering and in non-traditional forms of energy. The Report, though, rightly focuses its attention to the more immediate future and the extraordinary economic and political risks imbedded in the present economic crisis. its policy prescriptions in this respect are Keynesian.

In evaluating these policy recommendations one has first to concentrate on the fundamental assumptions upon which the Report is based. For the reasons presented in the section which follows we find the underlying assumptions of the Report's proposals on international Keynesianism to be quite false. Also the political chances for initiating such proposals are, in our judgement, a non-starter. Finally, the practical procedures for implementing them remain, in technical terms, unexplored and mostly at variance with the demands of power relations and established interests in the world economy. In the latter case interdependence between North and South does not imply mutuality of interests. There exists only a very small number of issues – the most important of which concerns the chaotic state of the present international monetary 'non-system' – where a resolution of conflicts can render interests to be compatible even if they are not common. The possibilities for enacting policies on international Keynesianism and their claimed implications, though, as they are presented in the Report, constitute more the product of wishful thinking than of an effective and visionary world policy alternative.

A more cynical interpreter of this proposal could see – in the guise of a 'mutually benefiting' North-South strategy – a veiled attempt by the North simply to get hold of and *control* the use of the mounting OPEC financial surpluses. In practice, the transfer of resources talked about in the Report, could end up simply not coming from the savings of the Northern countries but from recycled petro-currencies. This would, in turn, limit the chances of Third World initiatives to use the financial surpluses of the oil producers as a key source of leverage to negotiate a more effective restructuring in parts of the institutional machinery governing international economic relations. In this respect the Report's proposals – despite conscious attempts to include reciprocal concessions (like those presented in the Emergency Programme) – can be considered to be to the detriment of any fundamental North-South negotiations. The latter will lead to a change in the presently skewed nature of relations between the two parts, only if they are based on historical processes and situations which also imply a more diversified and balanced economic power base in the world economy.

The assumptions and political realities of international Keynesianism

There are two crucial assumptions on which the Report bases its proposals on international Keynesianism. Both of them are highly questionable. First, it argues that world peace and ultimately the security of the Northern countries are threatened by the continuing underdevelopment of the

South. Thus, it is implied that Northern interests, in this context, are homogeneous and that their major concerns relate to the evolutions in the South. The contours, though, of economic and political conflict now confronting the world community do not have their epicentres on the North-South axis. Instead, they basically concern the intra-OECD economic rivalry (where very serious differences exist) as well as the political and military rivalry between East and West. This does not, however, imply that conflicts involving the South, (e.g. Iran-Iraq, sub-Saharan African conflicts, convulsions in Central America and the Caribbean) will not be used as a convenient base for thrashing out North-North conflicts. The actual locus and the reasons for or origin of conflict need not coincide. The misplaced emphasis, though, for world peace and security on the North-South conflicting interests baffles the reader of the Brandt Report, particularly in view of the politically seasoned members of the Commission on matters involving international relations.

The divergence of interests within the North implies quite different attitudes by the OECD countries on restructuring the world economic system while using the South as a growth platform. In the case of the U.S. the cost of *in*action in international economic restructuring is much smaller as compared to the other OECD countries. In fact the U.S. will still wish to linger on the multiple privileges it has enjoyed in the system of 'Pax Americana', especially in the use of the dollar as an international reserve currency (to which General de Gaulle referred to as U.S.'s 'exorbitant privilege') and in the activities of its transnationals. It will, thus, avoid any hastening in changing the fundamentals of present international economic relations and concentrate its attention (including the use of Keynesian economics) on military issues vis-à-vis the U.S.S.R., *domestic* economic restructuring and investments in key high technology areas.

The two losers of World War II, who are the main growth economies in the North today, the Federal Republic of Germany and Japan, have much more serious vested interests in a controlled evolution in the world economic system. Such a change will be needed to accompany their own ascendancy to the club of world economic powers, in which the U.S. was previously the sole member. Also both of them, and especially Japan, are much more critically dependent than the U.S. on the markets and resources of the South. (It is no accident that a West German statesman of the stature of Willy Brandt was chairman of the Commission.) In contrast, other Northern countries with weakened internal economic structures, like the U.K., would hardly be willing to participate in a massive transfer of resources to the South from which other more dynamic economies withing the OECD will be the major beneficiaries. (This was amply demonstrated by Mrs Thatcher's position on this matter in the summit of Western heads of state last summer).

Finally, although the Eastern European countries are obviously hurt by the world economic crisis, they would not be likely to contribute to any serious softening of the intra-OEDC economic rivalry by opening up a massive opportunity through Northern stepped-up investments in the South. Anyhow, several of them (like Poland) find themselves in need of massive international capital transfers to and not from them. Also the direct economic advantages of the Northeast from such an evolution could hardly be compared with what the Northwest as a whole might gain. This is not only because the extent of involvement of Eastern European companies with international dealings in the Third World cannot be compared with the size of equivalent participation of Western originated transnational companies. Instead it also has to do with the nature of commitments within the COMECON, particularly vis-à-vis the USSR. These intra-Eastern European *economic* commitments condition the extent of corresponding interactions with the rest of the world.

Thus, the North is hardly homogeneous: it views its relations with the South in the context of quite different interests. Like the significant differences which exist in the national characteristics and in the resulting interests about international relations between Bangladesh, Kuwait and Brazil there are equally serious differences between the U.K., Japan and the U.S. or between them and Rumania or the U.S.S.R.

The second key and erroneous assumption of the Report is that a lower level of economic activity plus unemployment and a certain amount of relatively high inflation rates are to the detriment of all interested parties in the North. This assumption originates from the Northern heritage of a full employment growth with relatively low inflation rates of the first post-war quarter century which contrasted with the traumatic experience of the '30's. In fact, the present reverse situation – despite political rhetoric to the opposite – can be considered as a blessing in disguise for pivotal Northern interests. There are two main reasons for it.

First, a higher worldwide economic growth rate, with the present limits on energy supply, could have profound repercussions on the distribution of economic and non-economic power between the North and the OPEC countries. The fact that alternative scenarios approach in their implications some of the writings in political and economic 'science fiction', do not make them all that improbable if significantly higher growth rates are experienced in the world economy in the 1980's.

Second, in view of the fact that in a number of cases in the pre-mid '70's, wage increases in the North often tended to be higher than productivity increases, the present inflation rates could – if appropriately managed – provide an important monetary support for partially checking the falling rate of profit in industry. The impact of inflation on real wage rates could offset at least part of the forces which have led to a drop in profitability. Furthermore, slower economic growth rates and mounting unemployment could – within certain politically tolerable levels – alter the relative power of organized economic groups within the increasingly bargaining nature of Northern societies.

During periods of high growth rate, some groups can gain without this necessarily implying an absolute loss for others. However, during low growth periods, the preservation of certain economic performance (as in the level of profit) requires much more serious sacrifices by the rest. This is what is happening today with the real wage rate and the degree of acceptable unemployment in the North.

Within certain limits imposed by political realities, perceptions not only of the acceptability but also of the necessity of such levels of unemployment in the North have drastically changed from what was considered appropriate five or ten years ago.

The issue then of stepped-up Northern investments in the South is not just whether additional overall inflationary pressures will be absorbed by existing excess capacity in the North. (Incidentally the Report does not examine fully these implications and provides technically rather unconvincing arguments on the resulting net trade flows between North and South when it discusses these matters.) Instead, the key concern rests on much more precisely defined and strategic issues. They have to do with whether higher economic growth rates in the world economy will so alter the relative power internationally (with respect to OPEC) and nationally (with respect to the trade unions) that 'Northern interests' will find themselves in considerable jeopardy. More than the top management of business, the strongest supporter for higher growth rates in the world economy today should be the PLO. The former can at least console itself that settlements on higher wage rates can be checked both with respect to price increases (which effect real wages and real profits) and also with respect to productivity changes (which directly affect the profit rate, real and monetary). In contrast, the PLO will rightly feel that slower growth rates in the world economy will diminish the prospects for Palestine's independence. Since a significant part of PLO's political power comes today from the pressure that the Arab oil exporters can exert on the West, Palestine statehood is very much a function of the rate of growth of the world economy in the remaining years of this century.

There exists a number of examples - internationally, regionally and nationally - which demonstrate that the West has already examined and rejected any serious commitment for a Keynesian boost of the world economy whether along the lines proposed in the Brandt Report or otherwise. For example, four years before the Commission's recommendations, President Kreisky of Austria proposed in 1976 a major transfer of OECD resources to the South as a stimulus not only to development but also to the then faltering growth rates in the West. Similar proposals were formally made at OECD a year later by representatives of Norway and of the then U.K. government. These proposals were quickly lost without trace in the agenda of Western priority areas. Even intra - OECD Keynesian stimulus of the 'locomotive' type (using the Japanese and Federal German economics as 'engines') or later of the 'convoy' variety proved a non-starter. Furthermore, a proposal was aired in the mid-1970's by the Federal German Social Democratic party to use the occasion of the second enlargement of the European Community for a new Marshall plan type of activity in Southern Europe. Its objective consisted in firmly securing in political terms the southern flank of the Community which was emerging from years under dictatorial regimes. This was quickly shelved even by the Federal German social-democrat dominated government. Finally, the monetarist contracting policies dominating national economic thinking in practically the whole of OECD - even, as in the case of the U.K., to the detriment of needed industrial restructuring - hardly provide a receptive environment for Keynesianist expansionism. If such policies are rejected at home at the political risk of losing voters' support, how can they be implemented internationally where the first-round beneficiaries will be citizens of "other" countries?

The authors of the Report not only misread the political realities of the North but, on this subject, took some highly questionable positions on the meaning and requirements of the development process in the South. In a remarkable statement, on p. 43, the Report claims that 'the South needs, above all, finance'. In the context of the Pearson Commission a few decades ago, when North-South relations were seen exclusively under the prism of foreign aid and when the analysis of development requirements was dominated by Northern thinking', such conceptual blunders could be understandable. One wonders though how in the Brandt Commission, despite the content and sensitivity of some of its analysis of the political and organizational realities of the developing countries, it can be perceived that 'above all' more finance for the regimes of Pinochet, Mobutu or Marcos will promote development! Even on strictly statistical grounds, it would have been necessary – when the Report talks about capital transfers – to acknowledge that the North is presently a net capital importer from and not an exporter of financial resources to the South.

Far more important, though, than the quantitative aspects of capital transfers is another key concern of the North-South relations. The latter refers to the qualitative implications which such international linkages have for the way by which societies in the South organize the process of their accumulation and their productive capabilities. In this case the role played by the transnational enterprises is central. We turn now briefly to evaluate the proposals of the Commission on this topic.

Policy recommendations on the role played by transnational enterprises.

The implications of the proposed capital transfers from the North to the South bear with them a key concern on the operational *conditionality* imposed by such international financial flows. By conditionality we do not refer here to the known macro-economic policy constraints imposed characteristically by the IMF on borrowers. (It is a credit to the Report that, within the constraints of its membership and the need for acceptability in the seats of power, it explicitly recognizes and calls for a change in the management of international monetary relations. In this context it acknowledges the demonstrably discriminatory effects that the latter have had up to now on the process of development in the Third World.* It has also significantly called for an increase in programme rather than project

---

* In contrast, the hard line US policies on these matters continue to present a different perception of the functioning of the international monetary system. The Assistant Secretary of Treasury of the US, F.Bergsten, declared on the recent joint session of the World Bank- IMF that '[the Third World countries] are tragically misguided. These institutions are the ones that do the most for those guys'. Cynicism is undoubtedly one of the primary features of international politics, particularly when it is practised on the weakest members of the international community.

finance.) Instead we refer here to the link between the proposed financing of enhanced activities in developing countries, the stimulus to net Northern exports and the activities of the transnational enterprises.

As far as the North is concerned, the key areas – which appear in the package of policies recommended by the report to make operational use of additional finances granted to the South – are not likely to be covered by the small and medium sized firms of the North nor by the unemployed among its youth or certain regionally or professionaly hurt activities. Instead, the key beneficiaries – in energy exploration and exploitation, in mineral processing, in massive irrigation plans, etc. – are the large transnational enterprises and certain machinery producers, particularly those firms characterized by high capital and or certain skill intensity in their activities.

As far as the South is concerned, an internationally orchestrated financial flow which will bear the label of capital transfers from the North to the South *and* whose stated objective will be to promote export growth directly from the North, is bound to intensify the South's dependence on the transnationals. An unbundling of the foreign investment/technology package in, let us say, Malaysia which will promote the export of engineering services from India, capital goods from Brazil, steel products from South Korea and managerial services from Argentina, will hardly be consistent with the need to promote exports directly from the North. Obviously, the developing countries' exporters will in themselves be importers of goods and services from the North. Yet, these would have happened anyhow by alternative (including financial) strategies which could increase the import potential of developing countries. In this case there is need to acknowledge openly the existing conflict of economic interests between South and North.

The objective to increase the bargaining position of developing countries vis-à-vis the transnationals and the call for international action on this matter in the Report, appear to be more related to the re-negotiation of the 'terms of dependance' on the technology suppliers rather than to any effective altering of the structure of productive relations in the world economy. In fact, what is proposed involves the transfer of international financial resources to strengthen further the presence of transnational enterprises in developing countries.

There are, though, certain important cases with respect to which the Report acknowledges the need and calls for an increase in the share of developing countries in the operations of the world economy. One of them concerns the greater participation of the Third World in the processing of minerals and commodities. The implementation of such a strategy will confront the strong opposition of the transnational enterprises. After the wave of nationalizations in the primary production of a large number of minerals and commodities in the 1960's and early 1970's, vertically and internationally integrated enterprises consider as part of their strategic interests the need to maintain out of the control of developing countries several of their downstream operations. If the latter, like the processing activities, are shifted to and become subject to more effective control by the developing countries, the transnationals run the risk of losing their oligopoly control over key operations. Established firms will thus oppose such a shift and will only reluctantly participate in a process of relocation under economic pressure. Such a pressure can be effectively exercised if the currently operating firms are confronted with the risk of losing, including to other transnationals, their security of access to sources of supply of primary inputs. Other Northern interests might not be so adverse to the transfer of such activites to the South. These include interests in environmental protection in the North, transnational banks with high liquidity in search of investment opportunities, machinery and technology suppliers and policy makers who realize that in certain cases – as in aluminum production in Japan – a significant part of the reported value of output in the North involves the consumption of energy in which they are highly deficient.

In other cases though, also endorsed by the Report, the promotion of exports from the South, when they involve international sourcing activities by the transnationals, will be greatly supported by these firms in contrast to the opposition of other Northern groups, particularly organized labour. In these circumstances the South can be used as an intermediary to affect power relations within the North.

In both of the above cases (i.e. processing and international sourcing activities) the position of the North will reflect basically the outcome of intra-North political and economic positions. Whatever the Brandt Report or anybody else for that matter argues on these matters will need, in order to be pragmatic, to analyze first the preferences and pressures exercised within the industrialized countries and not simply the expressed needs of the South.

Proposed measures on the treatment of transnationals

Among all the sections of the Report, perhaps the least imaginative, and more limited in terms of the importance of specific proposals which will favour the South, is that which concretely concerns itself with the operations of transnational enterprises. In the proposed 'Regime for International Investment' and the related sections of that chapter, the Report endorses several of the hardest positions of the OEDC countries, particularly the inducement:

> to participate in intergovernmental agreements under which the governments of home countries insure foreign investment operations of their transnationals and thus, through a process of subrogation, elevate potential and actual conflicts between enterprises and host governments to the level of conflict between governments (a proposition which contravenes expressed decisions of several developing countries, such as those of the Andean Pact);
> to accept multilateral bodies for the settlement of disputes, 'in addition, or as an *alternative*, to national tribunals' (italics added), (a proposition which is opposed by several national and regional decisions in developing countries, e.g. the Calvo Doctrine);
> to formulate 'an international procedure for discussions and consultations on *measures* affecting

direct investment and the activities of transnational corporations' (italics added), (a proposition which will tend to place international pressures on national sovereignty when the latter is exercised through the introduction of policies which affect the interests of transnational enterprises).

In other cases which concern the specific practices and operations of the transnational enterprises, the proposals of the Report – depending on the subject matter – fall into categories which can be characterized as utopian, partial, concerned with the 'irrelevant alternative' or even of abstaining from adequately examining certain fundamental issues.

The utopian approach is most apparent in the call for 'sharing' technology between the North and the South, and for the effective 'transfer' of such technology. This simply does not recognize the meaning and origin of economic power in the structures of contemporary markets and the importance of control or captivity over the productive know-how. Also the proposal for international action to promote more extensive and effective disclosure of information by the transnationals does not recognize that any serious world cooperation on this issue has already been opposed by the North in view of the expressed negative reaction of its transnationals. Instead the initiatives of the United Nations in making operational such activities presently find themselves drowned in the swamps of endless international committee work.

One of the more inadequate analyses of issues on world business practices concerns the proposals of the Report on transfer pricing. They are largely circumscribed to policies of tax harmonization and the elimination of tax havens. No frank discussion is undertaken on how the substantial part of world trade which takes place through intra-firm exchanges, constitutes today an area of major conflicting interest. Such trade practices represent a well-organized and quantitatively very important channel for implicit income transfers internationally. It also covers one of the more important exercises of what is traditionally referred to as restrictive business practices.

Equally, no frank references are made to the discriminatory role played by these enterprises in confronting the needs of the world's poor, or to their absence of participation in other cases. Finally, the insistence on codes of conduct constitutes a misplaced emphasis. The primary contribution, if any, of such codes in promoting public discussion and awareness on issues concerning the transnational, has already been covered by United Nations initiatives. Its reiteration diverts attention from alternatives which are undoubtedly much more serious for Southern interests. Internationally agreed rules on 'savoir faire' on these matters simply do not touch the core of control and decision making which are central to the operations of transnational enterprises. The interminable negotiations on codes tend to blare the need for continuously bringing to the forefront the combined impact of requisite political will, technical knowledge and economic power to deal with these enterprises.

Concluding remarks

The Brandt Report needs to be judged according to the impact it is likely to have as a major opinion-forming and policy-influencing document in evolving North-South relations. Such impact will, in turn, depend on the relevance of the subjects it covers, the validity of its analysis and conclusions and finally the possibilities of influencing the perceptions and decisions of policy makers and those to whom the former are accountable. Novelty, which the Report lacks, is not a criterion here, since this is not an academic work; validity and effectiveness, though, are of central importance.

Contrary to the largely one-dimensional nature of the Pearson Report which preceded the work of the Brandt Commission, the latter was able to capture and convey the interdependence of several of the central problems facing developing countries. Thus, facile and evasively partial policy solutions, which have often dominated the agenda of North-South discussions in the past, are brought into questioning. Also the Report did not accept the institutional base as given but called for specific reforms. Its value then consists in lending its support, through an articulate presentation and the weight of the Commissioners' names, to these two notions: interdependence of problems and inadequacy of existing institutional mechanisms to deal with them. The usefulness of its impact is pedagogic. It 'legitimizes' some general concerns on development that have often been expressed in the past but which have not found their way into broader acceptance.

The validity of its analysis, though, and the political acceptability of its proposals in the two areas we examined (namely, the massive transfer of resources to the South and the activities of the transnational enterprises) are highly questionable. The Report misreads both the political realities of the North and the essence of some of the efforts of the South in asserting itself as an emerging force in international economics relations. In several crucial cases we concluded that the Report's concrete proposals, in the two above mentioned areas, will prove harmful to the interests of developing countries.

Poverty and power in international and domestic relations are not separable. Although the Brandt Report preoccupies itself seriously with the first, it only tangentially touches the essence of the latter. Thus, the analysis and positions taken did not address themselves to the field that, in view of their past experience, the Commissioners should know best but, in their attempt to reach a consensus in their positions, failed to present and analyse it as explicitly as they should have.

JOHAN GALTUNG*

> . . . all that is going to happen is that the internal gaps and contradictions will increase and that a good portion of the extra resources that come into a country in the South will be used to protect upper-class privileges, with the power that strengthened police and military can wield.

* Norway. Professor at the United Nations University at Geneva. Renowned peace researcher.

The Brandt Report is a gold mine for the internationally minded person, scholar or not, not only for all the information given but also for leading the trained or untrained eye straight to the basic point, with two important omissions to be mentioned below. The stands taken are morally irreproachable. The question is whether the analysis is of such a kind that it can lead to workable political proposals that together constitute 'a programme for survival', the lofty goal the commission has set for itself. What I shall try to show is that the answer is *no*, that the 'programme of priorities' (chapter 17) is (i) unrealistic and (ii) even if it could be implemented would lead to the wrong results, and that this is due to some severe flaws in the analysis of the workings of the contemporary world system. It goes without saying that this in no way reflects on the moral calibre of the members of the impressive commission, nor on their intellectual capacity. It is a reflection of their world views, though, ranging from conservative to middle-wing social democrat, with the report lying somewhere in-between, with all the compromises needed to arrive at a document with which all members can identify.

My own difficulty with the Report starts with its title and the map on the outside: a world neatly divided 'North-South'. I think this states the issue wrongly from the very beginning, because there is no North, hardly any South and it is hardly between North and South that the issue is located. Thus, the state capitalist countries, whether one wants to refer to them as 'socialist' or not, do not enter the world economy the same way as the market or private capitalist countries do: they are much less involved in the Third World because of the absence, practically speaking, of investments and the high level of self-sufficiency in raw materials in this region of the world, the Northeast. Second, there is no doubt an impact of deteriorating economic conditions in the Northwest on the state capitalist countries, a transmission of inflation and unemployment for instance; and there is little doubt that they prefer a strong Northwest to have something to catch up with in their propaganda, to use as a threat, and above all to import technology from.

But they have a different conception of what the Third World should do, more based on basic structural change, 'revolution' and less dependence on the countries in the Northwest. What remains of their marxist orientation would make them see this as a historical necessity, as something that is going to happen anyway, and to continue basing oneself on an essentially capitalistic international division of labour would be worse than a folly, it would be ahistorical. Of course they hope in the process to reap international trade benefits from socialist countries in the Third World, but they want to do this directly, not indirectly by having the First World resuscitate its 'interdependence' with the Third World at a new and higher level so that the First World still is strong enough to extend, for instance, soft loans to the Second World. Incidentally, it may also be in the Second World interest to have the First World more dependent on the Second than on the Third Worlds, investing in Siberia rather than in the Sahel or the Kalahari, for instance. The state capitalist countries, after all, are relatively reliable when it comes to servicing loans.

Then, the idea of a world 'South'. That there has been a largely successful voting and bargaining Third World bloc in the UN system is well known, and many of the Commission members have experience with this at a personal level. But the South is cut through by so many cleavages that expressions such as South and the Third World become increasingly misleading. To mention only some:

> the oil-exporting (OPEC) vs. the others (the NOPECs)
> the newly industrializing countries (NICs) vs. the others
> the Confucian-Buddhist-westernizing countries vs. the others
> the Islamic countries vs. the others
> the countries investing in other Third World countries vs. the rest

And then there are the usual continental/geographical divides and the socialist/capitalist distinction. All of this may not be so important at the level of UN resolutions; it is at the level of concrete political action that it starts becoming important.

To bring out the point clearly, let us for the sake of simplicity operate with a division of the South into three: OPEC, NICs and the REST. The Report's world model then looks something like this:

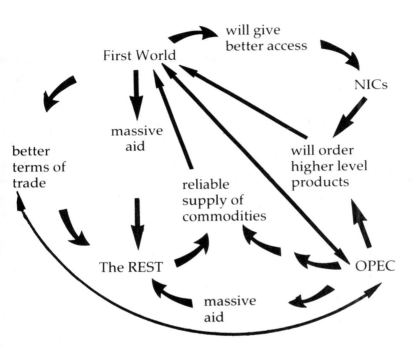

I shall comment on the scheme later, sufice it here only to point out how differently the various parts of the South enter the scheme. As will be indicated later there are considerable disharmonies of interest even within the South. Using the term 'South' mystifies this by making one believe that there is a bloc, even an actor with which one can have meaningful dialogues with a broad agenda of issues assuming that South will come to terms with South once North has come to terms with South. Even leaving the state capitalist countries out – which probably can be done as they are marginal to the key issue of the Brandt Report, emergency action to avert imminent economic crisis' – any presentation in terms of only two blocs of countries.

This becomes much more complex if we make use of the third cleavage alluded to above, introducing the Confucian-Buddhist-westernizing countries, in other words Japan, the four mini-Japans (South Korea, Taiwan, Hong Kong and Singapore) and – indeed – China. It can be argued that this is the coming triangle that will constitute the point of gravity of the world economy by the end of this century, much like the old triangle US – European Community – Japan has played that role, skilfully, to its own advantage and to the tremendous disadvantage of the countries underdeveloped by that process. If there is something to this then the figure above is wrong in a very important sense: in that triangle there is one country from the First World and at least four (possibly also oil-strong Indonesia and commodity-strong Malaysia) countries among the NICs, and then there is something rather big called China – if all this is able to come together in coordinated action then the rest of the scheme changes completely. For inside that new triangle, the world South-east, the Report's New Deal *could* already take place but aided by a shared civilizational ethos (the Report is very weak on history and culture). This is not what is most likely to happen, however. Japan will hardly open her markets to all the Southeast NICs, but prefer, together with them and China (that may one day become a NIC, and a major one) to dominate the world markets. But to the extent that is the case the economic conflict is not between North and South *but between a world Northwest* (ie., without Japan) *and a world Southeast* (ie., with Japan).

Mere semantics? Hardly, these are basic world realities. And the same applies to the second difficulty with the Report, also on the title page: 'of the Independent Commission on International Development Issues'. In what sense is it 'independent'? Of national governments possibly, yes. But they are not the only major forces in the world, and nobody can be independent of them all except through splendid isolation. Is the chairman, Willy Brandt independent of the German Labour movement and its natural concern with guaranteed employment in a society undergoing 'structural rationalization', with all kinds of automation/robotization, and increasingly exposed to competition with the world Southeast for markets all over the world, including in Germany itself? Would it not be strange if he did not weave the report around the theme of ensured employment by the old methods of predictable and guaranteed supply of commodities, including energy resources and markets, for products where the First World, including Germany, would have a comparative advantage?

Then the word 'international', in 'international development issues'. The rhetoric of the Report, the moral appeal, very well written and very appealing, is at the level of the suffering individual human beings of this world, and rightly so. But the analysis is at the international level and so are almost all the concrete suggestions about transfers and redistributions. Nobody, at least not the present author, will argue against international social justice. But there is a basic point about *time order* that is not taken into account in the pious references in chapter 8 to 'the task of the south' : 'national policies to alleviate poverty', 'social and economic reforms', 'elements of an anti-poverty strategy', 'the priority of agriculture', 'assisting the "informal sector"', 'social services', planning and participation. All of them very good points, but are they likely to come about when international distribution comes first?

This is a key dilemma in all development strategies, in theory and in practice: the proper time order. If certain changes have already taken place internally, creating strong people with ability to press for their fair share through appropriate institutions in a structure not too much biased against them, then there is no problem. Increased resources due to international redistribution would accrue to the people through welfare state measures (above all free schooling and medical services), better exchange relations between urban and rural, and formal and informal, sectors, and – perhaps above all – more opportunity to retain surplus produced at the bottom of the society, through cooperatives, communes etc. But such changes do not come about easily, and usually not through moral appeals to the élites. Hence, the problem is and remains whether *inter*national redistribution will increase or decrease the chances of *intra*national redistribution. The idea 'when there is more to share then more will be shared' is too naive for there is already more to share, and there has been for a long time (after all there has been positive growth in most countries), but nevertheless people are poorer than before. Conclusion: all that is going to happen is that the internal gaps and contradictions will increase and that a good portion of the extra resources that come into a country in the South will be used to protect upper class privileges, with the power that strengthened police and military can wield.

This is not a plea for 'revolution first, then international redistribution'. It is simply a reading of what has happened in most of the South during the 1960's and 1970's, with the accompanying idea that the time order matters. But the intra-project does not have to be completed for the inter-project to make sense. No social project is ever completed. A good start has to be made, the creation of institutions that are self-supporting and will continue to grow in the direction of steadily improving the condition of the people. Not even that is being done in most Third World countries. Hence it is very hard to believe that 'international development issues' really hold the key to 'survival'. They are important, but a necessary condition on top of the even more necessary condition of basic internal change. If the Report had some good ideas about how to set internal change into motion it would have been most welcome! – but for that purpose the composition of the Commission would have been rather different.

Let me then return to the international Keynesianism implicit in the figure above. It looks so convincing at the first glance. The First World gives to the Third World what it asks for: better tems of trade for those who want it, for raw materials/commodities (including energy); and access to First World markets for the industrial products of the NICs – and in addition to that massive increases in aid, including an emergency programme. Of course, given the present economic situation the First World can do this only if the Third World gives something in return, and that something is the old combination of raw materials and markets: a predictable, guaranteed supply of commodities/

raw materials, including oil, and a guaranteed and predictable market for more sophisticated products. That way everybody will gain, the economies of the First World will start running normally again, unemployment will decrease, perhaps down to close to zero, and the total process will generate enough surplus to help the rest of the Third World. What could be better than that!

But behind this, and in addition to the assumption that the time order for international versus intranational redistribution is immaterial, lurks the second assumption, of harmony of interests. To explore the validity of this assumption, let us look at what the three parts of the Third World are supposed to do, admittedly from a somewhat cynical, but also quite realistic angle.

From the OPEC point of view: obviously, better prices for oil was not a concession granted generously by the First World but simply something the OPEC countries obtained and continue to obtain by playing the market fairly much the same way as any (near) monopolistic seller can do. There was nothing mysterious about it, simply a question of announcing new prices on a take-it-or-leave-it basis. But this means there is nothing the First World can concede except willingness to continue buying. The only card the West can play is the threat of really developing alternative sources of energy, but that seems still to be for the future. The market will remain a sellers' market for some time to come and OPEC aid will probably mainly go to their Arab and Muslim brothers and in the fight against Israel.

As to the predictable price – why should OPEC prefer that to unpredictability, ability to play the market as new situations emerge? Why should they enter any kind of long term agreement, however dynamically formulated, that would tie their hands? Just to take an example: how could any long term formula take into account the possibility that two major oil suppliers, Iran and Iraq, might come close towards destroying each other's oil supply potential for some time, thereby pressing the prices up because of reduced supply?

And as to the demand for high level products – why should that demand necessarily go in the direction of the

Northwest? For passenger planes, military hardware of all kinds, and university study places the Northwest will probably remain the main supplier for a long time to come. But for many other highly sophisticated products the world Southeast may be both better, cheaper and just as close (the Southeast is bordering both on the Indian Ocean and on the Pacific). And if the socialist countries could offer something, why should they not take it if advantageous for some reason or another, eg if less expensive? After all, some OPEC countries do so already, or have done so, for military hardware, and to some extent for passenger planes and study places. To have been a colonial power is an ambiguous thing: there are ties, some of them positive, even partly nostalgic for the orderliness of the old days, but some of them are negative. The balance is bound to oscillate still for some time to come. But in general the OPEC countries would be stupid not to trade with the NICs, particularly those in the Southeast and Japan.

Then, the NICs. Here one may talk about concessions as the NICs by and large compete with domestic producers in the First World, e.g. in the field of textiles. The First World countries are in a better position here, they can demand a *quid pro quo*. But it is far from obvious that they will get what they want, for what they want is to maintain the old division of labour between the sophisticated and the more elementary, between the 'cooked and the raw'. And why should the NICs accept that division of labour, except for a small group of products and for a limited period of time? Why should they assume that they are only capable up to here, not a step further, e.g. that they can never make airplanes when they have already (South Korea, for instance) proved their ability to build highly sophisticated ships? If military hardware is the matter why should the NICs not also be able to make that, perhaps not at the same level of sophistication but sufficient for some wars, at least competitive with some of the left-overs from production cycles some generations old recycled to the Third World from the First and sometimes from the Second?

The answer to this would be that if they do not buy something they cannot sell anything either. But that is only an important answer as long as the First World is a (near) monopsonistic buyer. The First World has been in that position for some time, among other reasons because Third World countries may have prefered First World products to those of their fellow countries in the Third World, for reasons of quality, price and snobbishness. But this is rapidly changing, with increasing Third World solidarity and sales networks, and with decreasing faith in the assumption that everything from the First World is good by definition. Hence, again the harmony picture is based on assumptions that no longer necessarily obtain, or will not obtain for long.

However, the basic argument why the NICs might not like to enter into a new division of labour would be, to my mind, that by doing so they would forego the chance of developing their own industries in the fields reserved for the First World. After all these industries where the First World still has an advantage are not that old; they may actually be only ten to twenty years ahead of the most advanced NICs. How much time would it take to catch up? Enough to make it worthwhile tying oneself to an agreement of sufficient duration to be interesting for the First World? Maybe in a very few fields, but in general not. And one is reminded of the fate of Spain in the sixteenth century, very rich from the robberies in South America, 'recycling' their riches in the direction of England and the Low countries as it was not considered very becoming for superior people to make things themselves: they bought them. After some time Spain was made poor through her riches precisely because she did not have to learn how to make things, and England and the Low countries became, of course, the cradle of capitalism. The OPEC countries may be heading for this. The NICs are hardly that unwise.

Then, from the point of view of the rest of the Third World. Is it so obvious that aid is what they need most? Of course, any cabinet minister in a poor Third World country long on projects and short on funds, particularly after the loans have been serviced, will be in favour of aid, especially untied, and in the form of grants or soft loans. But did the countries with an adequate standard of living today develop that way? And was this the mehtod of the socialist countries that have ensured for their peoples at least the abolition of material misery, if not much more? In short, where is the country that actually developed the Brandt Report this way? Is there such a country anywhere? Or, did countries develop either the Japanese way by systematically substituting capital and research for labour until in the end highly capital-and research-intensive products could compete on the world market and the value added could flow into Japan, *or else* by withdrawing from the world market for a period, developing the domestic productive assets to the maximum? In other words, either by doing what the rich capitalist countries had done before them, or by being more self-reliant, socialist or not! But this is not the Third World country as envisaged by the Report: the Third World country participates in the market by delivering the commodities, fetches good prices for them, is a recipient of aid and obliges through internal reform. There cannot possibly be many such countries in the world, so participatory, yet with a humility the West never had.

From the First World point of view: is it so obvious that this really will solve their problems? If the problem is unemployment, then the approach seems ill suited, for the high level sophisticated products are generally not produced through sufficiently labour-intensive processes to be really helpful in countries with a big labour stock and an unemployment rate bordering on 10%. On the other hand, if the production process is made more labour-intensive, then, with current prices for labour, the products would hardly be competitive with what the NICs should be able to make relatively easily – for instance with some Japanese technical assistance. But even if it could work for some years it would only be a stop-gap measure. The Northwest can still for some time deliver capital goods, even factories with the key in the door, and make monies – but what happens when there are enough factories in the Third World to supply Third World markets, or even world markets? Moreover, if the demand from Third World countries, particularly OPEC and NIC countries, can be met through capital-and research-intensive First World production processes, is it not likely that the First World will find capitalist suppliers willing to sell even if unemployment is not alleviated in the slightest?

And is it not relatively reasonable to assume that this was the basis for the conservative-social democrat compromise, even harmony, that is the essence of the Brandt report: the conservatives thought that this could bring profits, the social democrats that it could bring jobs?

Thus, the conclusion becomes as stated in the beginning of this paper: the policy recommendations are unrealistic because they are based on an assumption of mutual interest, even harmony ('we grow together or we go down together') that is unrealistic given the general structure of the world economy, and the uneven development. But even if the recommendations could be implemented, and that is the second argument, the net result is likely to be continued increase in the gap between poor and rich in most of the Third World countries, reinforcement of the world division of labour, and no appreciable decrease in unemployment in the rich countries because the trend towards even higher productivity will be given a new lease of life with orders supposedly flowing in from the Third World. All of this because of the blatantly wrong implicit assumption that it does not matter much what comes first, inter- or intranational redistribution.

But this conclusion points a little further, to a more political conclusion. Are we not in the Report once more facing the idea that the Third World has to solve the problems of the First World? It started with the spices to keep our meat through the lean seasons, continued with all kinds of tropical products, then with soldiers during the First and Second World War to help the colonial powers win those wars against those who had none or very few colonies, then guest workers. Now the Third World is asked to become the engine of growth for a sluggish First World economy – an economy that seems rapidly to become the coloured man's burden? And given the overriding concern in the Report with international affairs that burden is even pushed on to the *poor* coloured man, or actually *woman*, since ultimately she is the one on whom the pressure falls most heavily as she runs the dwindling informal, subsistence sector that ultimately is the shaky basis of it all! Is this not a little too much in the old Western tradition when stripped of its humanist overcoat.

In conclusion: there are of course many positive elements in the Report even if the basic construction is faulty. The suggestions for changing the Bretton Woods system seem meaningful. To join UNCTAD and GATT into one organization is perhaps less so as this may deprive the Third World of its de facto secretariat – but then the Third World will probably come up with its own secretariat to counter the expertise of the OECD, the European Community and other bodies. And the GATT free trade assumption is probably totally unrealistic and will break down when the Northwest really starts building tariff and non-tariff barriers against the Southeast

Most positive, however, is the (old) idea of a world tax on governments as a source of revenue to carry out world social welfare tasks. This could be coupled with increasing multilateralization of all kinds of technical assistance. The current system, permitting countries and regions of countries to process human misery through the instruments of bilateral or regional assistance into foreign policy instruments should be scrapped for what it is: a continuation of colonialism with other means, combined with the usual Western missionary zeal in trying to form the societies of other peoples in our image. Bilateral aid agencies should be local branches of UNDP, just that. A world tax levied and disbursed collectively, through UN organs, would be an institutionalization of world solidarity. There would be obvious imperfections characteristic of heavy bureaucracies, but that may be a price we have to pay in order to get out of the current manipulatory practices, using technical assistance to aid the donor country and the recipient country élites more than those really in need. The Report should have developed this further, and certainly not in the direction of a tax on arms trade that will only serve as conscience money and increase prices to the buyer.

But all of these are among the things that will take place at the surface of the world, in the thin layer of negotiating and cooperating élites. And this is where the model fails: international Keynesianism may create some richer countries in the third World but not richer people, except at the top, the élites. All one can reach through international restructuring would be poor countries, not poor people.

Let us look at reality, not at sentimental and moralizing rhetoric: In the North of Malaysia Uniroyal Plantations (American Holding Company) has on one of its plantations, (Harvard Estate, 8,000 acres) 1400 rubber tappers, most of them Indians. Their salary is a little above $US 2 per day. The house of the manager and his private property covers twice as much ground as the plots of fifty of the tappers together. Fifty families share one public toilet; water and electricity are always scarce; unemployment is increasing; when they become too old they can no longer live on the plantation where they have worked all their lives, etc.

A little further north in Southeast Asia we find the same picture: in the south of Thailand, at Tombol Nogplap in the Hua Hin district, Dole Thai, owned by Castle & Cook, an enormous transnational corporation in agrobusiness, heavy industries and real estate, has a plantation – about 250 km from Bangkok – (ten thousand acres, 3000 workers) cultivating pineapple to be transported to the headquarters in San Francisco. First they bought the ground, squeezing out the peasants living off the soil, then they offered jobs to the landless, and they pay slightly below US$2 per day. Sometimes there is no work, then there is no salary either, only waiting. The local director earns thirty times as much as the workers. The work is heavy, the sun is burning, chemicals used for spraying burn on the skin. There are six workers in each room, machines make so much noise that they cannot talk together; managers have their own club with swimming pool, tennis, bar and golf – the company pays the golf bill, good for business. Vast sums of money leave the country.

Is there any hope for these workers in any of the proposals of the Brandt Commission? – apart from the pious hope that the developing countries will themselves initiate reforms, will there be socially just distributions of income, general participation in the development process? Nothing substantial as far as one can see. To fight hunger smacks of emergency and catastrophe help, not of lasting solutions that can only come about by giving the poorest direct access to soil, water, seeds, credit and technology.

Health and education are excellent but insufficient if the material basis is missing. To produce for export gives no guarantee at all for a better standard of living; it may even lower that standard as productive assets are absorbed in the export sector.

No. The West has to find other ways of coming to grips with its overproduction problem and sooner or later it will probably have to be by decreasing rather than increasing its productivity. And the survival of those really in need will continue to depend on their only real source of hope: their own self-reliant struggle.

SILVIU BRUCAN*

. . . the Third World possesses a formidable trump to be played in its battle for developments and that is OPEC.

The Brandt Report has not made much of a splash in public opinion. However, it stands a better chance of reaching decision-makers in both the North and the South than any other document of that kind. Indeed, never before has a group of such notable Western, Third World, and OPEC leaders participated in the elaboration of a substantive action-oriented programme dealing with the conflicts between the rich industrial states and the developing nations. What is more, the authors consulted with governments and officials in various countries on the ways and means of tackling so complex an issue. Briefly, the Independent Commission has been apparently concerned to meet an essential requirement of such a plan of action, namely *political feasibility*.

One

Although the Report's major goal is to resuscitate the world capitalist economy, it argues that such a goal can· be attained under present conditions only by a reform of the international financial institutions and a substantial transfer of resources from the North to the South.

* Rumania. *Professor of International Relations at the University of Bucharest. Co-author of the R.I.O. Report. Known for his books on international politics.*

Therefore, the Independent Commission and its final product represent a *crack in the wall of resistance* which central capitalism in the West has erected against the assault of Third World militant forces upon the present world economic order. Apparently, a section has emerged within the Western establishment which is becoming aware of the dangers inherent in the aggravation of the North-South conflict; to forestall a confrontation this section is advocating the necessity of accepting gradual change (that could be kept under control) in the world economy as a matter of self-interest. The Brandt Commission represents the enlightened wing of the Western élite and of its supporters in the South.

Throughout history, the division of the ruling class and the emergence within it of a section advocating reform to save the endangered system have always signalled the coming of social change. This may well apply to the social forces on an international scale involved in the North-South conflict. Whether the Third World will seize this opportunity and turn it into a *real change* in the international economic order depends on its unity and strategy and the support given by the Second World.

Two

Ideologically, the Report is a symbiosis of liberalism and social-democratism united by their common belief in the possibility of improving capitalism by gradual change and reform. At a time when the worldwide structure of dominance stabilised by central capitalism is challenged by the new historical forces struggling for a place in the sun, the Report responds with a subtle strategy based on the transplantation of liberalist models from the national to the international environment. Its fundamental message is that conflicting interests can be harmonized to the benefit of all parties involved.

Thus, North and South are being used in the analysis as conceptual entities while ignoring both their inner class divisions and the contradictions that underlie their relationship as a result of a century-long international division of labour between the capitalist metropolises of the

North and their peripheries in the Southern continents with the former becoming highly industrialized and the latter supplying raw materials and agricultural products. This division of labour was reinforced by a colonial policy adjusting communication and transportation to facilitate the flow of goods from the interior to the coastal ports, thus turning the economies of the colonies into subsystems of the metropolitan system. Even today, to reach Maputo or Dar es Salaam by air from a West African city you have to fly first to Lisbon or London. This is why radical economists in the Third World (Samir Amin for example) argue that developing nations must first unlink their economies before they can operate as truly independent nations.

The basic idea that runs through the whole Report is that the North and the South have a 'mutual interest' in getting the world economy out of the crisis – the South cannot grow adequately without the help of the North while the North cannot prosper or improves its situation unless there is greater progress in the South. The argument has a familiar ring recalling the appeal of Western governments to workers to join the national effort in overcoming the crisis by moderating their demands, creating a favourable climate for investments and working harder to make British or French or Italian industry more competitive. After all, workers and employers have a 'mutual interest' to prop up the Pound, the Franc or the Lira!

A big deal is suggested by the Report to the parties: the international financial institutions (World Bank, IMF) should be reformed so as to make more money available to poor nations on easier terms to expand their industry and modernize agriculture; in addition, decisions must be taken to make it easier for developing nations to export their new industrial products to the North. In return, the North should get stable prices on oil and other raw materials. Eventually, various measures would create in the Third World a huge market for the industrial equipment of the North.

This is a typical product of liberal promise in its popular version of the 'pie theory' – the larger the pie the bigger the slice for each of those sharing it, whether advanced industrial states or poor backward nations.

However, experience shows that the world economy does not work that way. Growth has its social limits. World industrial production in the last thirty years has grown faster than in any previous period. And yet, as we were told at the recent Special Session of the UN General Assembly, in the sixties the per capita income in the developed world increased by over $650 whilst in the Third World the increase was by only $40; in the seventies, the same indicator showed $180 to only $1. Even the economic crisis is not fair. The gap has been widening for the very simple reason that the whole mechanism functions according to the *capitalist logic*, namely that the accumulation of wealth by the few is based on the exploitation of the many. Capitalism generates inequality and thrives on its perpetuation. The fabulous boom of the fifties and sixties in the industrial North was largely facilitated by the fact that the relative prices of energy, food, and raw materials coming from the South fell rapidly after 1951 and remained low until the early seventies.[1]

The same logic applies to capitalist development as illustrated by the 'miracle of growth' of Brazil. In an impressive spurt from 1969 to 1974, Brazil's per capita output increased by a third to $1500 whilst the income gap among Brazilians still widened. In 1960, the affluent 5 per cent accounted for 35 per cent of the wealth and the lower 50 per cent for only 14 per cent of the wealth; by 1976, the division of wealth between these groups was 39 per cent and 12 per cent.[2] To sum up this point: the argument of 'mutual interest' comes into conflict with the very nature of captalism whose Holy Ghost presides over the North-South system.

Three

The present international economic order cannot be changed without affecting the political order and in the last analysis the world structure of power. Therefore, the Report rightly considers the issue in the broad context of international peace and security, including disarmament versus development.

Obviously, the present structure of inequity and

exploitation is a primary source of conflict and violence and it is a characteristic of our world that the structure of inequality extends to both socio-economic and politico-military dimensions. A formidable command over instruments of violence and military power is designed to support and reinforce a system of economic and political domination. At the heart of these structures of domination is their possession of nuclear weapons and their mainipulation of the nuclear threat. It is in this political-strategic context that one must view the reaction of various nations to the proposals put forward by the Report.

The strategy of the Seven Rich thus far has purported to strengthen the relative position of the First World on the assumption that taking steps within the OECD the industrial world will be able to stimulate growth and overcome stagflation. However, planning in a closed circuit has proved an utter failure. In an interdependent world, outside forces (e.g. OPEC) may easily frustrate the smartest anti-inflation policies. Besides, OECD countries are already saturated with industrial products and their feverish race for higher productivity and competitive prices among themselves looks like dogs chasing their own tails.

The ominous result of such a strategy has been growing protectionist tendencies and quarrels among the U.S., Japan, and Western Europe over import quotas and trade imbalances. There must be some reason behind this strategy. Let us examine what it is.

Had the establishment of a new international order been an exclusively economic issue, the U.S. would have probably taken a more sympathetic attitude toward the Report's proposal for massive financial help to the developing nations, particularly the poor ones. A very persuasive case is made that such assistance would put the developing nations in a position to order industrial equipment in the North, thus triggering the long-awaited non-inflationary expansion of the OECD economies that would get them out of the slump. But at the Venice summit of the Seven Rich the discussion of this item was practically killed. The reason is *political* and *strategic*, such considerations prevailing over economic ones. Apparently, Washington perceives Third World demands as a challenge to the present structure of power in which the U.S. holds a privileged position it does not want to renounce.

That such considerations prevail in US strategic thinking is evidenced by President Carter's decision to set up a mobile interventionist force for Third World disturbances. What official pronouncements could not possibly say is clearly spelled out by the Rand Corporation report to the US Department of Defense recommending such a decision. The report argues the need to evolve contingency plans to deal with the campaign waged by the Third World for a new economic order: 'Although its articulated demands are economic, the general thrust of the movement is political, aiming at a major modification of the power relations'. . . [3]

As for the Soviet Union, which is economically and financially at a disadvantage vis-à-vis the Western industrial states, it should logically have a vital interest in the creation of a new world order that would reduce such imbalances among nations; if, again, the issue were exclusively economic. In fact such a sweeping change is equally perceived in Moscow as altering significantly the present structure of power and, therefore, there is little enthusiasm for it. This goes for all great powers, irrespective of their social system; politico-strategic considerations take precedence over economic ones.

Four

The Independent Commission pleads for a deeper involvement of the socialist countries in the whole problem of international development, implying that their welfare and security depend also on North-South progress. At the surface the logic seems impeccable. And yet, the analysis reflects once again the limits of liberalism with its almost inherent inability to see the deep antagonisms that divide our world and make for such a diverisity of conflicts of interests.

To begin with, these days one could hardly view all socialist countries as a monolithic bloc displaying identical attitudes on world issues. Truly, political considerations have made all of them to vote at the UN in favour of Third World initiatives, particularly when they are directed against central capitalism, the common adversary. But from there on positions begin to differ; while those belonging to the Group of 77 (Yugoslavia, Cuba, Vietnam, Rumania etc.) are prepared to go the whole way for a new international order, others are reluctant, ideologically biased, or simply not interested.

Economically, the socialist countries have a common cause with the developing countries: asymmetric structure of trade with the West, inferior position of currencies in financial transactions with the West, lagging technology and productivity making for industrial products barely competitive. The resulting debts incurred by Eastern European countries with Western banks have reached an all-time high, showing that we are dealing here with a specific pattern of disparity in development whose origin goes back to the 18th century. The gap confronting the socialist countries of Asia, Africa, and Latin America is even worse. Moreover, the socialist countries have discovered lately that they too are affected by the crisis of the world capitalist economy; indeed, they dropped out from the capitalist system but not from the world market where central capitalism still dictates the rules of the game.

Politically, however, the workings of the East-West conflict are different from those of the North-South, though there seems to be a dialectical interplay between the two. Elsewhere,[4] I likened their motion with that of a seesaw. During the Cold War, *class-ideological* motivations prevailed in world politics and the East-West conflict was predominant. With the halting of the revolutionary process in Europe at the end of the fifties, the thrust of change shifted toward the underdeveloped continents. Against this background, the two superpowers discovered their common interest in maintaining their nuclear lead and the key-decision on war and peace in their hands. The two nuclear treaties jointly drafted by American-Soviet experts reflected this basic strategic policy. President de Gaulle's opposition to US domination in the West and the Sino-Soviet rift in the East along with the national resurgence of the developing continents are all signs that world politics has entered a new stage in which *national-strategic* motivations override ideological ones.

Hence, it was the redirection of the focus of conflict from the East-West to the North-South system that made détente possible. This basic appraisal ushered in the transition from the Cold War to the development decades, from confrontation to negotiation, from the doctrine of massive atomic retaliation to that of 'limited war' made to order for Third World conditions.

Now we are witnessing a strong outburst of *superpower rivalry* over spheres of influence and strategic positions. And yet, it is not possible to bring back the bipolar structure of power and the political climate of the Cold War, however great the nostalgia in Washington and Moscow for the good old days when everybody in the camp fell into line once they set it. For one thing, with the emergence of the Third World as a new political factor, the world is much more complex today than the 'two camps' of the fifties; the Iron Curtain is gone while ideological lines are crosscutting and overlapping the three worlds. With more than 150 sovereign states scattered over all continents it is no longer possible to run the world from two centres of power or even to exercise control over allies or clients. Whatever the geometry of power one considers whether triangular (including China in the big game) or pentagonal (adding Western Europe and Japan), one must now take a step further and recognize that in world politics there are now significant forces *outside* the geometric model. One of them is certainly OPEC, whose growing influence is something to reckon with not only economically but also politically.

All these may explain why the Brandt Report issued at the height of the US-Soviet tension did not make an immediate impact. Nevertheless, the superpower rivalry, lacking the old-time background, cannot hold too long the limelight of the international scene. While it is true that the North-South dialogue may make better headway when the East-West conflict is in abeyance, the problems raised by the Commission are too serious and urgent to be left on the waiting list. Major efforts have been made (successfully) to convene a selected North-South meeting in 1981, as proposed in the Report.

As a negotiations model the quid-pro-quo deal suggested by the Report seems to be tailored for such an occasion. It has the merit of showing awareness that in the act of negotiation short-term interests rather than long-term ones prevail. While the industrial North is beset by high inflation and unemployment coupled with recession, the Third World is in need of aid and credits for investments, and faced with mounting debts, deteriorating balances of payments and increased barriers against its exports. Out of this complex knot, the crux of the matter is energy and its price – the most important single problem of the North. This means that the Third World possesses a formidable trump to be played in its battle for development, and that is OPEC.

However, OPEC is struggling with its own inner contradiction: on the one hand, its political base is the developing world – on the other hand, most of the social élites running it have a vested interest in maintaining central capitalism in good shape. The interplay between these two contradictory tendencies will determine to a large extent the outcome of the coming negotiations.

References

1. Walter Rostow: Alternative theories of the 1970s (Canadian Seminar, May 22, 1979)
2. Editorial on the Pope's visit to Brazil in *International Herald Tribune*, 14 July 1980
3. Military implications of a possible world order crisis in the 1980s: A Project Air Force Report prepared for the US AIR FORCE (Santa Monica, Rand Corp oration, 1977).
4. *see* S. Brucan: *The dialectic of world politics* (Free Press, Macmillan, New York, 1978)

FIVE

BRANDT HELPS, BUT SELF-RELIANCE IS ESSENTIAL

CARLOS ANDRÉS PÉREZ*

> In face of the intransigence of the industrial nations, in face of
> the lack of political will for negotiations . . . the option of the
> developing world . . . must be in favour of seeking closer
> cooperation within its own ranks in order to strengthen its
> power of negotiation.

The Report of the Independent Commission on International Development Issues, presided over by Mr Willy Brandt, one of the most illustrious leaders of the social democratic world, constitutes the most serious effort made to date in seeking a solution to the crucial problem of humanity on which will depend the peace and well-being of the world: the New International Order, to be established within well-defined concepts of justice and equity. As Mr Brandt affirms in his incisive and optimistic introduction, the Report deals with 'the most important social challenge of our time,' emphasizing 'the conviction that the two decades ahead of us may be fateful for mankind.' The Commission, composed of such differing persons, unanimously believed in 'the certainty that the reshaping of worldwide North-South relations has become a crucial commitment to the future of mankind.'

However, despite this conviction conflict of interests has strongly dominated the political will of the industrialized countries and, unfortunately, it was nothing more than an honourable, worthy, yet pious aspiration of Willy Brandt when he conceived and succeeded in formulating the pledge to draw attention in the Report to 'the risks threatening mankind and to show that the legitimate self-interests of individual nations often merge into well-understood common interests.'

This does not mean that we must abandon ourselves to defeat, and have recourse to confrontation or continue the war of words which is leading us up a blind alley. The Brandt Report gives hope among so many frustrations and, despite the failures and persistent deafness of the North, we must persevere, explore new paths and continue the

* President of Venezuela from 1974 to 1978.

dialogue. At least it has been recognized that the North-South dialogue is the most important debate within the world community. Yet these long years of negotiations still do not permit any degree of optimism, especially after the failure of the XIth Special Assembly of the United Nations. The United States, the Federal Republic of Germany, and Great Britain obstructed fundamental agreements relating to global North-South negotiations, and the new development strategy was not adopted in spite of the support of the other delegations from the developed world. In face of the intransigence of the industrial nations, and their lack of political will for negotiations, publicly declared once again in the recent UN General Assembly devoted to the North-South dialogue, the option of the developing world, in our opinion, must be in favour of seeking closer cooperation within its own ranks in order to strengthen its power of negotiation.

'The anxiety engendered by the prevailing uncertainty in the relations among those who retain power, and the climate of restlessness created by the confusion predominant in the world economy would make way for confidence and peace, in the presence of real international cooperation in which the developing countries would derive the greatest benefit and to which they would contribute with their immense potential capacity.' This was observed in the Solemn Declaration of Algiers, which it fell to me to sign in the name of Venezuela. On the same occasion, emphasis was placed on the capacities of mankind and on the scientific and technological progress already achieved to overcome this crisis. 'The future of humanity depends ultimately' it was stated, 'on the capacity of man to mobilize his imagination and put it to the service of common interest.' A review of the progress of these five years which separate us from the Algiers Conference, years which carried us with determination and optimism to the Conference for International Economic Cooperation in Paris in 1975, to meetings of UNCTAD, to UN Special Assemblies, shows a frustrating aggregate result which affords very little encouragement, whilst the spectre grows of innumerable problems affecting the international community in general, and the countries of the South in particular.

Energy difficult to finance, the population explosion, unemployment, galloping inflation in the centres of economic power which is increasingly affecting all the developing countries in turn, crisis and instability in the prices of raw materials – these today constitute the most characteristic features of the developing world. To these can be added the political tensions: the struggle for spheres of influence, the rebirth of the cold war, the armaments race of many Third World countries, and the local conflicts which these armaments engender and glorify as has been the case in the tragic confrontation between Iran and Iraq.

Within this context, the Third World must seek adequate ways of resolving its crises and facing the challenges of its own development. And we within the Third World must do so without deviating from our commitments to solidarity, and without committing the error of thinking that we can advance alone as the industrial countries attempt to do with the thoughtlessness and egoism which incited them to invite the oil-producing countries to a unilateral alliance with the developed world so as to enjoy the advantages of an agreement which turned a reduced number of countries into the privileged ones of the Earth and which, in fact, only deepened further the gulf between wealth and poverty.

Latin America is and will continue to be solidly within the Third World, of. which it forms a part. But this does not mean that we must abandon the search for appropriate solutions in their geographical context, which can at the same time contribute towards the exploration of other global possibilities of understanding and make the industrial countries modify their attitude of resistance to comprehension. We shall endeavour to explore those possibilities. All are considered in the Report of the Brandt Commission: the latter's recommendations, although not exhaustive, represent the basic objectives of the New International Economic Order. It is, in fact, nothing more than the incomprehension and misunderstanding of the industrial nations which closes the doors to agreement. A simple statement of the problems and their solutions resolves nothing and inhibits the dialogue. And here, the

South-South possibilities have a unique transcendency, as was indicated in the appropriate recommendations of the Report.

South-South cooperation represents not only a possibility of more rewarding prospects for our countries; it represents something more: for countries having attained a certain level of development, with an old political tradition, with clarity of aims, and disposed to play a leading part in the community, cooperation among our countries can also become a commitment of historical significance.

In the face of world crisis and the stagnation of North-South negotiations, Latin America has a responsibility: that of looking inward, abandoning its old historic ways, and breathing new life into them by stimulating regional integration and cooperation on the strength of political will, determination, and faith in the possibilities of our countries. And we also have the responsibility of looking outward and contributing to world peace at a time when this is so seriously threatened.

In language which is discreet yet free of ambiguity, the recommendations of the Commission indicate the obstacles which make the ideal solutions impossible on an international plane when it mentions the changes and reforms required in international institutions and finance systems, and the practices to which the countries of the North have had and still have recourse such as their evil and degrading protectionism. The strengthening of South-South relations could eventually serve as a basis for multilateral negotiations which give strength to the intentions of the South and operate in support of cooperation and understanding. The Third World must increase its power of decision and Latin America has a role to play in a new strategy for dialogue.

The future of Latin America will depend on the understanding which all our countries – governments and people – bring to the integration and coordination of our policies. On the interest, determination and political will which organizations and experiments such as Latin American Economic System LAES and the Cartagena Agreement arouse in our people will depend their welfare, the achievement by Latin America of a significant position in the world order, and effective cooperation with other Third World countries, so that the example of institutions like LAES may be followed in other areas too.

It must be borne in mind that the satisfaction of the basic needs of Third World countries creates a serious problem of expansion in world demand at a time when world supply is subject to deliberate contraction imposed by the industrial nations. The distribution of this supply, one in which growth is stagnating, to meet the multiple demands of the developing world will generate many conflicts. These conflicts will be all the greater if we take into account the fact that the demands of about 1,000 million Chinese and some of the needs of the world within the Soviet orbit are included among those which have to be satisfied by this stagnating production. In addition, it must be realized that the intensification of the atmosphere favouring the reemergence of 'cold war' conditions between the two great powers and conflicts between countries which can lead to warlike developments must ultimately be reflected in a reduction of the proportion of this stagnant output intended to satisfy the needs of civilian consumption and investment. Thus, the first priority is to promote a policy of expanding world production of goods and services, starting with endeavours to increase the economic growth of the industrial countries which would allow an immediate expansion of the labour market in those countries and multiply their capacity to acquire the primary and processed goods produced in Third World countries.

The emergency summit meeting of 25 world leaders proposed by the Commission must have as its first priority the reaching of a decision to re-expand the world economy in the short term to levels which would make it possible to solve the problems of internal unemployment and achieve the transfers required to cover the most urgent needs of the Third World. The utilization of the unemployed labour of about 20 million people and full use of the capacity available in the highly industrialized countries could effect an immediate increase in production to the value of more than 200,000 million dollars. This would facilitate an increase in financial aid to the Third World countries, raise capacity to purchase their products, and permit reflection on the possibility of a remission in the debt of the poorest countries of the world, this as an act of justice and proof of the good faith of the countries of the North. The United Nations, through its appropriate organs, should set up a special study programme for the expansion of the world economy and establish standards condemning policies of economic contraction which are deliberately introduced by governments, as being prejudicial to the welfare of humanity and the enjoyment of economic and social rights, that is to say, of the human rights of nations and citizens.

Deliberate policies of economic contraction within every country represent an unlawful exercise of economic strength to weaken, by means of unemployment, the negotiating power of the working classes and to force economically weaker countries to sell their products at ridiculous prices in depressed markets. In this way, the more powerful and better organized economic groupings attempt to maintain their levels of profit at the expense of the suffering of thousands of millions of human beings, as much in the Third World as in the industrial world. Within this context it must be kept in mind that the first victims of unemployment in the industrial countries are the immigrants from the poorest countries. This constitutes a clear violation of elementary economic rights which must be heeded by the United Nations.

Economic expansion would reduce these social calamities to more manageable proportions. It is not disputed that an increase in economic growth rates could create disequilibrium in national balances of payments. This occurs, for example, when an accelerated rate of economic expansion in a country causes its imports to increase more rapidly than its exports. But if the economic expansion of the various nations were better synchronized, and if multilateral organizations like the International Monetary Fund, the World Bank and the Bank for International Settlements in Basle were to operate more effectively as mechanisms for compensation and the recycling of funds, such disequilibria could be minimized. In any case, the costs of such disequilibria would be less than the costs paid today by humanity in terms of unemployment, idle capacity, malnutrition and social conflict.

The gravest difficulties incurred by stagnation in the world economy relate to the solution of the debt problem of the Third World countries. Their most effective possibility of repaying this debt is to discharge their primary and manufactured products onto the principal markets of the industrial countries. Yet in conditions of recession on those markets, debt becomes a powerful mechanism of economic oppression. To service this debt, primary products must be sold at any price in stagnant and superprotected markets. This entails a further deterioration of the terms of trade of the Third World countries and intensifies the rate at which the developing countries are exploited by the industrial powers. But we have reached a point where a chain of economic failures in the public and private sectors of the debtor countries may prevent due settlement with the creditor financial institutions in the industrial countries. The assets of these institutions today incorporate a high element of risk from the funds committed to the financing of developing countries in serious financial difficulties. A situation of this kind could produce a chain of insolvencies among leading financial institutions in the industrial countries, creating a situation of panic and confusion which in turn would lead to a deep recession and economic disruption.

Deliberate policies of economic contraction within every country represent an unlawful exercise of economic strength to weaken, by means of unemployment, the negotiating power of the working classes and to force economically weaker countries to sell their products at ridiculous prices in depressed markets. In this way, the more powerful and better organized economic groupings attempt to maintain their levels of profit at the expense of the suffering of thousands of millions of human beings, as much in the Third World as in the industrial world. Within this context it must be kept in mind that the first victims of unemployment in the industrial countries are the immigrants from the poorest countries. This constitutes a clear violation of elementary economic rights which must be heeded by the United Nations.

Economic expansion would reduce these social calamities to more manageable proportions. It is not disputed that an increase in economic growth rates could create disequilibrium in national balances of payments. This occurs, for example, when an accelerated rate of economic expansion in a country causes its imports to increase more rapidly than its exports. But if the economic expansion of the various nations were better synchronized, and if multilateral organizations like the International Monetary Fund, the World Bank and the Bank for International Settlements in Basle were to operate more effectively as mechanisms for compensation and the recycling of funds, such disequilibria could be minimized. In any case, the costs of such disequilibria would be less than the costs paid today by humanity in terms of unemployment, idle capacity, malnutrition and social conflict.

The gravest difficulties incurred by stagnation in the world economy relate to the solution of the debt problem of the Third World countries. Their most effective possibility of repaying this debt is to discharge their primary and manufactured products onto the principal markets of the industrial countries. Yet in conditions of recession on those markets, debt becomes a powerful mechanism of economic oppression. To service this debt, primary products must be sold at any price in stagnant and superprotected markets. This entails a further deterioration of the terms of trade of the Third World countries and intensifies the rate at which the developing countries are exploited by the industrial powers. But we have reached a point where a chain of economic failures in the public and private sectors of the debtor countries may prevent due settlement with the creditor financial institutions in the industrial countries. The assets of these institutions today incorporate a high element of risk from the funds committed to the financing of developing countries in serious financial difficulties. A situation of this kind could produce a chain of insolvencies among leading financial institutions in the industrial countries, creating a situation of panic and confusion which in turn would lead to a deep recession and economic disruption.

Given the gravity of this potential danger, emergency measures must be taken to reorganize these debts and the assets of the relevant institutions. The World Bank and the regional development banks must cooperate with the principal private and public financial organizations in the coordination of a programme to provide a way out of so delicate a situation. They must make good use of the special interest of the financial institutions concerned so that, acting as a pressure factor within the industrial countries, they can facilitate the distribution of the primary and manufactured goods of the Third World countries on the most favourable terms possible. Understanding must be reached between governments on the issue of debt remission for the poorest countries, whose incapacity to pay is dictated by conditions beyond their control and whose indebtedness ultimately arises from the direct and indirect pressure exerted by civil or military exporting interests in the industrial countries. Agreements could be reached for prolonging the term of these debts, reducing or freezing the interest, and converting part of the capital into direct investment, that is to say, capitalizing part of the accruals with private institutions and converting them into bonds of the developing countries, thus giving private investors a greater opportunity of raising loans for development programmes in the Third World. The OPEC countries could prepare a programme of cooperation with the World Bank and the International Monetary Fund so as to create a Major Contingency Fund which would guarantee the debt created by the developing countries for specific investment programmes, especially those in the energy and agriculture sectors.

In the solution of the most urgent problems of the world economy and the restructuring of the international economic order, it is imperative that consideration be given to the importance of the publicly-owned multinational enterprise, an institution which is daily acquiring greater importance in world economic affairs.

The multinational enterprise engaged in the export of manufactured products from the Third World countries to the industrial countries can itself benefit from operating as a factor to neutralize and dismantle the protectionist policies which prevent increased purchasing of products originating in the Third World countries. The developing countries must modify some of their policies towards these enterprises in keeping with the function of the latter as exporting factors and as pressure factors in their countries of origin for the widening of markets and the abandonment of protectionist policies. Policies must be contrived to permit the participation of private and public capital of Third World countries which affords them the right to co-determine the decisions of these corporations and introduces a process to ensure their true multinationalization, that is to say, a situation of co-partnership at the level of nations.

At the present time, each day sees a greater participation of the industrial countries in multinational enterprises. In the petroleum, petrochemical and chemical industries can be found major transnational enterprises like British Petroleum and Elf-Aquitaine; the French state-owned bank has a great international coverage; in steel, British Steel, in the automobile industry, Renault. The subject of these transnational state enterprises must be integrated into agreements for restructuring the international economic order, with a view to applying the more innovatory rules to other enterprises which form the complex of transnational corporations.

It should not be forgotten that some of the Third World countries' markets in the industrial world are controlled by governments. This direct means of acquiring raw materials and finished goods held by the procurement departments of governments and state and para-state organizations can be put directly to the service of reorganizing the international economic order. Transfers to Third World countries from the industrial countries can be guaranteed by means of the best prices which they pay for direct acquisitions of primary and manufactured goods originating in the developing world. In the same way, the state enterprises of the industrial nations would assume an increasingly important role in the selling of capital goods and services to the developing countries. Therefore, possibilities must be explored for the conclusion of agreements which would allow a substantial part of these markets of a public nature to be reserved for the exports of developing countries and assure them the provision of capital goods on favourable terms, this serving as a model for relations with other private economic units which participate in international North-South trade.

Another factor of organized authority which must not escape the attention of world leaders in the reorganization of the international economic order is trade union power in the industrial countries. Trade unions are participating more and more in the process of economic planning in the industrial countries and in some nations, such as the Federal Republic of Germany, constitute important factors in the process of joint management within large private enterprises. The social welfare funds of the workers, such as pension funds, are managed by professional institutional investors who have employed them extensively for the acquisition of shares in large undertakings operating internationally. In many of the largest American corporations, the pension funds of organized labour are the principal individual shareholders. It is urgent that public mechanisms and inter-union cooperation be established at world level so that this powerful strength may be placed in the service of the reorganization of the international economic order. Agreements must be reached which ensure that trade unions in the industrial countries cease to be a protectionist factor in the productive sectors on account of their vulnerability to the import of goods from Third World countries.

The funds which belong to the working class movement could be used in the financing of new technological branches to absorb part of the unemployment which the import of manufactured goods from the developing countries might generate. The same funds could be employed in the financing of enterprises engaged in exporting from the Third World to the industrial countries. The trade unions of the Third World which operate in the branches dealing with the production of raw materials could reach agreement with the unions in the industrial countries which operate in the industries processing the materials. These agreements could be directed towards the coordination of policies to ensure the workers of both worlds a greater degree of influence over the decisions of the great international corporations and the harmonization of national economic policies.

Whilst the North-South dialogue is receiving new impulses and the Third World countries are overcoming the uncertainty created by numerous and absurd regional conflicts, like the one now bringing the Persian Gulf countries face to face in so suicidal a way, thereby inevitably affecting the world supply of petroleum and creating an unpredictable crisis not only in the economy but also in the security of all nations, our countries, the countries of Latin America and the Caribbean, must act with all possible good sense and prudence. The Brandt Report is more than an honest endeavour to create conditions which make possible productive understanding between North and South; it is a work which bears a dramatic warning, and testimony of the risks which threaten mankind at the present hour.

ADEBAYO ADEDEJI*

... the restructuring of the the world relations which constitutes the centre-piece of the Commission's recommendations will only be achieved when the South would have succeeded in achieving national and collective self-reliance which is not synonymous with autarchy.

1. *Introduction*

There are at least two important reasons why the Brandt Report deserves the serious attention of whoever is interested in the problems of economic growth in general, particularly in the present context of world recession, and in North-South relations in particular. Firstly, the composition of the Commission in terms of geographical spread and diversified experience and political orientation is such that the views of its members on the burning issues of North-South relations should carry a heavy weight in the world community. Secondly, the Report is so well researched that anybody who is interested in those issues

* Nigeria. Executive Seceretary of the U.N. Economic Commission for Africa. Former Nigerian Minister for economic development and reconstruction.

of world development, which have been subjects of serious discussion and even hot exchanges since the beginning of the 1970's, particularly in the global conferences organized by the United Nations and its specialized agencies – from food to water, from population to environment and human habitat – but has not had the opportunity to follow the conclusions of each of these meetings closely can easily follow such conclusions and recommendations in the Report of the Commission. Indeed, such a person will gain a better insight into those issues since the Commission has not only brought the issues and the recommendations on them together in this compact and readable Report but has also stressed the connections and linkages between them.

However, partly because of the comprehensiveness of the issues addressed and of the nature of development problems, and the associated issue of North-South relations, the Report and its recommendations will mean many and different things to many and different people. And the Friedrich Ebert Foundation is right in requesting people of various theoretical and ideological viewpoints to comment on the relevance of the Report and the recommendations therein not only to North-South relations but also to the development needs of the developing countries, particularly those of Africa, 'the continent which has suffered perhaps most from the North-South predicament', to quote some of the words in the letter with which I was invited to participate in this project.

This being the case, the rest of my comments will be organized as follows: North-South issues as seen by the Commission, including a discussion of the present world crisis, the assumptions and the realism and relevance of the major focus and recommendations of the Commission to the problems of economic growth and development in Africa; the possibilities of implementing the recommendations both in the North and the South against the background of the assumptions and the implicit major role given to external relations in the development process; and, some thoughts on a feasible and viable path for fruitful North-South relations. The last section offers some concluding remarks.

2. *The Brandt Commission and North-South Issues*

In commenting on North-South issues as seen by the Brandt Commission, the inevitable starting point is the terms of reference of the Commission. The Commission set itself the task to (i) 'study grave global issues arising from the economic and social disparities of the world community', and (ii) 'suggest ways of promoting adequate solutions to the problems involved in development and attacking absolute poverty'. In order to perform this task, the Commission identified three areas for study: record of development in the Third World and the influences on it of the *international* political and economic environment (emphasis added); prospects for the world economy particularly in the 1980s but also looking further into the future; and roads to a new international economic order, as a result of which the 'Commission will strive above all to carry conviction with decision makers and with public opinion that profound changes are required in international relations, particularly economic relations.'.

True to its promise, the Commission examined the record of development in the Third World with particular reference to the 'poorest countries' comprising the poor belts of Africa, South of the Sahara and Asia and related them to the low level of aid, trade, technical assistance and foreign investment particularly from the industrial countries of the West and Japan, which the Commission has identified as constituting the 'North' despite its acknowledgement that the North also includes the USSR and other Eastern European countries and the South includes China.

But, in my view, this approach is likely to invite from those who do not want a change in the present North-South relations (as it has already done) the charge that the Commission is taking sides with the Group 77 which represents the South in most international fora, particularly those of the UN and its agencies. And the situation is not helped by the decision of the Commission to limit its discussion of regional cooperation and regional projects, as measures to enable the poorest countries generate and sustain their own development, 'to those policy areas which can attract and use concessional finance without touching on internal national policies' and thus the discussions 'do not emphasize to the same extent many important ingredients of development, including education, administration and industrialization.' (p. 86) It is our view that without proper attention being paid to internal national policies and particularly to education, administration and management and industrialization, it will be difficult if not impossible to initiate and sustain regional cooperation and regional projects.

Similarly, while the Commission is quite clear about the absolute need for structural and ecological change through water and soil management for agriculture, afforestation and energy, transport and communications and mineral exploration; the provision of social services (housing, health and education); assistance to the 'informal sector'; participation; and planning as basis for generating and sustaining development, all of which can only be initiated at the national level, it is apologetic in mentioning them. (p. 126) True, domestic policies lie within the national domain. But international and national policies are intertwined and in many instances 'the case for an international order conducive to development and both equitable and rational in terms of relations between countries' will 'rest on the contingency of particular national policies whether social, economic or political'. Indeed, many of the causes of the poor performance of many developing countries derive from poor domestic economic, social and political policies.

But perhaps the most significant aspect of the Report of the Commission as far as the issues in North-South relations are concerned is its special concern with the current world recession with its attendant problems of unemployment and inflation in both North and South. As the Commission sees it, 'the industrial capacity of the North is under-used, causing unemployment unprecedented in recent years, while the South is in urgent need of goods that the North could produce. Rapid inflation, erratic exchange rates, and unpredictable interventions by governments are seriously disrupting the trade and investment on which an immediate return to world prosperity depends. (p. 267) In other words, the present world crisis is seen by the

Commission as being amenable to orthodox macroeconomic policies of effective demand management with emphasis on demand for investment goods in the South and on new materials and other intermediate inputs in the North. Despite the central elements of the call for a new international order, this view is not in total agreement with increasing emphasis in the South on national and collective self-reliance, which demands not only the creation and development of productive and distributive capacity in the South but also the utilization of their natural resources for initiating and sustaining self-reliant and self-sustaining development.

Indeed, this preoccupation with the present world recession and the associated concentration on global aggregate demand management have underplayed the problems actually facing the developing countries especially those of Africa, South of the Sahara, namely the ability to generate and sustain development and economic growth. Yet in a number of areas in the Report and particularly in Chapter 4 – The Poorest countries – and Chapter 8 – The Task of the South – the emphasis is clear that the problems of these countries are more of long than short-term nature.

The emphasis on the massive transfer of resources for the development of food and agriculture and minerals, while pertinent, in a way ignores the fundamental problem of lack of productive capacity in these countries. In saying this, I am not unaware that the Commission emphasizes 'that human needs can only be met by the productive efforts of the society which strives to meet those (basic) needs' and that 'the only way to make this possible for developing countries, particularly the poorest ones, is to enable them to build up and develop their own productive capability'. (p. 16) I am saying it because the Commission stresses the immediate more than the long-term problem which this statement reflects and the greater importance of external than domestic markets in its emergency programme.

Another problem which the Commission ignores in its report is how the North sees the present crisis. This may be because the Commission does not share such a view.

However, in view of its importance to the South, I believe we ignore it at our peril. This is the view that the root cause of the present crisis is 'structural' rather than 'conjunctural' and hence will only be seriously attacked in the long-run through the development and application of appropriate technologies that will respond to the changing social values and aspirations of the peoples of the North. Indeed, if social values and aspirations influence technological and innovative development and this in turn influences the structure and direction of development and economic growth, as I believe it does, then to ignore this view will be detrimental to the development and economic growth of the South. For while the North will be changing its scientific and technological policies to shape its needs in the fields of economic, social, political and cutltural development, the South many be running after technologies that many not be available and which it may not be able to import and adapt because it does not have the necessary infrastructure.

To end this section of my comments and suggestions, I should like to say that I share the view that the underlying causes of the present crisis are more problematic than the Commission believes. Thus, as Reginald Herbold Green says, [1]

'in retrospect, the present tempest can be traced back to the end of the 1960s. The collapse of the Bretton Woods monetary system; the first steps (largely against garments) of the New Protectionism; the narrowing of global food and energy 'margins' to knife-edge balance; declining real growth rates in socialist industrial economies; increasing problems in managing unemployment, inflation and investment simultaneously through neo-Keynesian techniques in capitalist industrial economies; dependent, unequal and often immiserizing development or disintegration in a majority of southern economies and for a majority of southern human beings . . . the objective trends and events were there. Similarly, the death of the growth and modernisation paradigm as a global intellectual idology has not been sudden. The still-birth of the Pearson Report (*Partners in Development*) was an early sign, but the questioning of the adequacy and sustainability of the old intellectual order which has led to a cornucopia (or Pandora's box) of approaches from Friedmania to the Khmer Rouge, from Redistribution With Growth (World Bank) to the IFDA Dossier, from Limits to Growth (Club of Rome) to basic human needs was much broader than rejection of 'development aid plus free trade equals progress' or even than any reassessment of North-South or capital-labour relations'.

I believe that the present crisis for the developing countries, particularly those of Africa, dates back to the early 1960's when most of them on achieving political independence embarked on planned socio-economic development. Then development aid plus free trade equalled progress. What we are trying to do at present is to go back to first principles as far as initiating and sustaining self-reliant development are concerned. And despite the various statements in the Brandt Report (vide chapters 2, 4, 5 and particularly the section entitled 'What Does Development Mean?' in the Introduction by the Chairman of the Commission) which supports this approach, the main emphasis of the Commission is on the idea that development aid plus free trade mean progress.

3. *Problems of Economic Growth and Development in Africa*

In the foregoing, I have already touched on some of the necessary and sufficient relationships between the major concerns of the Commission and the real development and economic growth problems facing African countries. The main purpose here is to deepen this discussion and identify those recommendations that may be of benefit to African countries.

The Commission dwells on access to markets for commodities and manufactures and the transfer of technology. As far as African countries are concerned, the capacity to benefit from all these measures is at present at a minimum. In that context, to talk of massive transfer of resources is tantamount to advocating a continued wastage of resources. If mass poverty is to be frontally attacked, the focus will be on the development of the domestic and regional markets. In the context of low-level productivity, this means that little if any will be left for exports to pay for loans and the purchase of foreign inputs into the development of agriculture, industry, energy, and transport and communications.

One other implicit assumption in the Report is that the North is capable of solving its own problems while the South can only solve hers through the assistance of the North. There are many sentences in the Report which support this view. Thus 'industrial countries face a major challenge: solving their own employment problems, including the "restructuring" of production to meet their domestic needs and the needs of the international economy' (p.35) 'But if the North fails to adjust, it will be more difficult for everybody'. This is despite such statements as 'the poor will not make progress in a world economy characterized by uncertainty, disorder and low rates of growth; it is equally true that the rich cannot prosper without progress by the poor'. (p.270) 'The economies of the North need to regain economic vitality but their intimate dependence on world markets makes it impossible for them to do this by trying to put their own house in order while forgetting about the rest of the world'. (p.273) The reaction of the North to the call for a new international order as expressed in their continuing efforts to 'delink' at least in the areas of energy and raw materials indicates clearly that such sentiments are not shared by the North. And if the South is to save its neck and provide for its future, it will learn more from the implications of this reaction than by believing its demands under the call for a new international economic order will be met.

In this connection, it is important to reflect briefly on the major assumption of the Report, namely 'that mankind wants to survive'. The Commission stresses the crucial role of disarmament and the overcoming of world hunger, mass misery and alarming disparities between the living conditions of rich and poor. This simple assumption is buttressed by the argument based on mutual interests in the areas of energy, commodities and trade, food and agriculture, monetary solutions and inflation control, financing of projects and programmes, technological innovations, ground and space communications.

There is no doubt that the developing countries are interested in all these issues and areas. But the question is in what capacity – as consumers only or as both consumers and producers? If they are more interested in both consumption and production aspects as are commonly expressed by their statements on self-reliance and self-sustainment, then one has to re-examine critically the meaning of 'mutual interests' in the long run and how to sustain them. In this context, I should like to say that the transfer of massive resources to develop energy and mineral resources in the South to maintain the existing level of industrialization in the North cannot promote such mutual interests. This is because the South wants to step up her own industrialization as the Commission stresses in various places in its report.

In the light of the foregoing, how realistic and how relevant are the recommendations of the Commission as far as the development and economic growth problems of African countries are concerned? One can only say that the Commission identified the problems but only marginally touched on the required solutions.

Obviously, external capital and technology have a role to play. But the question is what role? I believe that the basic problem is how to use external capital and technology to develop domestic capital and technology. The answer is not massive transfer of resources if this means continued purchase of foreign technology and equipment for the development of domestic natural resources for export. The issue is the internalization of the factors of production, distribution and consumption, i.e. the 'growth' of entrepreneurs, the establishment and use of training institutions for the development of scientific and technological, managerial, administrative and marketing manpower, the development of national and regional markets and other institutions of development of national and regional markets and other institutions of development at the national, subregional and regional levels for the purpose of establishing and managing self-reliant and self-sustaining development. For the purpose of emphasis, it is important to say that while external relations whether economic, social, political, cultural or technological have a role to play, such a role will have to be supplementary. Otherwise, we shall not be able to get out of the present vicious circle, i.e. export of raw materials for the purchase of technology, technical manpower and other services, and/or borrow money for such purchases, followed by intensified exports to pay for such loans. Another corollary of such a situation will be the continuation of the debt burden syndrome.

This conclusion has implications for the North – the need to reduce production to a lower level in those goods which depend mainly on raw materials from the South. And this should not cause any disturbance to the North since more and more people are becoming worried about the continuation of the present industrial and life styles. Moreover, it is the only way by which true independence can be built. And as far as future markets for industrial goods are concerned, they are to be found in the South. Thus following the accepted principle that production and distribution are better organized near the market, more industrial activities should be sited in the South.

4. Implementation of the Recommendations. Prospects and Possibilities in both North and South

There is no doubt that the Commission believes that its recommendations are realistic and sound and deserve to be implemented in the North, the South and in the international community where the two groups interact. In this connection, the Commission appeals to the self interest of the North and to human compassion and/or world solidarity with the poor – the South. Yet there are a lot of statements, ideas and recommendations in the report which may make it difficult if not impossible for its recommendations to be implemented by the North, the South or the international community.

Firstly, beacuse a great number of the recommendations are identical with or similar to those that have been made in international fora particularly those organized by the United Nations and its agencies and those associated with the Third World, the North is likely to be indifferent if not hostile to them. In any case, this has already happened at the Nice (France) meeting of the seven western most industrialized countries and the comments of the leading individual countries of the North manifest this attitude. Secondly, although Reginald Herbold Green has described the recommendations of the Commission as 'constituting "the only game in town" with all that it implies about the costs of refusing to play, seeking to upset the table, or proposing the substitution of one's own (marked) pack of cards', [2] it is important to note that to be able to play a game, the rules must be clear and understood by the players. In addition, the rules must indicate who should play first and the gains which will accruehich is synonymous with autarchy. In any case, the North, both East and West including Japan and China, does not believe that its survival depends on the South.

Thirdly, it has not been indicated clearly how the East and China should be integrated into the team. In fact, all references to the role of these two groups have been extremely marginal. Fourthly, while Reginald Herbold Green again realizes that 'a purely southern analysis and call to action is, objectively, most unlikely to provide a viable rallying call in the North', [3] and rejects the 1979 Arusha Programme of the Group 77 for UNCTAD V as a candidate in the group of 'unified proposals for next steps and interim directions based on a political analysis of political, economic necessity and possibility', the Chairman of the Commission agrees that 'certainly ideas from the Arusha Conference have found their way into our report'. [4] The fact that the North was represented in the Commission by Olof Palme, former Swedish Prime Minister, Edward Heath, former British Conservative Prime Minister, and American Banker Peter Petersen, a Canadian Union leader, Haruki Kori of Japan and Willy Brandt himself, a German Democratic Socialist, is not likely to convince the rulers of the North who see the issues and crisis differently. On the other hand, the Report has been well received in the South.

In any case, the difficulties encountered during the 11th special session of the United Nations General Assembly (held in August/September 1980 and devoted to the examination of the progress made in the implementation of the Programme of Action on the New International Economic Order, the establishment of arrangements for global negotiations to be initiated early in 1981 and to adopt the International Development Strategy for the Third United Nations Development Decade) in the discussions between the North and the South and the failure of both sides to reach any agreement on the agenda and procedure for the global round of negotiations confirms that the North is yet to be convinced by the argument of the Brandt report. The fact is that the North still believes it can solve her problems to a large extent without the South, while the South believes that it always needs the North. No peace, justice and jobs will be available until the South realizes that equitable, just and equal relations can only be established between it and the North when it has established the capacity to produce, distribute and feed its own people. And as the Commission has aptly said 'the journey will be long and difficult, but it must begin now if it is to meet the challenge of the next century'.

The danger is that the South may continue to dissipate her energies in the wrong direction instead of, firstly, understanding that it is not as poor as it sometimes thinks and, secondly, that if it is to make a purposive move, it has to initiate the actions. As I have already indicated, we believe that if the developing countries are to benefit significantly from external economic relations, they must first put their house in order in the crucial areas of capability to identify their national resources, develop their people and technology to utilize such resources for their own benefits. Such advice is given in many places in the Report although its heavy emphasis on development finance particularly from the Western industrial countries gives the wrong impression that domestic development finance has only a marginal role to play.

Finally, the more one observes the international cooperation scene, the more one is convinced that the restructuring of the world relations which constitutes the centre-piece of the Commission's recommendations will only be achieved when the South has succeeded in achieving national and collective self-reliance which is synonymous with autarchy. In any case, the North, both

East and West including Japan and China, does not believe that its survival depends on the South.

5. *A Feasible and Viable Path for Fruitful North-South Relations*

In my comments and recommendations so far on the Commission's report on international development issues, I have indicated that while it clearly recognizes the necessity for the developing countries to initiate and sustain endogenous development, it has nevertheless placed more emphasis on action at the international level than at the national level to sustain such development. Yet 'in a sense, the world is a system of many different components interacting with one another – changes in one affecting all the rest'. (p.268) And it is necessary to add that the final shape of the international order is determined over time by the strength of the strongest subsystem or groups of subsystems based on their internal strength as determined by their natural resources, manpower, institutions, technology and the capacity to initiate and take autonomous decisions vis-à-vis others. The old order was created in this way and I do not see how the new one will be differently created. True, the world has gone far towards globalization of the discussion of development issues but it is also true that it is still far from globalizing the implementation of decisions arrived at during such discussions. This is because nations participate in international discussions and negotiations because of their interests as determined by their constituencies, that is their peoples. Moreover, as the Commission itself has indicated, there is no uniform approach to development. There are different and appropriate answers depending on history and cultural heritage, religious traditions, human and economic resources, climatic and geographical conditions, and political patterns of nations. Unfortunately, this point is exactly what the developing countries have not understood, or if they have understood, they are not prepared to accept and follow it. And this is what the Commission has not followed up in its emergency and long-term programmes because it was concerned with the present problem of world recession.

Yet another point which the Commission made in the earlier part of its report and which was lost sight of towards the end is that behind the differences between the North and the South lies the fundamental inequality of economic strength as measured by manufacturing industry, patents and technology which make Northern countries dominate the international economic system – its rules and regulations, and its international institutions of trade, money and finance. It should be added that this possession of economic power is the main fact that makes the North see the North-South issues differently from the way the South sees them. Further, it is the equitable sharing of this power that makes cooperation and dialogue easier in the North-North circle whether among the OEDC countries or between them and the East. The South needs to understand this point and begin to prepare the ground for its acquisition and management.

Thus, as we in the Economic Commission for Africa have been saying over the years and particularly in the past five years, any change in the international economic and hence political system will depend seriously on the extent to which the developing countries are determined to gain a knowledge of their natural resources, determine the profile of their manpower, including entrepreneurial needs according to this knowledge, plan to obtain such manpower needs both by using domestic and external institutions and use such manpower and their scientific and technological capacities to develop the resources for the satisfaction of their peoples. This is the way the West including Japan has developed. It is the way the East has developed. It is the way China is developing. It is very doubtful if the South can escape it. So far we have succeeded in taking our constituency with us and we intend to pursue faithfully this course. [5]

The Commission has talked much about the apparent success of a handful of countries in the South – the Brazils, the Taiwans, etc. But except in the case of the Republic of Korea and Taiwan such successes have not been accompanied by a direct attack on poverty and an equitable distribution of the benefits of development.

Now taking into account the population problems in the

South, how are all these needs to be provided without a change in life styles? If the goods and services, particularly capital goods (equipment, fertilizer, etc.) and services (expertise, finance, etc.), are to be imported, how are they to be paid for when productivity at the national level is very low? Assuming the financial resources which the Commission has called for can be generated (apparently in the West), how are they to be paid for since official development assistance cannot take the lion's share in view of the growing problems and demands for more attention to them in the countries of the West? The developing countries in general and the African ones in particular do not have a choice but to be prepared to generate their own resources. In saying this, one is not necessarily advocating 'delinking' as currently understood nor saying that external resources have no role to play in the South's determination to initiate and sustain a self-reliant and self-sustaining development that will enable its people both to satisfy their needs at home and to participate equitably, equally and effectively in international relations.

But if external resources have a role to play, what does that role mean? As far as Africa is concerned, whatever external resources that may be forthcoming will have to be provided on the understanding that they are to be used in the development of projects with a long gestation period and as resources that are to be used for producing those goods and services that are meant for the domestic and regional markets. In effect, the resources will be used to develop those basic goods and services without which there is no meaningful development. In this connection, I should like to say that the most appropriate recommendations of the Commission's report are those that deal with the activities of the transnational corporations, particularly with regard to their transfer pricing practices since the evidence is becoming clearer that Africa in common with the other areas of the Third World is a net exporter of capital to the North as a result of the activities of the transnationals. Another fruitful area for the mobilization of resources is the effective utilization of the services of the United Nations agencies by the developing countries in their development efforts. The Commission has talked about the need to rationalize the activities of the United Nations and other agencies. Unfortunately, it has failed to talk about the need for the South to use more efficiently the services being provided by these agencies. It has also failed to talk about the use of past aid in general.

Now if the South is determined to pursue the course outlined here and the external resources to assist it are forthcoming, will these necessarily impoverish the North? I do not think so. Firstly, it is in the North's interest to help the South so as to relieve itself of much of the existing pressure. Secondly, the North is already aware of the futility of the continuation of the present approach and is therefore veering towards changed life styles that are bound to affect the composition of its output of goods and services with consequent changes in the level and rate of growth. This is why one is particularly unhappy about the Commission's concern about the need for the North to regain its vitality by exporting to the South. There is no doubt that there must be a change and the siting of economic activities and the development of markets in the South constitute parts of that change. But they do not necessarily need to be linked to exports to the North and vice-versa.

6. Concluding Remarks

In conclusion, it is necessary to emphasize again the excellent job that the Brandt Commission has done. But if the countries of the South are to benefit from the recommendations of the report, they will concentrate more on those chapters that put emphasis on action at the domestic and regional levels, particularly chapters 4, 5 and 8 for it is when the measures addressed and recommended there are achieved that they will be able to penetrate the markets of the North with their manufactures and commodities if they need to; stabilize the incomes from their commodities; import and adapt technology; benefit effectively from the activities of transnational corporations; and participate equitably, equally and effectively in the deliberations and negotiations that go on in international fora while at the same time satisfying the needs of their people at home. The journey will be long and hazardous. But it is the only sane way.

References

1. See Reginald Herbold Green, 'Gale warnings: fragments of charts and charts for navigators', in *Development and dialogue* 1980: 1, pp.35-54
2. Reginald Herbold Green, *op. cit.*, p.39
3. Reginald Herbold Green, *op. cit.*, p.39.
4. See *Development and Cooperation* (Published by the German Foundation for International Development) No.2/1980 (March/April), p.25.
5. For full information on this course, see Plan of Action for the Implementation of the Monrovia Strategy for the Economic Development of Africa recommended by the ECA Conference of Ministers responsible for economic development at its 6th Meeting held at Addis Ababa, 9-12 April, 1980.

BENJAMIN R. UDOGWU*

I see no real prospects for a radical change in the attitude of rich countries, even though the élites of these countries do recognize the problems quite clearly.

FRIEDRICH EBERT FOUNDATION: The Brandt Report proposes in essence those changes in international economic relations which have been demanded by Third World countries for years. It maintains that they are necessary to allow faster economic development in the South and that they would be, therefore, in the interest of the North as well. Does this brighten the prospects for the poor countries in Africa, Asia and Latin America?

MR. UDOGWU: The international community is now at a

* Nigeria. African Regional Representative of the International Trade Union Federation

crucial stage economically and politically. Therefore, the proposal the Report on this question strikes rightly on the crux of the issue, considering the growing impatience of the countries in the South about the unjust international economic forces which continue to work against their interest. The countries of the South have for years been demanding fair trade practices. It is up to industrialized countries to recognize that the solution to the economic problems of the North is inevitably linked to the solution to those facing the South. This, I think will lead them to think about structural changes that could help facilitate faster economic development of the South. If the expected changes can be carried out they would obviously brighten the prospects for the poor countries in the interest of the North as well. However, the success of these measures would demand more than just fast economic development since this is concerned with quantity and cannot promise the necessary qualitative improvements.

FRIEDRICH EBERT FOUNDATION: Can the poor countries hope for a radical change in the attitude of the rich countries, as advocated by the Commission? Or can only increasing bargaining power on the side of the South force concessions upon the rich nations?

MR. UDOGWU: I see no real prospects for a radical change in the attitude of rich countries, even though the élites of those countries do recognize the problems quite clearly. Some of the reasons for this pessimism are:

1. the élites who are aware of this need are often powerless to bring about changes,
2. a good number of leaders of economically powerful nations tend to regard their economic superiority as a special advantage which should not be surrendered.

A close look at the history of diplomacy in the past three or more decades can show clearly that the economically powerful nations have tended to resist any major change in the present economic setting between the South and North. Most of them completely disfavour the idea of multi-lateral aid in preference to bi-lateral arrangement simply because they would like to maintain the disequilibrium, while pretending to support the idea of rapid development in the Third World. Unless and until the donor countries commit themselves genuinely to international cooperation and bury the concept of using aid as a means of dictating or exerting disproportionate political influence in the internal affairs of recipient countries, the aid crisis will continue and the opportunities offered by the Brandt Report as well as other UN recommendations before it, would be meaningless.

3. consciousness of instability (often exaggerated) prevailing in the poor countries, making some leaders of industrialized countries assume that the idea of proper economic management in most countries of the South is still a dream.

In view of the above, it stands to reason that stronger bargaining power on the part of Third World countries could force concessions upon the rich countries. But they have to act collectively, regardless of their internal policy divergences, to be able to achieve positive results. A useful start would be to explore the possibilities of common approach, analyse the factors that have so far impaired their solidarity and identify the areas wherein lie their strengths for concessions from countries of the North. Unneccesary rivalry coupled with structural weaknesses in the United Nations system have combined to erode the bargaining power of the developing countries in their dialogue with the North. The Brandt Report has opened up new areas which the South could use to convince the North that genuine and steady development in the Third World could in the long run work in their own interest.

FRIEDRICH EBERT FOUNDATION: According to the Brandt Report, a substantial increase in financial transfers to the less developed countries is a major precondition for their economic development and for the eradication of poverty. Others attach more importance to the way a society makes use of its resources and organizes the process of capital accumulation.

MR. UDOGWU: Financial transfers to less developed countries are desirable but should be arranged in a way that would guarantee development to meet the targets for which they were meant. Experience shows that financial transfers often end up in the hands of those who have power without meeting the needs or bringing the desired benefits to the ordinary people.

It is also a fact that some financial transfers have strings attached. In such a situation, the financial aid is known only to the leaders who alone could meet the demands of the strings. This in turn breeds and encourages corruption which are the sources of constant unrest and chaos in most developing countries. I would agree with the Brandt Report in this respect provided the transfers are made:

> in a manner that does not become a disincentive to national initiative for the countries to generate their resources.
> with no strings attached
> with a guarantee that financial flows are controlled and channelled to the targets.

FRIEDRICH EBERT FOUNDATION: The Brandt Report focuses on international action in order to promote development in the South, that is to say in agreements between governments. Does it sufficiently take into consideration the role of the people and their organizations?

MR. UDOGWU: I agree that there is the need for international action and agreements between governments since such actions need political will to succeed. It is, however, a fact that given the nature of political organizations and governments in many developing countries, the views and role of the people are often not taken into consideration. Take the case of trade unions. Most governments of the developing countries merely tolerate them while in others they are not allowed to function independently. The same applies to other groups withing articulate the views and aspirations of the masses because they understand better their needs and expectations. To answer this question, would say that this obviously depends on the political system obtaining in each country and on the extent to which people and their organizations have the right to function freely and are accepted as partners in national development.

FRIEDRICH EBERT FOUNDATION: Do those measures which the Brandt Commission proposes imply fundamental improvements for the people in the poor countries?

MR. UDOGWU: I see the measures proposed by the Brandt Report as very realistic. Much will depend on how the measures are carried out, taking into consideration the prevailing economic and political diversities. I believe that each case and measure must be viewed on its own merits.

But the measures will be negative if the industrial countries resort to a neo-colonialist approach in both negotiations and implementation of agreements. The role and activities of the transnational corporations is yet another factor. Since these corporations wield great influence both in their countries of origin and in the Third World where they operate, there is the need to check their activities and bring their operations under strict codes of conduct.

FRIEDRICH EBERT FOUNDATION: The Brandt Report asks for a 'development based on the genuine needs of Man, not on the transfer of development models which focus on machines and equipment'. Does that correspond to the aspirations of the working people in Africa? Are there forces which tend to push the economic process into the opposite direction? What could the rich nations do about that?

MR. UDOGWU: Any anti-poverty oriented programme that does not take cognisance of the needs of man based on his environment, history, culture and geography would be cosmetic, even negative. The Report's recommendation on this question is unquestionably correct because it corresponds with the aspirations of the working people of Africa. For anti-poverty strategy to succeed, we must think in terms of what the people can do by themselves to uplift their living standards. Any assistance given must be viewed in this light. Transfer of development models focusing on machines and equipment will negate rather than foster progress. Rather than transfer models of development, the people must be trained to acquire the skill to mobilize, organize, tap, accumulate and manage their own resources.

There are, unquestionably, forces in most of these countries which tend to push the economic process into the opposite direction, simply to suit their own ideology or to keep themselves in power for material gains at the expense of the impoverished masses. The rich countries can and should influence a change in this direction. A pragmatic start would be to develop the kind of aid policy that cannot be influenced by political considerations, but rather by the needs of man – education, shelter, food, clothing and gainful employment.

FRIEDRICH EBERT FOUNDATION: The Brandt Commission deplores the particularly low level of financial aid coming from the socialist countries of the North. What kind of support would the people in the Third World countries expect from the socialist bloc?

MR. UDOGWU: If the past aid pattern after the Second World War of the socialist bloc (I mean the socialist countries with heavy leanings to the Soviet Union) is anything to go by, one would be pessimistic about any significant finance aid from those countries. In the past, the socialist countries have tended to be influenced by political rather than economic factors in their relationship to developing countries i.e. their aid was geared more to military matters rather than investments that would generate development. The prevailing world political tension cannot convince anyone that the quest for spheres of influence will not continue to dictate the aid attitude of the socialist countries.

Assuming, however, that the East European countries remain constant to their declaration in regard to international initiatives without political strings, their support to the Third World would be welcome more in the field of medium level technology since they are unlikely to afford much financial transfer for investment.

FRIEDRICH EBERT FOUNDATION: The Report has been especially concerned with mass poverty. Nonetheless it seems to neglect the role of social movements, namely trade unions, by rather stressing the task of governments. How could the trade unions fit into the framework of the Report's recommendations?

MR. UDOGWU: The rapid growth of industrialization or the need for it is evident in most countries of the Third World. These developments and/or the aspiration for them have brought in their wake heavy challenges to the leaders and workers alike.

Dealing with the task of the South the Report recognizes the shortcomings of the Southern countries on development policy problems and the need for reform. Among other points, it also recognizes that in the majority of developing countries, better distribution of incomes is yet to be undertaken. Thus, there remains massive injustice in the incomes policy, agrarian reform and in general delivery of social services. These are the evils the trade unions in the South have been fighting so as to improve the lot of the working man but with little success.

As already pointed out in my comments, trade unions enjoy freedom and independence in only a few countries of the Third World. The political stresses that have impeded their freedom and development into strong and viable entities should receive greater attention. Any reforms that will create a climate for the application of global anti-poverty strategy must include those dealing with trade unions since they are the legitimate vehicle for the realization of workers' aspiration.

Unfortunately, the Report placed no stress on the important issue of trade unions, i.e. the necessary reforms that would enable them to function effectively to articulate workers' views on government policies regarding national development as well as on the distribution of national wealth. It is difficult therefore for any trade unionist to see (without a fuller discussion of the role of trade unions in the Report) how the proposed measures would meet the promise or the aspirations of the working man strictly from a trade union point of view. Experience teaches us that no amount of benevolence can bring about equity in income distribution without pressure from the trade unions.

The Report, however, dealt generally and extensively with measures to alleviate poverty in the Third World. These measures are designed to enable equitable sharing of the fruits of technology based on goodwill between the advanced and the developing countries. One can only hope that the implementation and sustainability of the new thrust of strategy as envisaged by the Report can meet some of the aspirations of the working man on the following assumptions:

1. The economic prosperity to be attained from the measures will uplift the standard of living of the masses, i.e. working people in general of the Third World, most of whom live in abject poverty.

2. New trade arrangements are likely to give the Third World countries not only access to markets but better terms for their products. This, in turn, will make possible the acceleration of investments, thereby more or better paid jobs.

3. The Report's views on trans-national corporations provide food for thought in seeking ways and means to remove the existing malpractices by these corporations against workers of the Third World. The powerful trade unions in the economically powerful North countries should desist from their protectionist stance and realize that only combined action can stop the corporations' applying of double standards in their treatment of workers in their poorer host countries.

ALBERT TEVOEDJRE*

> As long as the economies of the developing countries are externally oriented they will continue to occupy an inferior position on the world market.

Broaden the Consensus

Everyone who is labouring for the advent of an international order in which justice and solidarity prevail is now aware of the necessity of an unceasing struggle to mobilize public opinion against the inequality in all its guises which constitutes the foundation of contemporary international relations.

I have always maintained that this traditional order, which has been perpetuated into our times, incorporates a living symbol which finds strong support in all quarters, namely apartheid. On a world scale, apartheid appears first and foremost in the marginalization of that major part of humanity which the peoples and nations of the Third World represent. It also appears in the condemnation of millions of men and women in that part of our planet to die in poverty of hunger and disease.

Within this context it seems absolutely justified that the Brandt Report raises such crucial issues as (i) the low price commanded by the raw materials produced in developing countries (with the exception of oil) and its predisposition to fluctuation; (ii) the underrepresentation of these countries in the decision-making organs of international institutions in general and international finance institutions in particular; and (iii) the inaccessibility of the industrial countries' markets to products manufactured in the South. However, the Report goes further: it proposes solutions which are not far removed from the demands made by the

* Benin. Director, International Institute for Labour Studies of the ILO at Geneva. Former Minister of Information of Benin (then Dahomey) and Secretary General of the African and Majegassian Union. Author of 'Poverty, Wealth of Mankind'.

developing countries for many years now in the course of protracted and fruitless negotiations. This is a significant change which indicates that the consensus is broadening. Reason enough for celebration – yet not before raising the question as to whether the industrialized countries will now meet demands which they have unremittingly rejected for the past two decades.

To justify such demands vis-à-vis the leaders of the industrial countries and public opinion there, the Commission emphasizes primarily the mutuality of the interests of North and South. Throughout its deliberations, the Commission stresses that the essential condition governing whether or not the countries of the North will be able to sustain their present prosperity is the speeding up of development in the Third World.

Nobody can fail to be aware of the reciprocal nature of the interests of the various countries of the world in the establishment of a new international order. However, the countries of the Third World do seriously question the validity of the relations of dependence on which international 'cooperation' in its present form is based. Any argument or innovative measures aimed at reorganizing the world should, we maintain, be designed to ensure that North-South relations breed true partners with equal rights and equal responsibilities.

The Commission does not examine all the contradictions with which the West now finds itself confronted: internal contradictions between countries or groups of countries which are competitors in the economic field (USA, Europe, Japan), contradictions between capitalist countries and socialist countries, contradictions between North and South.

By camouflaging the internal dissension in the West, the Commission gives the impression of a kind of 'sacred union of the North'; this latter would be justified by a mission which consists of safeguarding the development level of the industrial countries on the one hand while manifesting solidarity, in the name of justice and peace, with the hungry, disadvantaged populations of the South on the other.

For history, throughout all its major periods, has shown

that dominant groups are always able to overcome their internal dissensions in order to preserve their privileged position (abolition of feudalism and slavery in the 19th century, termination of direct colonization during the first two decades after World War II). To supplement this observation on conduct, it should be noted that, despite every effort and a number of appearances, the countries of the South do not yet constitute one front; the industrial powers can therefore play on their divisions and their internal instability in order to perpetuate inequality in North-South relations.

A 'Marshall Plan' for the Third World?

Accordingly, the massive transfer of financial resources to the Third World which the Commission recommends as a solution to the problem of underdevelopment might appears to some to illustrate an intention on the part of the industrial countries to maintain their hegemony in international cooperation.

First of all, the notion of 'transfer' of financial resources is itself a notion which merits revision: the state of abundance characterizing life in the developed countries and their technological and scientific advance would undoubtedly not have been possible without the enforced participation of the peoples of the Third World. These latter provided gratuitous labour during the era of slavery, cheap labour during the colonial era, and provide the immigrant labour of today. They continue to supply cheap raw materials and now represent a greater market than ever before for the sale of the manufactures of Western industry at high prices. To the detriment of their own national cultural values, they have developed into agents for the diffusion of Western culture. The issue at hand should not be termed the 'transfer' of financial resources – we should be speaking of restitution or compensation.

There is now a widespread fear that the new 'Marshall Plan' mentioned in the Report would in fact conceal a deliberate political attempt to establish for the North a moral, commercial and economic empire over underdeveloped Latin America, Africa and Asia. Within this empire it would be possible, with the aid of massive financial resources, firstly to develop and consolidate local élites which would organize themselves as defenders of those of their interests which are most closely linked with those of the dominant groups in the North, and secondly to promote a policy of social reforms to orient the major part of the various populations towards acquiring non-durable material wealth to the detriment of aspirations to initiate the structural changes which are essential if underdevelopment is to be vanquished.

Restructuring the International Market

In the chapter dealing with trade in commodities, the Commission analyzes in detail the distortions and counter-performances which characterize the exchanges between North and South. It affirms that between the industrial countries and the developing countries there exists a 'mutuality of interest in stable and remunerative prices for commodities.' It is on the strength of this affirmation that the Commission speaks in favour of a Common Fund for commodities and International Commodity Agreements. Although the authors of the Report acknowledge that grave doubts have been expressed as to the adequacy of the arrangements to finance the Common Fund and the advantages which exporting countries would derive from International Commodity Agreements, they nevertheless speak in favour of a greater integration of the Third World into the world market. Such an integration, the Brandt Report contends, would enable Third World countries to increase their earnings.

I, personally, had the opportunity to observe the slowness with which the negotiations on the Integrated Programme for Commodities proceeded, a slowness which was nothing more than the expression of the delaying tactics to which certain developed countries had recourse in their attempt to safeguard their privileged position on the world market and postpone for as long as possible the conclusion of agreements which would allow Third World countries to commercialize in situ their surface and underground resources. As long as the economies of the developing countries are externally oriented, they will continue to occupy an inferior position on the world market, to produce goods which are not consumed on the domestic market, and to consume goods which they do not manufacture. In other words, they will continue to be unable either to change their contemporary consumption models or implement the strategy of endogenous and self-sustaining development which they elected to adopt as the sole alternative for freeing themselves from their state of dependence.

Endogenous Development – a Necessity for the Peoples of the Third World

It would be erroneous to claim that the path of endogenous development which the countries of the Third World are struggling to pursue would signify a break with the world market. Numerous studies have shown unambiguously that it is the laws of unequal exchange (deterioration in the terms of trade, transference abroad of production, low degree of local commercialization of raw materials) which the 'underdeveloped' countries are contesting. It is these which are in fact negating all efforts to effect a development process which would satisfy the basic needs of the populations of the Third World.

Recourse to a strategy of endogenous development thus appears to be a decision enforced by the counter-performances of international cooperation and the internal production structures of our countries whose extraction practices are the generators of an increasingly tragic pauperization process. The share of only 14 per cent of total world production held by the countries of Latin America, Africa, and Asia with their populations accounting for 67 per cent of the world population; their low level of per capita income and national income; their increasing number of illiterates (756 million in 1970 as opposed to 701 million in 1960); their high unemployment and underemployment rates, these, inter alia, all reveal the gravity of the present situation and, by extension, the necessity of introducing radical changes. And it is precisely a definition of new priorities which bear greater relevance to the cultural dimension of the national environment which endogenous development seeks to bring about.

Technology in the Service of Mankind

The Commission affirms that the Third World countries' most important requirement is 'a development based on the genuine needs of man and not on the transfer of development models which have machines and equipment at their centre'.

If this formula implies that the development process to guarantee harmony and progress among the societies of underdeveloped countries should be centred on the individual within society, we cannot fail to support its authors. However, we should point out the contradiction between this affirmation and the recommendation made elsewhere by the Commission in favour of an increased transfer of technology to the developing countries.

It should be emphasized that the peoples of the Third World are not backward peoples opposed to all technological progress. That which they reject is a technology which alienates, pollutes, which is inappropriate and brings domination. In effect, the very concept of technology transfer asphyxiates every will to innovate among the peoples of the southern hemisphere, inculcating a widespread lack of confidence in their own abilities and respect for their cultural heritage. This ideological and no less psychological weapon allows the developed countries to preserve their supremacy in the field of technology and consolidate their monopoly on the markets of the Third World countries which they encumber with products which are non-essential and often ill adapted to the development needs of these countries. A number of figures illustrate this point. Ninety percent of machinery and transport equipment imported by Third World countries come from industrial countries. Only six percent of the 3·5 million patents currently in force were granted to applicants in Third World countries. Furthermore, five out of six of all patents issued to developing countries were in fact granted to nationals of industrial countries. And one could hardly expect this situation to be otherwise when one considers that, according to UNIDO, 97 percent of expenditure allocated to technological research and development throughout the world is invested in developed countries which employ 87 percent of the world's complement of researchers.

Nonetheless, there is an abundance of examples which prove that traditional techniques, suitably improved, could not only adequately cover the needs of the Third World but also represent a means of economizing on foreign currency. In the late 1970s, the Makulu Centre in Zambia finalized the development of a 'ferrumbu,' a one-ton-capacity maize silo constructed with locally available, inexpensive materials which costs only $US 20. The Fisheries Authority of the Philippines has invented a piece of equipment capable of determining the hormone content of fish destined for consumption which costs only $US 2 as opposed to the $US 500 required for an electrical centrifuge for the same purpose. In Botswana, the Brigade movement, which is responsible for technical training, has produced a multi-purpose agricultural device called the 'makgonatsotlhe,' as well as its own machine for fertilizing and planting; the National Society for Industrial Development in Swaziland has sponsored the development of a low-power tractor called the 'tankabi' suitable for use on small farms which is marketed at $US 2,000 as opposed to the $US 10,000 required for a medium-power tractor imported from the West. A technician in Sri Lanka has invented a rice-processing machine which is simple to operate, space-saving, and costs only one tenth of the price charged for imported equipment. The imported machine furthermore has a higher energy-consumption level.

The technologies cited in the above examples are all simple pieces of equipment which can contribute to terminating or at least reducing the developing countries' dependence on our economies. What is needed is a technology of liberation generated from mankind's capacity for innovation which responds primarily to the exigencies of a development process which does not aim to satisfy the needs of a society of the urban privileged.

Popular Participation – an Indispensable Factor

International cooperation is primarily an affair which operates between governments acting in the name of their peoples. The role of intergovernmental organizations such as the United Nations is significant insofar as these organizations represent a platform on which all nations may express their aspirations and render their contributions towards safeguarding peace and building a more equitable world. However, the overrepresentation of the North in the decision-making bodies of these institutions should be corrected in favour of the Third World countries.

Thus it is with good reason that the Commission places emphasis on the importance of the role of governments and intergovernmental organizations in endeavours to build a new international order.

In the countries of the Third World, endogenous development implies first and foremost a democratization of national development, i.e. the adoption of policies and establishment of structures which facilitate the organized participation of the national population, especially that part of it living in the rural areas, in the execution of development measures – in their conceptualization (determination of priorities), their administration (decentralization of structures and de-bureaucratization of procedures), and their evaluation. It furthermore implies a guarantee of equality for all as regards access to the means of production and access to the fruits of development. At a more general level, endogenous development presupposes a democratization of civic life, that is to say, the guarantee of basic freedoms.

In the industrial countries, it seems that the popular organizations in whose names the governments act should realize that their long-term interests do not lie in narrow, nationalist attitudes but in solidarity with the peoples of the South in working towards the establishment of a new international order with new rules for cooperation and new modes of consumption which are neither alienating nor destructive.

It is appropriate in this context to refer to the privileged three-way forum which the International Labour Organization represents, a unique international institution bringing together the representatives of management and labour and governments in its quest for that justice in the social order which is the sole guarantor of lasting peace. Once again, this is but one example. The need for other groupings to give hope to the people of the world is now making itself felt with increasing intensity.

Towards a Deadend in the North-South Dialogue

The Commission recommends that summit conferences be held periodically to bring together a limited number of heads of state and government from both North and South. The purpose of such summit conferences would be not to negotiate but to seek a consensus on the main orientations of a solution to the most pressing problems of our time. The conclusions of the summit conferences would subsequently be transmitted to the General Assembly of the United Nations for deliberation by all UN member states.

This proposal is undoubtedly to be welcomed for practical reasons. Nonetheless, an article published in *The Economist* of 7 June 1980 contained information which cannot fail to provoke concern among the countries of the Third World. According to this article, the conference of major Western powers held in Venice in June 1980 was to examine the Brandt Report and submit its opinion on a tripartite agreement on the basis of which the industrial countries would agree to increase their development assistance contributions in return for a commitment on the part of the OPEC countries to guarantee stable oil prices and regular oil supplies while non-oil-producing countries would use their financial aid to purchase goods from the industrial countries.

I am not aware of the minute details of the results of the Venice conference but the opinion cited above, which has found support in numerous Western circles, demonstrates that the North-South dialogue is about to embark on a very dangerous course. The expansion of the cartel of major powers into a club which would conjoin capital and oil would not in fact offer a viable solution to the problems of the Third World and would instead contribute towards reinforcing the status quo.

Thus the greatest obstacle to any real progress in the North-South dialogue seems in essence to be the lack of political will among the leaders of the North to introduce the changes in the structure of the traditional international order which would guarantee relations of solidarity among true partners.

Against this background, the Report of the Independent Commission on International Development Issues brings an element of hope into our times. And it is with joy and pride that we should read the proclamation of faith expressed by Mr Willy Brandt himself in his introduction to the Report: 'Together with my colleagues I believe that the nations of this world not only have to but are able to live together in peace. We think that the task is to free mankind from dependence and oppression, from hunger and distress. New links must be developed which substantially increase the chances of achieving freedom, justice and solidarity for all. This is a great task for both the present generation and for the next.'

SIX

THE LIMITS TO REFORMISM

CARLOS RAFAEL RODRIGUEZ*

. . . the international atmosphere has been so much contaminated recently that, undoubtedly, it is not the most auspicious moment to discuss this topic with the calmness and depth required, even in a limited summit meeting.

North-South: a programme for survival is a timely document. In terms that are both exact and easily understood, it sums up and illustrates the great problem of our times: backwardness. Backwardness is underdevelopment, and – as the Report indicates – underdevelopment is hunger, lack of education, disease . . . in a word, poverty. But such poverty, which still prevails in certain areas of the so-called North, is concentrated, however, in the area that is called the South – a term which could be the subject of discussions. It is overwhelming specially in Southern Asia, in most of Africa, in the Caribbean and Central America, but it is also present in countries that in spite of being economically strong have not really achieved full development, such as Mexico, India and Brazil.

The Report's diagnosis of backwardness and poverty in the developing world and of the relations between it and the developed countries is an almost complete one. We can accept it, without too many objections, as a description of current reality. What is lacking, however, is an analysis about *the causes* of this unbearable situation. If such an analysis had been made, the primitive colonial plunder of the 14th to the 19th to the 19th centuries and the subsequent neocolonial exploitation of the imperialist period, continued in today's transnationals, would immediately appear at the roots of present-day backwardness. The core of the North-South problems would then be more clearly

* Cuba. Vice-President of the Council of State, Member of the Political Bureau of the Communist Party of Cuba

visible in their true historical perspective.

However, I do not want to be too demanding. The Brandt Report describes the present day situation without disguise and in much clearer and bolder outlines than its predecessor, the Pearson Report. The extent of agreement with which this initial description of North-South problems has been received in Third World circles is due to the fact that it objectively and specifically presents the crushing circumstances facing our countries. I do not believe the Commission claims originality. Most of the topics the Report underlines, so as to stress existing situations in the developing countries, have already been pointed out and given considerable attention. In this regard, the coincidence of the basic points in the Report with the speech delivered by Cuba's President Fidel Castro at the United Nations General Assembly, a few months before the Report was published, is illuminating. The importance of the Report lies in the fact that it is endorsed by a number of well-known personalities who can hardly be called radicals.

If the diagnosis of the situation is acceptable to us, we can also approve the premise upon which the solutions proposed by the Commission are based. It claims that there is a common interest, shared by North and South, in eliminating poverty and underdevelopment as world phenomena. Until now, the North has been unwilling to accept that promoting development could be something more than just an act of altruism. Meanwhile, up until now, the revolutionary forces in the South in their turn have emphasized, struggle as the best, and almost only, means of achieving our aims. Nevertheless, we consider that to admit the existence of such common interest does not necessarily lead us, as Marxists, to lose sight of our conviction that, in the long run, the contradictions are insurmountable and will end only when imperialism disappears as a system. However, it does enable us to accept the possibility that such disappearance may be attained not through permanent crisis and confrontations that could lead to a nuclear holocaust, but by a less dramatic readaptation.

It must be recalled that this idea also exists in Fidel Castro's speeches as a historical *possibility*. The arguments presented in the Report show that it is technically *possible* that cooperation for development given by so-called 'post-industrial' or 'late' capitalism to the Third World could provide such capitalism with a reanimating market for its industrial plants and equipment which can no longer be found so easily within its own system, worn out by periodical and ever more frequent crises.

The question we must pose ourselves is: Are the Western developed countries willing to accept that *possibility*, even when it implies facing immediate sacrifices in order to obtain advantageous and lasting results in a later stage?

The historical reply to this question has always been a negative one. In ancient times it was stated that 'God blinds those He wants to lose'. In modern times, we have found, in Marx, a less theological and more scientific explanation: the ruling groups – classes – do not voluntarily admit that the hour has come for them to hand over their domination; they refuse to relinquish their privileges until they are swept away by the new forces. So it happened with slavery, and again during the time of the feudal lords and absolute monarchies. The behaviour of the big capitalist industrialized countries seems to be a repetition of their predecessors' blindness. So far, it has been the lack of political will on the part of these countries – as the Movement of Non-Aligned Countries and the Group of 77 have repeatedly pointed out – that has caused the failure of successive UNCTAD and UNIDO meetings, global negotiations and the North-South Dialogue. While these lines are being written, this obstinacy is threatening to turn the United Nations Special Assembly, at which the global negotiations for development are being discussed, into an equally barren debate.

The way in which the Report has been received by those circles – which I should rather not call 'rightists' – is one of rejection, or at least, of mistrust. A typical approach is found in *The Banker*, a circumspect British financial publication, which pointed out with disdain what it called 'The Commission's tendency to accept naive suggestions, rather than to engage in careful analysis'. (April-May 1980).

'*E pur si muove*'. Nevertheless, the problem remains. The Commission recognizes that the alternative to dialogue is too risky, when it states: 'Change is inevitable. The question is whether the world community will take deliberate and decisive steps to bring it about, or whether change will be forced upon us all through an unfolding of events over which the international community has little control'.

In that same spirit we, Cuban revolutionaries, have stated that although we do not fear confrontation we prefer negotiation, if it could save the world from a nuclear holocaust. This option arises from our belief that the problems of underdevelopment are so serious and spread such danger over current events that 'without development, there can be no peace'. Therefore, we must persist in the efforts for dialogue. And the Brandt Report is a contribution to this end.

North-South presents a 'Programme of Priorities' and a 'Summary of Recommendations'. We believe that both provide an adequate basis for future discussion. The 'priorities' gather the main demands of the Non-Aligned and the 77. But, in spite of these valuable contributions, it is necessary to re-examine some of their proposals more closely. Let us refer only to financial questions, as well as to monetary ones, which are so closely related to the former.

The book rightly emphasizes that financing is at the heart of developing, and it recognizes the need for a considerable increase in the flow of resources to the developing countries. Fidel Castro has proposed at the United Nations that 'no less than $300 billion' – in terms of 1977 prices – be injected into the world economy in the coming decade in the form of additional resources over and above what the developing countries are already receiving. The Commission mentions figures that may be considered similar; they are even a little higher. From our point of view, it stops short of the complete change that must be made in the international monetary system and also takes for granted that the World Bank and the IMF can be adequate instruments – and almost *the* adequate instruments – for this necessary financial transfer. We, on the contrary believe that these institutions are not capable of so doing because of the Bank's structure and to the ominous policy of the Fund. We consider that in addition to a totally new international monetary system, the world needs new financial instruments, not those which, like the Fund, have been scourges of development. These instruments, both in their structures and in their decision-making, should be real bodies of the 'international community' in all its varying richness.

But, in the end, these are matters to be discussed. What we are interested in, now, is in finding out whether this necessary discussion is feasible and, if so, in organizing it in a fruitful manner. The Report proposes that the dialogue be carried out through a 'summit of world leaders' of both the industrialized and the developing nations. The first thing we must take into consideration is the fact that the international atmosphere has been so much contaminated recently that, undoubtedly, it is not the most auspicious moment to discuss this topic with the calmness and depth required, even in a limited summit meeting. In talks with the United Nations Secretary-General, Mr Waldheim, the Cuban Government had proposed that combined efforts should be made in order to hold the Special Assembly on the Third Development Decade at a level of Heads of State. The increase in tension prevented Cuba from fulfilling this initiative.

The more limited meeting that the Brandt Commission proposes can prove less difficult. However, we must speak out against any implication in the sense that such a limited meeting might replace the global negotiations in which all countries participate. No matter how carefully the participants are chosen, there will always be some sectors that will not consider themselves as adequately represented and which cannot be ignored in international life.

Therefore, we conceive this limited meeting as a forum in which the absence of publicity prevents any playing to the gallery and fosters serious, systematic analysis. Evidently, a true and careful *negotiation* is necessary. Not just a simple gathering of high-level personalities, in which – as someone has sarcastically stated – 'a twenty minutes speech is delivered, a banquet is attended, and then one goes back home'. Any attempt to organize such a meeting disregarding the socialist countries and without the presence of the most representative personalities of the Movement of Non-Aligned Countries and the Group of 77 will lead straight to failure. It is not a question of compromising positions among a group of countries in order to impose them later on others. That stage has been definitely overcome in international life.

The Report charges the Socialist countries with not having maintained a continuous and systematic participation in the discussions to solve the problem of underdevelopment. As a matter of fact, the socialist countries regard with suspicion situations in which they claim – due to their ideology – they are being pressed to adopt measures that developed capitalism is not willing to undertake by itself. They insist that this would place the socialist system at a disadvantage in economic competition. If, however, the question is finding common solutions aimed at putting an end to the lack of equity in international economic relations and helping the most backward countries, we are sure that the socialist countries cannot refuse to give their support.

If the Report does not attain to this necessary continuity of action through the discussion it proposes, it will only remain as a reference work in the great struggle to improve international political and economic conditions – but that would be a rather fruitless fate. We hope, therefore, that those who are organizing these deliberations – a task that Chancellor Kreisky and President López Portillo seem to have assumed – will devote all their talents and tact in order to get together a group of Heads of State who can present the international community with solutions that can be adopted by all the countries and, at the same time, provide answers to the problems summarized by the Report, before it is too late.

EVARISTO ARNS*

> . . . the North . . . bears responsibility for the pauperization
> and marginalization processes which its decision-makers
> induce by their support for an uncontained form of capitalism
> in the South.

FRIEDRICH EBERT FOUNDATION: In its Report, the Brandt Commission speaks as a rule in terms of merely North and South, without making much distinction between the various social groupings existing within each country. Yet a minority group enjoying a considerable degree of prosperity is a salient feature of the social structure in developing countries. To what extent should a redistribution of wealth take place at national level before demands are made for an international redistribution mechanism to operate a transfer of resources from North to South?

CARDINAL ARNS: Here, we must examine the complex of international relations characterizing the capitalist system. A state of economic dependence is self-evident. Each national minority enjoying greater wealth is the product of this state of economic dependence and does all in its power to preserve it. The population of the developing countries is made up of a very wealthy minority group accounting for five per cent of the total population, a larger group accounting for 15 per cent having some share in the national income, and an 80 per cent majority living in poverty on the margins of society. The roots of the income distribution problem reside in North-South relations. Accordingly, our attention should be directed towards the politico-economic aspect of North-South relations: multinational concerns,

---

* Brazil. Archbishop of Sao Paolo and Cardinal of the Roman Catholic Church. Important advocate of the political and economic rights of the Brazilian lower classes

transfer of profits, raw materials exploitation, second-class markets for the countries of the South, paralysis of any incentive for genuine economic independence for national productive forces.

Perhaps we should devote less attention to a transfer of resources from North to South and instead take steps to halt the extraction of resources from the South for the benefit of the North. For the North bears responsibility for income distribution, capital accumulation, and development wherever foreign capital is invested; it likewise bears responsibility for the pauperization and marginalization processes which its decision-makers induce by their support for an uncontained form of capitalism in the South.

FRIEDRICH EBERT FOUNDATION: If the volume of the capital flow to the South were really to increase as the Report recommends, what proportion of these resources would actually reach the poor and marginalized strata of the population, especially that of Latin America?

CARDINAL ARNS: The capital flow affects monetary policy and the production and export market. It operates in the interest of the aforementioned 5 per cent and 15 per cent groups. To speak of a capital flow towards the South is almost an illusory irony. It should be observed that the flow of profits and raw materials from the poorer countries to the richer countries is much greater than the capital flow in the other direction. If we were to choose to reflect on concepts such as justice, a number of theses, some utopian and others more realistic, might be advanced: freezing of foreign debts, national regulation of profit, and the international capital flow of multinational concerns. To make the capital flow benefit the poor, it would be necessary to create real opportunities for raising the per capita income, upgrade wages and salaries and social security, ensure a more balanced distribution of income, and initiate direct aid programmes which take account of the situation of the marginalized population groups (migrant workers, landless agricultural labourers, farmers with insufficient production, etc.).

How does one reach the poor? By resolving the land tenure problem and increasing economic productivity in the focal areas of emigration and repression. And this on the assumption and condition that the benefits therefrom remain within the country and accrue to the weakest.

FRIEDRICH EBERT FOUNDATION: The Report proceeds from the assumption that the developed countries of the North have a self-interest in the development of the South. It contends that continued underdevelopment in the South would ultimately endanger further development in the North. Yet critics would say that the North's interest lies merely in political and economic stability for the ruling élites of the South. Does the experience of the past twenty years prove that an increasing pauperization of ever greater population groups in developing countries has had little influence on the North?

CARDINAL ARNS: The influence of economic power on the political power of the First and thereby also of the Third World appears to be a relevant factor here. The poverty witnessed over the past twenty years has exerted an influence on politics in Latin America, where dictatorial regimes emerged to isolate the population and deprive it of all opportunity for political participation and, after an aggressive period of repression, democracy became formalized without any genuine popular participation or organization. The programme for a substantial democratization process includes the problem of North-South relations as well as that of genuine national organization within the various countries. The contemporary political organization serves to maintain these countries as sources of raw materials and cheap labour, and as consumer markets. A change in this relationship would afford the peoples of the Third World the opportunity to take decisions on their own economic policy and influence the decisions taken in the North as far as these affect the South (and, if possible, the peoples and the system in the North).

FRIEDRICH EBERT FOUNDATION: The negotiation partners for the measures recommended by the Commission are almost always governments. Yet should not a programme aimed at eliminating poverty elect to have primarily the organizations and the representatives of the poor as its negotiation partners? What role could the Church play in the realization of the Programme for Survival?

CARDINAL ARNS: Within the framework of a structural solution, this type of programme would be of a palliative nature only. But if it were to be implemented, it would, of course, be best if it were to have a real impact. Its effect should be directed towards the hardest hit areas – the focal points of emigration, areas in which conflict prevails over land tenure and exploitation by major national and international industrial units. The work of the Church in this respect could be to deploy its organizational units as agencies to assist the population in organizing its production forces and freeing itself from its marginalization and poverty predicament. The Church could also review the 'policy' pursued by certain institutions in the North (governmental and ecclesiastical alike), which distribute funds on the basis of dubious political and economic criteria.

FRIEDRICH EBERT FOUNDATION: The Report deals exclusively with economic and political issues, that is to say, with the material well-being of mankind. By so doing, does it not draw a distinction between these and cultural, religious, and social requirements?

CARDINAL ARNS: No, not if structural justice is the ultimate objective. The North could cease exporting to the South a subculture which is a by-product of the economic system of the North and a source of income for only a small minority, a subculture which pollutes the countries of the Third World as much with cultural refuse as with industrial refuse. Insofar, economic exchange cannot be isolated from the cultural and social dimension. In the field of religion, too, one should not ignore the fact that some religions, even the Christian religion, have recourse to a type of religiousness and 'Christianity' which weakens the reactive capabilities of the population in the interest of maintaining the economic status quo. In such instances, religion assumes the form of an ideological instrument of political and economic forces and sometimes even proffers its services for strategic and informational purposes.

FRIEDRICH EBERT FOUNDATION: If one considers the power of a religious consciousness such as that which has developed during the Iran crisis, one has to ask what role religion will assume in the processes of change which will confront the Third World. Undoubtedly, the Report seeks to spark off not a revolutionary but simply an accelerated development process in the developing countries. What role would religion and in particular the Catholic Church of Latin America play in such a process, and what repercussions would such a process have on religion?

CARDINAL ARNS: Religion plays a major role. There is already talk of there being two forces in Latin America – the military and the clerical. The military placed itself at the disposal of economic forces; the influential and powerful military élites dissociated themselves from the populace. Some elements, however, are concerned about the social problems and are beginning to question the validity of this authoritarian system of government and the alliance with the technocrats of the economic sector. With the historical insurgence of the poor and the organization of popular movements, the Church has become a significant force during the past twenty years. The Church's alliance with the disadvantaged classes is indeed a historical power factor which should not be overlooked and which will undoubtedly exert a strong influence on the future of Latin American countries. The struggle for justice is a struggle which preceded the schism into different creeds and which, drawing on the historical strength of the poor, will be able to create unity, thereby giving reason for renewed hope to the large majority of the peoples of Latin America.

FRIEDRICH EBERT FOUNDATION: Economic growth and material prosperity have often led to alienation from religious traditions. Is such an alienation process likely to occur within the rapidly developing societies of Latin America?

CARDINAL ARNS: The materialism of the economic system, whether in surfeit or in dearth, is one of the contradictions inherent in that system. It would be sophistic to contend that the living conditions of the majority could not be improved without incurring the danger of a cultural revolution. This is an 'ideological' consideration which serves to preserve the privileges and prosperity of a small minority of the population. The struggle of the majority of the poor for justice and a united society creates a mystique and engenders values which are those of humanism and evangelism. As long as this struggle and societal change remain in line with a concept of participation in an order created by the populace, the likelihood of such a cultural revolution remains slight.

FRIEDRICH EBERT FOUNDATION: The Report advocates an active demographic policy. Yet the Catholic Church maintains a rather conservative attitude in this respect. On the other hand, it is indeed doubtful whether, given the contemporary population growth rates, each and every individual can be guaranteed an existence which is worthy of mankind. What solutions do you foresee with respect to this problem?

CARDINAL ARNS: I would not say that the attitude of the Church is conservative, but rather that it is realistic and is supported by the majority of the population. Population control programmes again operate in the interest of a minority and to the detriment of the large majority. Such programmes, projects and solutions always incorporate the seed of injustice and the problem of overpopulation is not always accurately portrayed. Even the statistics are 'ideological,' designed to ramify the logic of production and the market in the capitalist system. For example, it is now possible to eliminate the 'distress' in the world, yet the poverty will remain a challenge. But is overpopulation in a country such as Brazil really a problem or an 'ideological' expedient to justify certain economic measures? If this issue is to be resolved, it must be formulated in more realistic, more equitable, more 'just,' and less ideological terminology.

PEDRO VUSKOVIC*

> [The Report] . . . continues to be, in effect, a message which developed capitalism directs to the Third World with all the benevolence which may be desired but without renouncing in the slightest its own aim and, ultimately, its own long-term interests.

The Brandt Report represents, without doubt, the most complete and systematic expression of a style of presenting the problems of international relations; and its recommendations indicate, very probably, the ultimate – yet, in my opinion, very remote – possibility of reaching transcendent agreements within the framework of that conception of international life.

The Report has much in its favour: the sense of dramatic urgency in its appeal which is accentuated by its very title: 'A Programme for Survival'; the form in which it appears and establishes its legitimacy as a demand of the prevailing institutional system, which remains committed for that reason to accept it as its own work; the significance of the names of those who subscribed to it; and the very extensive diffusion of its text sought by various media. Therefore, it will not be surprising if in the years to come it represents a principal and obligatory testimonial of the great international forums.

It also has much against it: indisputably because it appears like just another act in the already well-known ritual of international debate which every so often comes to seek other terms of reference for very similar contexts; far from benefiting it, its predecessors are prejudicial to it: the reports of UNCTAD or the Club of Rome, the documents

* Chile. Prófessor at the Centro de Investigación y Docencia Económica in Mexico. Former Chilean Minister of Economy. Former Director of Development Division of the UN Economic Commission for Latin America.

elaborated under the direction of Leontieff or Tinbergen, of which the Brandt Report appears more like a legitimate heir than an alternative formulation charged with its criticisms and frustrations. Thus its first obstacle will be, in all probability, that of a scepticism which on these levels is not unwarranted.

Nonetheless, more than the favourable or adverse elements in the formal plan, and more than the intuitive and subjective reactions of optimism and pessimism which the Report arouses, that which counts and will decide its fate is the degree of objective validity manifested in its main contents.

On this there appears to be something pertinent to be said. In the first place, attention should be drawn, with all the emphasis necessary, to the obvious incongruity between the forcefulness and clarity with which the problems are denounced in that which could be termed the 'diagnosis,' and the feebleness and ambiguity of the proposals for action put forward to combat them. In short: there is no correlation between the magnitude of the problems taken into account and the measures suggested for overcoming them. There is thus a danger that the Report will serve as a text singularly useful as a reference for the 'facts' of the world situation (indeed, an exceptionally rich summary of antecedents), but not as a suitable reference for arriving at decisions which are in keeping with the true nature of the problems concerned.

For example, the call for change in the various fields appears to be reiterated with justifiable vehemence; warning is given regarding the major risks of the present time, the alarming disparities in living conditions throughout the world, the threats to mankind's very survival; and, on the strength of such invocations, appeal is made for bringing about the appropriate internal changes, for voicing the crucial commitment to redefine world relations, for staving off resignation to assistance or aid in favour of working to build new structures. But such noble calls become muted when it is time for the recommendations and propositions, since these do not extend far beyond the forms of negotiation already conventional.

The expressions of goodwill, of that which could be ideal, are numerous; expressions which are indeed supported by figures, diagnoses and denunciations, but which end by remaining more as a display of hypothetical calculations of that which would be if things were different, than as the driving force of proposals for action. An illustrative example presents itself in connection with the suggestions arising from the affirmation that military expenditure is more than twenty times the total amount of official development aid: from the Report can be inferred a fundamental accusation against a system which reaches such extremes in the allocation of resources, but no trenchant condemnation of such a system nor a viable proposal for significant correction is forthcoming.

In the same way, it deals forcefully with the 'diagnosis of poverty'. But this is very much simplified when poverty is reduced exclusively to its economic dimension and it is affirmed with a note of apparent optimism and an implication of bitterness that 'mankind has never before had such ample technical and financial resources for coping with hunger and poverty.' If this is so, who is responsible meanwhile for the hungry ones?

The Report underlines the need for 'fundamental corrections to the existing system of international institutions': comparison is made between the majority of votes of the South in the General Assembly of the UN, which affords the South a capacity for defence, and the position of the North in the World Bank and the International Monetary Fund, which affords the North 'control of key areas in the monetary and financial field'; and the Report echoes the justifiable protests against the IMF for the pressures it exerts, 'beyond its legitimate interests,' to impose certain policies. But in the end there is passive acquiescence to the reality of its existence, and no positive challenge is made to the significance and implications of the objectives pursued by McNamara with respect to removing international negotiation from the forums of direct representation in the United Nations to other more circumscribed forums. Indeed the Report ends by collecting arguments for locating the Brandt Commission itself as a further part of the 'complex' constituted by the World Bank, the International Monetary Fund, GATT, and the Trilateral.

There is no concealing the charges against the transnationals: ' . . . heavily criticized for unethical political and commercial activities. The attempt to bring down the Allende régime in Chile; the illegal payments by oil companies to governments in different parts of the world; the support given by certain corporations to unlawful régimes in Africa . . . ' But all these acknowledgements do not culminate in a final condemnation, merely in a demand addressed to them for more discreet and reasonable conduct, with a more generous contribution to 'universal interests.' Furthermore, limiting the attention drawn to the moral ambit leaves concealed the essential function of the transnationals as instruments of a system which assiduously seeks the maximum degree of internationalization of economic life in the interest of imperialism.

Calculations are compiled on the impressive magnitude of external indebtedness and what this represents in obligations for debt servicing. But these are followed by calculations even more exorbitant on the 'transfers of funds' necessary in the near future. In fact, a direct confrontation of the problem of accumulated indebtedness is sidestepped. What inevitably has to be said at this stage is not said: that the international debts accumulated by many countries today cannot be paid and are unrecoverable; that the acknowledged interest of neither the debtors nor the creditors would now be served by their settlement, inasmuch as in reality the debts would imply a long period in which commercial interchange would have to register a surplus in the export of primary goods, that is to say, a period during which the creditors would be obliged to buy more than they sell. But in this line of argument specific mention must be made of 'acknowledged interest,' for no one would be disposed to recognize that the only way in which the debt could be reduced or cancelled would be by means of transferring property in national assets as a form of payment to foreign creditors, bringing about a phase of accelerated and excessive denationalization in the national economies of the underdeveloped world.

A plea is made regarding the need for planning in terms as unequivocal as the following: 'The importance of efficient planning and economic conduct can hardly be exaggerated.' But the whole of the Report is impregnated with a 'liberal philosophy,' with expectations depending on a 'private initiative' which has the advantage of full decision-making capacity with the minimum of disturbing 'interference,' under the banners of the supposed theoretical rigorousness of Milton Friedman and his school.

Behind contradictions like those already indicated is another basic characteristic of the Report: the extent to which it brings uniformity to problems, anxieties, and interests. The Report speaks continuously of a world responsibility, of mankind as one big community, of a globalization of risks and challenges, of dialogue and compromise. The result of such universal conceptions is only little scope for the acknowledgement of many opposing national interests, and even less for any consideration of 'class' or of harmony and conflict of interests among social classes and groups at national and international level.

This supposed 'mutuality of interests' results, with regard to many of the problems dealt with, in insurmountable difficulty in reaching truly effective solutions. The Report similarly ends by falling victim to that same illusion of globality: the authors seize upon any common ground rather than recognize differentiation and conflict. Because in the event, and nowithstanding the carefully planned composition of the Commission to ensure a certain regional equilibrium, the content of the Report does not correspond with that of a 'universal message': it continues to be, in effect, a message which developed capitalism directs to the Third World with all the benevolence which may be desired but without renouncing in the slightest its own aim and, ultimately, its own long-term interests.

As to responsibility for ecological damage by the destruction and exhaustion of resources, it, too, appears 'universalized.' In the terms of the Report, it would be treated above all as a problem of the responsibility of this generation in relation to future generations, rather than of the responsibility of certain dominant nations in relation to other dominated nations, or of certain privileged social strata in relation to others dispossessed.

It is very difficult to hope that significant progress can be made with such conclusions. For it is most important to recognize, as is done, that we are in a world which squanders in military expenditure more than is necessary to eliminate the most distressing problems of the human condition, in a world which has reached the point of uniting all the capacity and availability of technical and financial resources for the eradication of hunger and poverty but which nevertheless continues to generate a heritage of unemployment and misery for future generations. But to such acknowledgements must be added the most elementary and immediate observation that this is also a world in conflict, with sharp contradictions, and that these universalistic conceptions cannot ignore the coexistence of opposed social systems, nor the relations of domination and dependence between nations, and also between social strata, superimposing national categories on class categories, in terms much more complex than the reference to an 'international community.'

If such differences are not made explicit and treated as important questions in need of answers, then the result will be not only inefficiency but confusion. This is already happening with the 'new international economic order,' where discussions terminate with confusing demands or requests, with concessions or grants, and where, as regards its introduction, there is an increasingly clear divergence between the dimensions of negotiations which do not progress, and the dimension of reality, in which a 'new order' takes shape, imposed by those who have the strength to do it.

From this now arises a need for a fundamental decision referring precisely to whether the plan in operation has to be considered as an immovable 'fact' or whether, on the contrary, it is necessary to define and promote an alternative plan.

The disequilibrium between such options is evident, and unfortunately the Report contributes little to mitigate it. On the one hand, a strategy of internationalization is in progress, capitalist and regressive, completely rationalized, capable of expressing itself in terms of theory and in terms of economic policy proposals, with a long-term view, operative guidelines, and the support of powerful and relatively homogeneous forces. On the other hand, the alternative appears more in the phase of evidencing a need, expressed in very general conceptions and not conducive to the elaboration of more or less integrated proposals of economic policy, and of which the potential impelling agents are relatively heterogeneous.

Those who act in the sense of 'capitalist internationalization' are also those who hold the formal, conventional image of the national interest: it is the strategy which suits the ruling classes. In contrast, in a considerable part of the underdeveloped world the interests of those who retain power do not favour an alternative strategy, but the same internationalization. This confirms that the problem is not solely of national interests, but also of class interests; and an effective strategy must be capable of considering both.

Whilst increasing attention is given, deservedly and necessarily, to such simple facts as these, more weight will have to be directed to that subject which the Report does not handle with the necessary commitment: that of the relations between an 'external strategy' and the standards of internal development. Because 'internationalization' implies an industrializing strategy in the underdeveloped countries oriented towards the demand emanating from the capitalist world market; such an orientation can be alien and even in contradiction to the development of the domestic market; industry itself assumes a character somewhat complementary to the industry of the 'central' countries. An alternative strategy, on the other hand, can involve an industrial orientation which is more 'horizontal' and more dependent on the expansion of home markets, and consequently other aims in international economic relations.

Perhaps it must also be said that the first road is not accessible to all, far from it. This is being illustrated by the tragic experience of Chile under military dictatorship, with the conviction increasingly more widespread that the enormous sacrifices imposed on the Chilean people in the name of a redefinition of the terms for returning the country to the world economy have been and continue to be sterile.

All that the Brandt Report contributes to the discussion of these subjects will be of great benefit. But, within its content, the real import of the discussion is not concluded in any way. It thus runs the risk of being the final report in a series which has not succeeded in breaking down traditional and conventional barriers, nor overcoming the stamp of patent paternalism on the part of the 'North.' Meanwhile the Report on the underdeveloped world, which, in the final analysis, is that of the workers of the North and the South, remains still to be written.

PAVEL KHVOINIK*

> . . . the Report appears to proceed above all from the interests of the capitalist West in a quest to reconcile contradictions, to avert a confrontation with the developing world, and to identify new, more flexible and, where possible, mutually acceptable means of integrating the young states into the capitalist world economic system . . .

The interest displayed in the Brandt Report is attributable not only to the eminence of its authors but also to the fact that it claims to formulate a comprehensive programme for the solution of the problems confronting young, independent states regarding their own economic development and their relations with the industrial countries, as well as for the solution of the problems of international economic cooperation. The first question which arises in this connection is whether issues of world development can today be approached exclusively or even primarily on the basis of a classification into 'rich countries of the North' and 'poor countries of the South'. A number

* USSR. Member of the Institute of World Economics in Moscow. One of the leading Soviet experts on international economic relations. This article first appeared in Novosti/Rundschian 23 January 1981. Reprinted by permission of Wladimir Miljutenko.

of fundamental objections can be advanced to such an approach.

This method of procedure has less to do with terminological simplification than with the fact that the authors took advantage of a highly dubious concept according to which all the developed countries, capitalist and socialist alike, are contrasted with the 'poor South,' without any distinction being made as regards the fundamental divergence in the formers' respective socioeconomic models or their attitudes to and the nature of their economic relations with these young states. Such an approach, irrespective of the motives dictating its adoption, objectively operates primarily in the interest of the Western powers insofar as it effectively obscures their responsibility for colonial oppression and the contemporary imperialistic plundering of the peoples of the developing countries.

The strongest element of the Report is its endeavour to take into account the entire complex of present world problems, which complex forms the framework for the struggle of the young states for economic independence and an upgrading of their position in the system of the international capitalist division of labour. The authors do not restrict themselves in this connection to purely economic aspects but also touch on a number of social and political issues. The Report distinguishes itself from the majority of the works previously published in the West on this subject insofar as it devotes a large measure of attention to the tasks of guaranteeing peace and security, disarmament, and détente as the most important preconditions for the creation of a world climate which favours the economic advancement of the liberated nations.

It is no easy task to summarize the general impressions transmitted by the Report. Despite its premeditated simplification, the Report is just as complicated and contradictory as the problems dealt with within it. On the one hand there is evidence of an endeavour to assess the situation realistically and without prejudice, to examine the tasks which confront mankind today within the framework of the scientifico-technical revolution and the struggle of the two world systems, and to cast light on the future fate of the national liberation movement within the overall context of world development.

In this respect, the magnitude of the attention devoted to the problems of peace and security, peaceful coexistence, détente, and disarmament, especially in relation to the liberated countries' prospects of economic development, is of characteristic significance. As Willy Brandt emphasizes in his Introduction: ' . . . reshaping worldwide North-South relations has become . . . equal in importance to counteracting the dangers of the arms race . . . '(p.8)

On the other hand, the Report is guilty of a mechanical juxtaposition of diverse and to some extent very contradictory concepts. An attempt is made to camouflage the antagonism between the imperialist powers and the developing countries by bearing the standard of the struggle for an improvement of these young states' economic situation. The deliberations extend even to the solutions popular in the developing countries regarding the new international economic order and collective economic self-reliance, to some elements of the concept of satisfying mankind's basic needs, and to the most recent doctrines regarding the modernization of the methods of international expansion of monopoly capital.

For the uninitiated reader it is not easy to determine exactly where the emphasis in the Report lies: in the illusions regarding the possibilities of harmonizing the antagonistic interests of the exploiter and the exploited or in the pragmatic approach of various countries which refers to the developing countries the task of raising funds from abroad and securing the position of transnational monopolies.

The fact that such very different views are represented side by side reflects, of course, the real image of the complicated relations between the imperialist world and the developing countries. The fact that both groups of countries are equally represented on the Commission is of subordinate importance when one looks to see whose interests the Report defends. Of course, the participation of representatives of these young states did afford the document a certain character of compromise. This notwithstanding, the strategic objectives of modern neocolonialism are clearly enough in evidence.

It is no coincidence that the Report contains indications of an endeavour to steer the 'dialogue' between world imperialism and the developing countries along a path which is acceptable to the West and, accordingly, to regard the new international economic order as a 'continuously changing process in which forethought and negotiation operate constantly to establish an overall balance between all its elements'.(p.268)

Under the prevailing circumstances, however, the realization of such neocolonialistic objectives meets with ever more daunting obstacles. All in all, it is difficult to dispel the impression that the authors of the Report are less concerned about the destiny of mankind and its poorest representatives than about the possibilities open to the West of adapting itself to the new conditions governing their relations with the developing countries. Even the description of economic backwardness, of hunger and poverty in large areas of the developing world, of the widening cleft between the 'prosperity' of the Western powers and the low standard of living of hundreds of millions of individuals in the countries of Asia, Africa, and Latin America pursues, in my opinion, a very specific objective. This objective consists, as the entire content of the Report and its conclusions and recommendations in particular reveals, firstly of convincing the West of the necessity of adopting a more flexible policy vis-à-vis the developing countries, and secondly of demonstrating to the developing countries how difficult it is to bring about such a change without their taking appropriate steps. One can trace in this approach an attempt to diminish the bitterness of the struggle of the developing countries against imperialism and to persuade them to be more 'accommodating'.

The mutual interest observed by the authors resides above all in exploiting the genuine interest of the developing countries in expanding the inflow of financial resources for a massed attack by international monopoly capital on these countries. It is by no means coincidental that all questions concerning the young states are viewed exclusively from the perspective of finding new methods and spheres for the investment of foreign capital.

In the final analysis, the Report presents an alternative which can be summarized in the following terms: if the West fails to receive a guarantee of access to raw materials at 'forecastable' prices for the servicing of Western countries and for the free deployment of foreign capital, there will be no 'massive transfer of resources' to the developing countries.

The contradictoriness of the Report also finds expression in the fact that the criticism contained therein of the contemporary system of relations between the developed capitalist states and the developing countries reflects an audacity which is not evident in the – by and large – very modest proposals for guaranteeing these young states equal status within this system. This applies in particular to the transnational monopolies and pro-West finance institutions of the IMF calibre, the unmasking of which is followed by an appeal for the granting of a range of guarantees to support their work in the 'interest' of the developing countries. An incidental observation in this connection: the measures outlined by the Commission to curb the transnational monopolies do not go further than those which are already being deliberated within the framework of the United Nations.

Even in its most audacious recommendations the Report remains within the bounds of a reformist concept according to which it is possible to effect a fundamental restructuring of the capitalist system of international relations without removing the basic causes of socioeconomic inequality. It is again no coincidence that issues of a policial or social nature are usually dealt with only in passing, and the task of bringing about a genuine restructuring of international economic relations to conform with progressive democratic principles is not even mentioned.

It would of course be an oversimplification to regard the Commission's Report merely as a testimony of a culmination having been reached by the contradictions of international capitalism, a testimony in which, moreover, concern is expressed that 'at the beginning of the 1980s the world community saw itself confronted with considerably greater dangers than at any other time since the end of the

Second World War'.

The Report not only discloses the concern of the West regarding the state of its relations with the developing countries and the deterioration in the general conditions governing the capitalist reproduction system. It also discloses the concern of the young states regarding the ever greater accentuation of economic inequality, and their disappointment at the slow pace adopted for realizing the programme for the new international economic order, in which they had placed so many hopes and whose realization is hindered by the policies of imperialist states, seeking to turn both the objectives of this programme and the 'new partnership' slogan to their own advantage.

To me, the Report appears to proceed above all from the interests of the capitalist West in a quest to reconcile contradictions, to avert a confrontation with the developing world, and to identify new, more flexible and, where possible, mutually acceptable means of integrating the young states into the capitalist world economic system within the framework of the changed situation. The developing countries are called upon to take part in a 'dialogue' because the days of dictating now belong to the past and because, as it is now acknowledged, 'there is no alternative to dialogue itself and to further negotiation'.(p.264)

The broad-based approach to the problem adopted in the Report and the numerous initiatives it contains suggest that this document should be regarded less as a stocktaking survey of the world economic relations of capitalism and the needs of developing countries than a kind of programme declaration. The past decades have witnessed numerous attempts to outline ways of updating the strategy of the West vis-à-vis the developing countries to the former's advantage. Many of these documents have openly borne the stamp of pro-imperialism.

However, times are changing. Today, it can hardly be expected that the liberated young countries would lend their support to recommendations elaborated unilaterally under the aegis of the industrialized West. This explains the adequately generous representation on the Commission reserved for the young states. At the same time, the tendentious character of the Report and the prominent position accorded therein to respected representatives of the Socialist International suggest that this document is to a certain extent to be regarded as an attempt by western Social Democracy to convert the young sovereign states to their cause.

Time will permit the real nature of the recommendations to manifest itself more clearly. But even today it is obvious that many of these recommendations would merely serve to increase the dependence of the developing countries on the capitalist world economic system. Despite all the distraction manoeuvres, it is self-evident that the principal obstacles confronting the young states in their quest for economic liberation and social advancement are the residual elements of colonialism, neocolonialism, racial discrimination, and all forms of foreign aggression and occupation, hegemony, and imperialist exploitation.

ANDRE GUNDER FRANK*

> . . . contrary to the apparent belief of the Brandt Commission, the present crisis is not a Keynesian under-consumption crisis of demand deficiency but a classical overproduction crisis of accumulation.

The Brandt Commission Report poses many paradoxes. To appreciate the significant problems and new solutions in the Report and to distinguish them from the merely important but humdrum incantations, it is necessary to distinguish the very different, albeit related, parts and purposes of the Report. In a sense, the 300 page Report is four reports in one.

1. The *ideological* message of North-South 'mutual interests' set out in four general chapters totalling 100 pages and including Willy Brandt's personal appeal and personalistic introduction,

* Germany. Professor of Development Studies at East Anglia University, England. Renowned and controversial theoretician of the 'development of under-development'. Revised version of article which first appeared in *Economic and Political Weekly* (Bombay).

2. A series of financial emergency solutions for the *short term* from 1980 to 1985 (in two chapters totalling 40 pages),

3. A 'new approach to development finance' for the *medium term* based on global Keynesianism and set out in one chapter of 20 pages, and

4. The analysis and *long term* recommendations for the many global development and other problems of long standing (set out in ten chapters averaging 13 pages each).

The number of pages per item that the Report devotes to each of these four different problems seems to be proportional to the real importance that the Commission attaches to its recommendations. We may examine these in reverse order.

Long Term Problems and Programmatic Recommendations

Collectively the greatest, but individually the least, amount of space is devoted to each of the long standing development problems of the poorest countries, hunger and food, population and environment, arms and disarmament, various tasks for the South itself (like agrarian and institutional reform, provision of basic physical and social needs, and Third World cooperation), raw material commodities, trade and prices, energy supply, access to Northern markets for Southern manufactures in the face of new Northern protectionism, transnational corporations and technology, and mechanism for North-South negotiations through international organizations and summit meetings.

It would be surprising indeed if the Commission could offer any startlingly new analyses or significantly new recommendations on all or even any of these serious and long standing problems that require a long-term solution. These problems have already been dealt with by many previous official and officious reports and 'world order' studies. One might almost say that these world development problems have been researched and talked to death already, so why still another highflying report?

Indeed, examination of each of the chapters about these

problems and programmatic recommendations of the Report summarized above will show that point for point they repeat the specific demands made by the South in the call for a New International Economic Order (NIEO), that was formally introduced at the United Nations in 1974. In none of these has the North (often including the East!) been willing to accept the demands of the South, which the Commission now makes its own through its recommendations.

On the contrary, although perhaps less obviously to the general public, in the real world outside the conference rooms, the tendency throughout the 1970's has been for events to move in exactly the opposite direction from those that the South demanded and the Commission now recommends. For instance the poorest countriesn or socialism (indeed many of them built their political careers on combatting such revolution). But the Report never explains how other wise to eliminate the paradoxes in their mixed bag of recommended measures. For these contradiction, and the hunger of the poorest has increased instead of decreased; population has continued to increase and the environment to deteriorate ever faster; world arms expenditures and arms imports as well as production by the South have multiplied despite all appeals for disarmament; commodity prices have fluctuated widely and terms of trade of the non-petroleum exporting South have deteriorated since 1974; Northern protectionism especially against Southern manufactured exports and processed raw materials has grown contrary to all interested demands and wise counsels; and so on with regard to all the NIEO demands and Brandt Report recommendations.

Moreover, the Report itself observes this deterioration of reality in many cases and uses the observation as a justification for its recommendations to the contrary, though it leaves the paradox of why it hopes that yet another recommendation of the same should produce a significant turn-around. Indeed, paradoxically for this very reason, this part of the Report on long-term problems and recommendations is not and perhaps is not really intended to be the significant contribution of the Commission.

These basic recommendations for long standing

problems pose some important additional paradoxes or contradictions that the Commission itself is unable to sort out and that a capitalist system, no matter how reformed, is unlikely to be able to resolve. Like those of the NIEO demands, the implementation of these recommendations would imply and require an even more extensive and deeper integration of the South and its population into the operation of the world capitalist market. The operation of this market and productive organization has already generated the very international polarization between the North and the South, and regionally or domestically within the South, that the Commission deplores. Even if the implementation of some Commission recommendations, like higher and more stable raw materials earnings or more earnings from exported manufactures for the South, could reduce the international North-South polarization, implementation of these same measures would be likely to increase the polarization still further within the South. Indeed, the new export promotion and export-led growth in some parts of the South and especially in the 'new industrializing countries' (NICs) increasingly differentiates them from the other and especially from the increasingly marginalized poorest countries, for which the Commission expresses concern in a special chapter. However, the same process also increases the polarization and marginalization *within* the NICs themselves, to which the increase in infant mortality and massive poverty in Brazil during its economic 'miracle', the growing unemployment and wetback emigration from Mexico, and the political regression and revolt in South Korea, only to name some manifestations in the three most important NICs in the South, bear eloquent testimony.

The South's demands for NIEO have recently been supplemented by the ILO's and the World Bank's proposals for measures to serve 'Basic Needs' (BN) of food, shelter, health, education, etc. in the South. The Report echoes the debate among those who claim that NIEO and BN are competitive and those who claim they are complementary.

The Report, not surprisingly, takes this second side but argues that while all measures are to the good and the more the better, no advance on any – it explicitly mentions internal reform – is necessary before beginning with any other measure. Nonetheless, the Report's emphasis on social services for BN is very slight, though the provision of these BN has been a major strength of the countries like China and Cuba that have made a socialist revolution. The members of the Commission, as social democrats and capitalist statesmen, of course do not recommend political revolution or socialism (indeed many of them built their political careers on combating such revolution). But the Report never explains how otherwise to eliminate the paradoxes in their mixed bag of recommended measures. For these contradictions have so far been resolved in the South – and even then only partially so – by development efforts that followed socialist revolution.

Medium-Term Problems and Recommendations: Global Keynesianism for a North-South Marshall Plan

The major significance and innovations, if any, of the Brandt Commission are in the technical fields of economics and finance, to which the Report devotes fully 60 out of 190 programmatic pages, or 30 per cent of its attention on all of the dozen major problems put together. In one of these chapters, entitled 'A New Approach to Development Finance', the Commission makes a major recommendation for the medium term. The principal problem that occupies the Commission's attention here is not so much in the South as in the North and in the two put together. This problem is – as the Report notes in its subtitle on p. 240 – that 'the world economy is slowing down' into a world economic crisis. This problem appears to the Commission to have begun with the recession and the oil price increases since 1973, but the crisis is deepening at this very moment in view of the recession of 1980 and further increases in the price of oil. This problem is really so serious and so relatively new as to demand a significant contribution from the Commission which makes special mention of 18 million registered as unemployed (and twice that many counting the part time and underemployed workers) in the industrial capitalist countries of the North, although permanent unemployment is of the order of 300 million in the South. Growth rates have declined from more than 4 per cent a year in the 1950's and early 1960's to 2 per cent a year in recent years and in many countries 'growth' rates have been *negative* and threaten to decline futher in the immediate future. What is the reason for this new turn of events and what can be done about it?

The sometimes explicit and often implicit Keynesian economic analysis of the Commission attributes the source of the problem to inadequate effective demand on a global level (or to a problem of realization to use a Marxist terminology, which is foreign to the Commission). The Commission's solution, therefore, is to provide or stimulate additional new demand through Keynesian measures to prime the pump on a global level. Herein the Commission seems to combine orthodox Keynesianism – the effect that a redistribution of purchasing power can stimulate increases demand – with post-Keynesian fears that an overall increase in purchasing power would be inflationary. Therefore, in the subtitle immediately following the one about economic slowdown the Commission speaks of 'the need for 'massive transfers' ' of purchasing power from North to South. Lord Keynes and Lord Beveridge recommended massive redistributions of income from high income savers to low income spenders and the provision by the welfare state of social services to the latter in Britain and other countries in the North in the 1930s and 1940s. Now the Commission's 'New Approach to Development Finance' proposes to do the same internationally from North to South on a global Marshall Plan basis. To that end, the Report recommends 'the creation of a new institution, which might be called a World Development Fund' to function in the absence of a supernational welfare state to redistribute income, international taxes on arms expenditures and exports, and other institutions and measures to redistribute purchasing power from North to South. The Commission believes that this 'new approach' would increase global demand that would be in the 'mutual interest' of everybody in the North and the South, because it would increase income in the latter and thereby stimulate demand for the products of the former, who then could put their now underutilized productive capacity and unemployed labour to more productive and more profitable use. The world economy would be on the medium term road to recovery from its present growth recession and crisis.

This new approach of global Keynesianism by the Commission (to supplement if not replace Keynesianism on each national level separately) is of doubtful value and efficacy, because it rests on a number of minor analyses and major assumptions which are very questionable. From the point of view of the members of the Commission, who represent the élites of their respective countries, it may be a relatively minor matter that the proposed 'massive transfer' would be to the states and through them to the high income receivers in the South and not to the massively poor masses. If there is a global consumption function, such a financial transfer of purchasing power to the state and the rich in the South could indeed help satisfy the real and increase the effective demand of high income receivers in the South for high wage goods that the North want to export in order to be able to produce them with some of its underemployed capital and labour. The Report itself emphasizes how increasingly important Southern import demand has been to keep Northern industry afloat during the 1970's. Without new demand from OPEC countries, from the rich in the South and not incidentally from the socialist East, production and employment in the North would have sunk even faster and deeper during this crisis. The Commission want to institutionalize global Keynesian measures to ensure that this Southern lifesaving action for the North should continue and increase. That surely is a significant proposition.

However, paradoxically, in the distant and recent past this Southern import demand has been at the expense of meeting the basic needs of the poor in the South, to whom the supposed mutual benefits of this arrangement have not yet trickled down. Foreseeably, the implementation of the Commission's new approach of global Keynesianism would not allow the benefits to trickle down to the poor any more than in the past but would instead result in a further exaggeration of their exploitation and oppression, just as the implementation of the South's NIEO demands would. Moreover, a careful reading of the Report reveals that these Keynesian measures are not even designed to be translated into basic products and services for the moneyless poor but rather for the moneyed spenders in the South.

Whether intentionally or not, the Commission's recommendations rest on some sound economic analysis in this regard. For if there really were to be a massive increase in the income of the poor masses, they would demand basic food, housing, clothing and services. The productive apparatus in the South cannot now provide these goods in rapidly increased quantities (as the Allende government found to its regret after it raised the income of the poor by 50 per cent in 1971), and the productive apparatus of the North by and large does not want to supply them. The reason is that the economic crisis and its solution lies not in northern technological downgrading to low wage consumer goods for the South, or even to machinery to produce them in the South, but in Northern industrial upgrading to more advanced technology in the capital goods and technology producing industries. Thus, paradoxically, even if there were a big increase in Southern demand for low wage goods, this demand would soon encounter a supply constraint; and yet this demand would be unable to solve the *apparent* demand problem of productive overcapacity and idleness. The Commission seems to avoid this paradox by not really proposing to increase the effective demand of the really poor, but therefore paradoxically it also does not in fact really tackle many of the problems which it treats rhetorically in its non-financial programmatic chapters.

Moreover, the Commission and its new approach to development finance encounter another fundamental contradiction and paradox, to which they offer only an *apparent* solution. The main problem that the Commission tackles and the main weakness of its recommendations in this part of the Report are that the medium-term problem of the crisis in the world capitalist economy is only apparently one of insufficient demand but really one of overaccumulation of excess productive capacity, especially in industries and locations, like labour-intensive textile and clothing industries and also capital-intensive automobile, steel, shipbuilding and petrochemical industries in the North, which have to be phased out and replaced by new leading industries based on more advanced technology. Profits are low and new investment is unattractive both because of existing overcapacity in existing industry and because of low profitability in potentially new industry. In the medium term the needs of capital and its profitable investment are not served so much by immediate new expansion on the heels of increased demand as by temporary retrenchment and other measures to reduce costs or production, *before* increased demand can become useful and new investment possible. That is, contrary to the apparent belief of the social democratic members (including the conservative Edward Heath) of the Commission, the present crisis is not a Keynesian under-consumption crisis of demand deficiency but a classical overproduction crisis of accumulation.

That all Western government leaders and ministers as well as their leaders of industry behind them do not promote expansive Keynesian demand creation today but retrenching cost reductions to increase productivity instead cannot be laid at the door only of wrongheaded economic theory or squareheaded political ideology. These policies really do respond to the present medium-term exigencies of capital in the North. In one Western country after another, and now even in the most social democratic Scandinavian ones like Commission member Olaf Palme's Sweden, Keynesianism has been abandoned and is replaced by monetarism, if only for lack of any better alternative yet at hand.

The world press objectively reflects that 'the world goes monetarist' (*Financial Times*, October 13, 1979) and that 'the world needs a recession' (*New York Times*, May 3, 1979). The reason is that depressing costs of production, if necessary through retrenchment and exploitation (in Marxist terms through centralization of capital and increased surplus value), must take temporal if temporary medium term precedence over demand expansion at least in each capitalist country taken individually, and in the South on the Chilean and Israeli model of Milton Friedman all the more so than in the North. Yet the Commission harks back to old Keynesian analysis and remedies that have been universally discarded as inappropriate to the present crisis in each country taken individually, and proposes that they be applied instead through a global Keynesian policy applied to all of the North and South put together. There is no objective evidence, however, and the Report does not even try to offer any, that international Keynesianism would now be any more appropriate or effective than national Keynesianism.

In fact, there are good objective reasons to presume that medium-term Keynesian analysis and remedies in the South and all the more so on a global basis of North and South put together, are and will be even less appropriate and effective than they are on a national basis in the North. The very fact that Northern states are no longer willing to use Keynesian remedies for their national ills at home suggests that they will not find it in their mutual interest now to apply them globally abroad and, for instance, to spend in the South what they are unwilling to spend at home. The Achilles heel of Keynesianism is its inapplic- ability in a monopolized economy in the North that per- mits and generates unemployment of capital and labour with simultaneous inflation expecially in the monopolized sector. Therefore Keynesianism is *a fortiori* useless in the South, where foreign and domestic monopoly, structural unemployment, and continuous inflation are endemic and now acceleratingly deepened by the world economic crisis. But if Keynesian analysis and remedies are no longer useful in the North and increasingly useless in the South in each country taken separately – and yet another weakness of Keynesianism is precisely that its efficacy is limited by the also limited autonomy of any national economy and state in the contemporary world economy – then what objective reasons are there to suppose, as the Commission does, that international Keynesianism will work on a global basis in which the monopoly structure of polarization is far stronger and anti-monopolistic controls are far weaker to the point of non-existence than in the national economy and state in either North or South. The Report certainly offers no such objective evidence. Though its subjective appeal to an ideology of mutual interest may convince some people to think so, this ideology is hardly likely to persuade any decisive powers to act on this basis – with one short-run exception, which offers the saving grace of real significance in the Commission's recommendations.

Short-Term Emergency Measures

The most practical and significant recommendations of the Report are in chapters 13 and 14 on 'The World Monetary Order' and 'Development Finance : Unmet Needs' rather than in the catalogue of basic work problems and remedies that attract wider popular attention. But it may be suggested tha the relatively large amount of attention that the Report itself devotes to this single immediate problem and its proposed solution (40 pages or one fifth of the 200 pages of wide-ranging programmatic analyses and recommendations) is a better indication of the real significance that the Commission itself does – and we should – attach to this most technical part of the Report. Another reason for the real significance of this section of the Report is that it is really the one that has the greatest possibility of acceptance and implementation, precisely because it is in the mutual interest of all those who are directly concerned, although most general readers and the press generally will scarcely notice it.

The particular financial problem that concerns the Commission in these two chapters, although of course related to all the others, is that the new world recession, which started in 1979-80, and the new increases in the price of oil will again significantly aggravate the balance of payments of the South, which will have to borrow more money to service its existing debt and to cover its new deficits. The problem is that the institutions and mechanisms that covered the South's deficits by recycling OPEC and other surplus funds through the American and European banks to the South (and the East) since the recession and oil price increases of 1973-75 (while investment and profitable credit opportunities declined in the West) cannot be as available or as effective in the new balance of payments and debt crisis that is just beginning. The trouble is that the South will have to borrow new loans from Peter to pay off old loans to Paul; and the problem is that if there are no Peter finances to loan this new money to the South, one or more major debtors in the South may have to default on the old debts to Paul, thereby immediately threatening Paul – and through a domino effect chain reaction ultimately Peter as well – with banruptcy.

The financial and popular press all around the world commemorated the fiftieth anniversary of the October 1929 Wall Street crash by publishing alarm signals about the impending possibility of another crash, which this time could bring the entire highly fragile international financial system down like a house of cards. This anniversary was before the December 1979 oil price increases and before the accelerated decline of output in the United States and Britain in early 1980 (whose cause is sometimes wrongly attributed to oil), and which now aggravate balance of payments deficits and make major defaults on loans and a crash all the more possible. (In the United States the Chrysler Corporation, the Philadelphia National Bank, and the Hunt Brothers silver speculators have had to be bailed out with one to two billion dollars each, not out of brotherly love or Christian charity but out of a realistic sense of self-preservation to prevent bankruptcies that might start a chain reaction.) Brazil and Mexico already have debts outstanding of about 50 billion dollars each, and a default on only a minor part of their annual debt service of 6 to 10 billion dollars each, or even by debtors in the 10 billion dollar category like South Korea, Turkey and Peru, or for that matter of socialist Poland, could be enough to start a worldwide financial avalanche. Obviously there is a mutual interest of debtor and creditor alike in preventing that; and appeals to ideology apart, all those who are immediately concerned are earnestly engaged in seeking and implementing emergency measures to forestall impending disaster.

The Brandt Commission has evidently participated most seriously and actively in this endeavour, and it is in this hard-nosed area of world finance that the Report makes its most practical and therefore significant contribution. Paradoxically again this immediate danger did not even exist in such threatening degrees when the Commission received its terms of reference in 1977; and also paradoxically this major new recommendation by the Commission – as it observes itself on page 212 of its Report – is not really so new, since it only revives the proposal to 'link' the creation of money, credit and reserves in the world economy to the extension of development finance to the South. The 'Group of 77' developing countries had already asked for such a link after the Smithsonian Agreement, that patched up the Bretton Woods monetary system that Richard Nixon destroyed on August 15, 1971 when he took the American dollar off gold. This Southern demand for a 'link' between world money creation and credit creation to the South was unceremoniously scuttled by opposition from the North at the meeting of UNCTAD III in Santiago, Chile in 1972, but its essence has now been resurrected by the Brandt Commission.

The Report is naturally reluctant to recommend a significant increase in the world supply of money, credit and reserves, because like monetarist governments and central bankers it regards a deliberate increase in the money supply as inflationary. Of course the supply of money, credit and reserves has vastly increased since 1971 through printing of money to cover government deficits, uncontrolled Eurocurrency market credit creation, and the spectacular increase in the price of gold, which has resisted all attempts at 'demonetarization' and has instead multiplied the real or potential value of central and other banks' gold reserves. Almost all of this new money was created in and for the North, however, and only a small portion of it has been loaned to the South on increasingly onerous terms.

The most significant and practical recommendations of the Commission are that on an emergency basis beginning right now the creation of new sources of money, credit and reserves be 'linked' to transfers of funds to the South through a whole series of financial measures and institutional reforms, which the Report itemizes. These recommendations include reform of the IMF and easing the conditions of its loans (which have been provoking 'IMF riots' in the South), reforming the flexible exchange rate regime, modifying the international monetary reserve system and the use of gold, renegotiating Third World debt, increasing programme lending and export finance, and other measures.

Perhaps the Commission fires these recommendations off like buckshot or launches them like multiple warhead missiles to make sure that after another goodly number of them are shot down by recalcitrance in the North at least some of them will land on target in the South.

But paradoxically, it is precisely some of these technical recommendations that have the greatest chance of getting implemented, because they are demonstrably and self-evidently the ones in which governments and financiers, if not the people, in both North and South have the greatest mutual interest in self preservation.

Paradoxically, also, one of the now most practically plausible mechanisms based on mutual interests to channel financial resources to the South is not mentioned by the Commission, perhaps because it finished writing its Report before a new alternative became plausible. This alternative is now to cycle part of the new OPEC surplus, derived from the 1979 and 1980 price increases, directly to the deficit and debtor countries in the South without using the banks in the major capitalist countries as intermediatries of their states to back them up. There may be new mutual interests for South-South cooperation and development finance beyond those that the Commission mentions or that it would perhaps even like to contemplate.

Thus paradoxically the most practically significant recommendations of the Commission are in the areas of technical financial arrangements that are controlled by a charmed inner circle of powerful decision makers. The Commission consulted many of these eminent persons according to the Report's Annexe 2 on 'the Commission and its work', but broad appeals to ideology are the least necessary and useful to persuade these few persons to act, since they know full well what their mutual interests are. Indeed, one may be led to suspect that these eminent financiers have been telling the Commission a thing or two so they could use the prestige and ideological cover of Mr

Brandt and his Commission for their purposes. On the other hand, the wide projection of and broad appeal to a North-South ideology for the promotion of a wide-ranging programme for survival is perhaps necessary but in no wise sufficient to convert these visionary proposals into significant practical recommendations, which most of them are not.

Finally, we may observe another triple paradox. The Commission includes the Soviet Union and Eastern Europe as part of the North and sets China apart in a category of its own; but paradoxically the conservative social democratic and other members of the Commission did not include a single representative from any of these Eastern countries. Yet the Commission repeatedly includes the leaders of the socialist East in its ideological appeal to mutual interests. The last paradox is that the Commission is probably right to believe that its members share with the leaders of the socialist East, and most obviously with Deng Xiaoping, an ideological mutual interest to propose – though they also share the practical difficulties to implement – a Keynesian programme for the survival of the capitalist world, North and South.

IMMANUEL WALLERSTEIN*

> . . . the world is going through a reshuffling of alliances in the North which, until it is completed and stabilized, doubtless renders politically impossible the realization of the reforms advocated by the Commission, even were they all desirable.

The Brandt Report is a classic document, the kind that future archaeologists of knowledge will read to understand the mentality of the modern world. It is in a sense a quintessential testament to Kantian or Enlightenment liberalism. It touches all the bases, not once but over and over. It talks of moral imperatives, worldwide moral values, and a global civilization. It asserts the objectives of

* USA. Director, Fernand Braudel Center for the Study of Economies, Historical Systems and Civilizations, State University of New York at Binghamton. Known for his analytical work on the world economy.

equity and justice. It insists on the moral obligation to survive and wants to bring the world from chaos to order. It asks that we aim at a global community based on contract rather than status, on consensus rather than compulsion. It exhorts us to aim at a global community, or at least a global responsibility. It reminds us that for development to be meaningful, the focus has to be not on machines or institutions but on people.

And throughout the Report, like a litany, comes the refrain that justice and mutual self-interest are, if not identical, at least not contradictory. It argues that what is good or necessary for the poor and very poor nations is good for the better-off areas as well. It admits that the 'restructuring' for which it calls will create minor pains but insists it must be done because it will prevent or remedy greater pains.

Nor does the Report merely remain at this level of generality. It is an extraordinary review of virtually every specific issue related to global development that has been analyzed and debated over the past 30 years. No question of any importance has been evaded. On each issue, almost without exception, the Commission comes down on the side of reform, on the side of global liberalism if you will, albeit always in the prudent, rational tones of a patient, persistent advocate. In the welter of specific recommendations, one is often hard-pressed to know from this sober document what are the real priorities. At a few points however the Commission allows itself absolute modifiers, and in these the theme is the same. On page 43, the Commission says: 'The South needs, *above all*, finance.' And on page 237, it says: 'The *most urgent* need is for the programme of large-scale transfer of funds to be stepped up substantially from year to year during the final two decades of this century.' And in its Emergency Programme for 1980-85, the first item on the list is 'a large-scale transfer of resources to developing countries', although it adds that such a global transfer forms an interlocking programme with three other items – an international energy strategy, a global food programme, and a start on some major reforms in the international economic system – the four items being of equal importance.

Who is the audience for a report like this? It is claimed that the Report is addressed to everyone, North and South, the West of the North and the East of the North. But it is clearly not so. The Soviet Union is adjured from time to time to realize that it too must be involved in this process of 'restructuring' – as one of the great protagonists in the control of armaments the Commission sees as essential, as a part of the North in North-South negotiations. But these repeated pleas, as well as occasional assertions about the important role China must play, have a perfunctory air about them. The fact is that none of the major thrusts of the report depend on Soviet collaboration; the most they require is the absence of intensive, active hostility – a posture the USSR has already adopted in the discussions concerning the so-called new international economic order.

Nor is the audience the South. To be sure, every once in a while, when the report has called for some specific policy on the part of countries in the North, the Commission adds that the South must do something or other; or else they reassert the right of the South to find original paths to or definitions of development. But these passages read like apologies, to fend off know-nothing critiques in the North about the South not pulling its weight, or angry protests in the South about the paternalism of the liberals of the North.

The report is clearly addressed to public opinion in the North (and to be more specific, in the West of the North). Indeed the Commission says so in explaining to the leaders of the South why they too must be liberal:

> Leaders in the South shoulder the bulk of responsibilities. They should also be aware how important it is that public opinion in the North is convinced that measures of international reform which need support will really affect the living conditions of their people as a whole (p.17).

Of what is this Commission trying to persuade public opinion in the North? They tell us their problem at the outset: 'Many people in government, and elsewhere, may consider this to be the worst possible moment for advocating radical changes' (p.12). But, says the Commission, on the contrary, prolonged recession is the very moment for 'bold initiatives.' In any case, the Commission reassures us:

> Our proposals are not revolutionary; some are perhaps a little ahead of current thinking, others have been on the table for many years. We envisage them as part of a process of negotiated reform and restructuring. And we hope that the understanding of their interrelationships will strengthen the will for change (p.66).

The Commission is right. Their proposals are not in any way revolutionary. They are determinedly reformist in nature. Quite aside from the question of whether reformism is an appropriate or plausible remedy to the many social dilemmas the Commission describes so clearly, there is the question as to whether this is a moment when reformist measures will in fact be adopted. Does the Commission itself believe their proposed reforms are practical politics? They say they believe it, but permit me to be sceptical.

In a striking self-image, the Commission asserts: 'It is not enough . . . to sit around tables talking like characters in Chekhov plays about insoluble problems' (p.47). Yet, speaking about population projections, the Commission remarks: 'It is easy to feel a sense of hopelessness at these prospects' (p.106). And speaking of the history of North-South discussions, the Commission is sober: 'We were conscious . . . that many negotiations on these issues had ended in stalemate. . . . There is no alternative to dialogue itself and to further negotiation' (p.264). Finally, most wistfully of all, the Commission avers: 'Both North and South have an interest in the preservation of hope' (p.77).

Are we in such a bad way then, that we must assert as our objective not the achievement of the good society or the transformation of the world but merely the preservation of hope? So it seems, or so it seems at least to this intelligent, sophisticated, and informed group incarnating world liberalism.

I believe myself that the next 20 years of North-South negotiations are not going to be more significant or efficacious than the last 20 years, and I believe the evidence for this belief lies in the very structure of the Report as I have analyzed it. An appeal of the liberals among the powerful to their compeers to make reforms in the interest of equity, justice, and heading off worse has never had any significant effect in the past several hundred years except in the wake of direct and violent rumblings by the oppressed, and it will have no more effect now. Furthermore, I believe the Commission members must know this too.

Nor do I believe that if all the multiple reforms that the Commission advocates were in fact carried out the process of world polarization and ecological and human disaster that has been the *increasing* reality of the capitalist world-economy over its history would in fact slow down. I suspect in fact it would increase still further.

Let us look at one of the Commission's casual and orthodox generalizations which is, I believe, profoundly wrong. The Commission says of industrialization that Latin America, Asia and Africa are today following in the footsteps of Europe and North America, 'a development which is already beginning to change the pattern of comparative advantage in the world economy' (p.172). The Commission further argues that this industrialization 'involves a profound transformation of society' and that the 'transition from the country to the city and the adoption of new lifestyles and attitudes have far-reaching consequences' (p.173) – consequences which we are led to infer are beneficial.

In fact, the involvement of various parts of the world as peripheral zones of the capitalist world-economy has not been historically beneficial to their populations, and the fact that some of these zones are being restructured today to become 'newly-industrializing countries' is no more beneficial and has *not* changed the pattern of comparative advantage in the world economy. All that has happened is that, in the normal cycle of events, productive activities that once were high-profit, high-wage, high technology activities like textiles, later steel, later electronics, as they lose this quality, are shuffled off to peripheral zones of the world-economy, while today's core zones are seeking to develop the leading industries of the next era – biotechnology, microprocessors, advanced forms of energy production. Far from reducing unequal exchange, this 'new international division of labour' will increase it. And it is very doubtful indeed whether it can be said that the quality of life of the 18-23 year old girls who man the factories of the newly-industrializing countries is better than that of their mothers' 30 years ago.

For a report that was written by a Commission largely composed of political figures, politics is strangely absent from it. Nowhere is there a hint that the world is going through a reshuffling of alliances in the North which, until it is completed and stabilized, doubtless renders politically impossible the realization of the reforms advocated by the Commission, even were they all desirable. And since this reshuffling is not adumbrated, obviously the Commission could not treat its implications for the North-South division of labour.

Nor does there figure in this report in any way the existence of vast social *movements* – socialist and/or nationalist in character – that have been the motor force of much that has happened in the past 30 years and whose role is bound to increase. One would think from the Report that the 'negotiations' are and will be exclusively between states. This seems very poor political prognosis to me.

The Commission seems to know this but wishes it were not so. Speaking of the 'search for increased self-reliance and economic independence,' the Commission asserts: 'This thrust does not imply that the South wants to dissociate or 'delink' itself from the North' (p.134). No doubt this is true for some in the South, but surely not for many others. The Commission must obviously have been talking to different persons from the South from me, but I have heard a lot of demand lately precisely for 'delinking'.

This is perhaps why this Report is more than an exercise in Chekhovian futility. It is a message to the West that the ideology of 'delinking' – an ideology that is profoundly antisystemic – has in fact been gaining ground over the ideology of 'development.' The Commission's 'programme for survival' may be that of the survival of the system. But Chekhov was describing a social situation that was in fact resolved (or if not resolved, then profoundly affected) by first disintegration and then revolution. The only programme for survival is the creation of a socialist world order, and 'negotiations' between North and South will only have a marginal effect upon achieving such a world order.

SAMIR AMIN*

... the Third World countries ... will only begin to free themselves inasmuch as they are capable, through their own internal transformation, of 'delinking' to the utmost from the world system ...

One

It is now universally acknowledged that the world system has entered a lasting structural crisis which has invaded every quarter of social, economic and political life. This crisis has called into question the conditions of the international division of labour on the basis of which the extraordinary boom of the years 1945-71 took place, just as it has challenged the national growth and development models of the different segments of the world system, both North and South.

It is not my intention in this article to dwell upon the nature and perspectives of this crisis, a question to which I have already addressed myself at least four times since 1974[1]. It is rather to examine the 'solutions' proposed by the Brandt Commission report as they concern North-South relations.

Needless to say, however, it is my hypothesis – implicit here, explicit elsewhere – that this crisis, whose pivotal factor is situated within the international division of labour, is the natural consequence of the changes in economic and political power relations accumulated as a result of the growth of the years 1945-70. Moreover, the most significant changes have taken place along the 40th parallel and involve:

* Egypt. Director of the UNITAR Programme of Strategy for the Future of Africa at Dakar, Senegal. Leading theoretician of unequal world development. Author of *Unequal development*.

(i) intra-Western economic relations, marked by the end of American hegemony and the emergence of Japan, on the one hand, and Europe (and particularly Germany) on the other as partners which were henceforth competitive, if not outright capable of unseating the United States from at least some of its prime positions.

(ii) military relations between the West and the Soviet East, marked by the equality of the two superpowers since 1960; and political relations between the West, the Soviet East and China, distinguished by the emergence of China as an autonomous nation capable of submitting its international strategy to the imperatives of its development options.

On the other hand, North-South relations have undergone only slight modifications. The victim of an externally-oriented development which was pursued and expanded during the 1945-70 period, the Third World entered the crisis as a weak partner, bearing the brunt of its consequences. It was for this basic reason that the plan for a 'New International Economic Order', expressing the aspirations of the Third World countries, did not even begin to be implemented. Under the circumstances the Third World countries, caught in an impasse, will only begin to free themselves as far as they are capable, through their own internal transformation, of 'delinking' to the utmost from the world system, 'stepping back' and concentrating on the construction of a national, popular economy and society. Will they be up to the task? It remains to be seen whether they can enhance their capabilities through mutual support which could constitute the progressive content of a 'collective autonomy', thus complementing their efforts at national autonomy. In any event there is no alternative. For failing this solution, the most likely prospect is that of the total subjection of these societies to the strategies of the transnationals, thus implying an aggravated political dependence.

Or yet again, popular explosions of the 'populist' type which, though forcefully expressing what the people in question reject, prove incapable of defining the content of a positive and coherent strategy for national and popular development and, consequently, trigger a series of processes of collapse and disintegration whose aftermath cannot be foreseen. But then, history has largely been made this way.

Because it is global, the crisis is therefore naturally one of 'theory' as well, whether it be the theory of central growth and capitalist accumulation (where the policies inspired by Keynesianism or classical monetarism are inadequate and unable to account for new phenomena such as 'stagflation'), or the conventional theory of 'development-modernization'.

The New International Economic Order, the recommendations of the Brandt Commission report and the United Nations strategies for the 1980's decade are attempts to respond to the challenges of our time while safeguarding what decision makers deem to be essential: the 'global interdependence' of contemporary societies.

Two

The Brandt report shares the general philosophy – which its very title, 'programme for survival', suggests – according to which interdependence is synonymous with the partners' mutual interests.

It is apparently, therefore, this threatened 'global interdependence' which is to be saved. The world system – a world system (capitalist implied?) – must be maintained, and the various national societies must find their place and situate their development within the system's development as a whole. The entire Report, its recommendations and its analyses (or more precisely, its lack of them), are based on this choice. The hypothesis that the common interest shall override conflicts of interest smacks of 'wishful thinking' if only all the governments in the world were willing . . .

Naturally, we do not share this philosophy. We feel that it has too frequently been contradicted by history to continue to be acceptable. History has thus far been one of both interdependence and a concomitant asymmetry (the very term interdependence is thus incorrect, and that of dependence more appropriate). The history of this unequal development is that of the unequal evolution of the powers of the respective partners.

Modifications in power relations are rooted in both the accumulated effects of unequal interdependence and in the societies' internal transformations. In the final analysis it is the evolution and change in the internal orders which dictates to the international order, and not the reverse.

The 'cure' for the global crisis proposed by the Report is that of a 'global Keynesianism', to use the tidy expression of André Gunder Frank. 'A massive transfer of resources from the North to the South would get the machine going again (and, by the same taken, resolve unemployment) in both the South and the North . . . '[2]

Within the same perspective what the NIEO proposes is better and sounder, and avoids the unnecessary and questionable detour of the 'transfer of resources'. Indeed, what the NIEO is proposing is simply an industrialization for export from the South toward the North, based on low wages and abundant natural resources. The effect of such a massive delocalisation of industry would undoubtedly be to give an overall boost to the profit rate. In this area, Keynesianism simplifies things: it attributes the crisis to an insufficiency of demand which may be stimulated by a redistribution of income. It avoids tackling the question of the organization of production, which is specifically aimed at by the NIEO.

Obviously, delocalization involves both a redistribution of productive forces, and hence revenues, and an increase in the profit rate. Furthermore, far from appealing for a supplementary 'transfer' whose limitations and characteristics – largely pernicious – have been illustrated by history, the NIEO foresees an increase in the prices of the South's traditional exports (and to do so urges unilateral action through cartelization, following the petroleum example) and the mobilization of the additional resources thus obtained (and particularly mineral and petroleum earnings) to finance the new stage of 'transfer-free' growth.

Naturally, the partners in the redistribution in question are not 'peoples', but countries. The NIEO is not so naive as to confuse the two. In fact, an export industrialization based on cheap labour presupposes: (i) a developed agricultural sector which supplies the cities with both an overplentiful labour supply and inexpensive food-stuffs, and (ii) urban unemployment, a working class and poor, subordinate middle classes. The project is therefore one not of 'development for the poor', but of capital accumulation.

Naturally too, since the allies in the conflict are not 'peoples' but the ruling classes, the battle for the redistribution in question pits the capital of the North against the States of the South against a backdrop of the division of a growing surplus. And here two conflicting interpretations of the NIEO emerge: one advanced by the Northern transnationals (redeployment under their guidance) and the other by the Southern states (export industrialization, yes, but also nationalization of revenues, producer cartels and the concomitant setting up of an economy and an industry which, if capitalist, are nonetheless self-reliant; its exports permit and prolong domestically oriented production by infusing it with massive imports of technology).

That the states of the South lack the strength to impose a redistribution today seems clear.

The failure to provide an analysis concerning the causes and mechanisms of 'underdevelopment' leads the Report to propose inadequate and misleading solutions for each question which comes up.

With regard to the 'least developed' countries, the report portrays them as a homogeneous group, whereas an historical analysis had led us to propose several types of countries which are 'less developed', for a variety of reasons having to do with their integration into the world system as 'peripheries of peripheries' supplying either migrant labour (for example: (i) the 'second degree' trading economy, such as Upper Volta in relation to the Ivory Coast, or (ii) 'labour reserves' such as Bantustans, or Lesotho), or food products (for example: the Sahel countries which export meat, and formerly exported cereals, to the Coast of Benin . . .).

The report's 'recommendation' – that of giving priority to agriculture – is for this reason superficial. Undoubtedly such a priority is called for. But the models of colonial exploitation, similarly founded on this priority (the trading economy, concessionary economy and the labour reserve economy are at the historical root of the current massive poverty in the African rural areas[3]. And the 'new' policies advocated by the World Bank: bureaucratic assistance, kulakization or agribusiness, by reducing food priority to that of simple food projects without calling into question the global policy of world integration, are thus inevitably destined to aggravate the peasants' misery.

'Food priority' – which is imperative not only for the 'less developed' countries 'but for the others as well' (i.e. the NIC's: newly industrializing or 'semi-industrialized' countries) – demands something quite different:

> (i) the challenging of global policy at all levels (income distribution, real wages and agricultural prices, financial and fiscal policies, etc. . .)
>
> (ii) the setting up of industries supporting the agricultural priority (and not exportation or the satisfaction of the effective demand on the basis of current structures);
>
> (iii) the autonomy of peasant communities in the conception and execution of their development projects (and this goes far beyond the agrarian reforms advocated in the Report); and finally
>
> (iv) a critical distance taken from the criteria of profitability, it being understood that the setting up of a national, popular economy and society is in contradiction with the demands of 'international competition'.

What is said for agriculture also holds, mutatis mutandis, for the other sectors of popular interest: the activities of small enterprises and artisans to satisfy popular consumption. The Report advises 'assistance to the informal sector', but it ignores the fact that this sector, articulated as it is with an economy which is not oriented toward the satisfaction of popular needs is for this very reason, exploited. And the classical discourse on the 'social services' in unacceptable as a substitute for the requirements of genuine autonomy for popular communities.[4]

The construction of an economy oriented toward the

satisfaction of the people's needs certainly calls for 'domestic reforms'. But history – and politics – have shown that such reforms are rarely compatible with the constraints of integration into world system. One wonders why the Report shies away from condemning the policies of 'destablization' of popular regimes implemented by international powers and institutions such as the IMF. Under these conditions the Third World governments are correct in considering this recommendation to be demagogical since it attributes responsibility for the current situation to them alone.

One detects a certain bashfulness with regard to the capital of the major transnationals in the chapter on trade. Yet it seems absurd to recommend joint Funds and other means of trade stabilization without taking account of the failure of negotiations. Why overlook the possibility, envisaged in 1975, of a cartelization of Third World producers?[5] Perhaps this is the only way of altering power relations in favour of the South.

Concerning mineral resources and energy, areas in which the interests of the North are specifically at stake, the Report contents itself with: (i) proposing the acceleration of mining research in the South through the creation of a special Fund; (ii) attributing the grinding poverty of the 'Fourth World' to the rise in petroleum prices. One wonders why the plunder of the natural resources of the South should be accelerated so that the North might pursue its wastefulness. The Report's failure to relate the political economy of mining revenues to the international division of labour[6] should be questioned, as should the total disregard not only for the historical responsibility of the North in the unequal development of the South, but that of its strategy in the contemporary crisis as well.

Concerning industrialization, the report appears to consider the result obtained in the 'NICs' – semi-industrialized countries (Brazil, Mexico, South Korea, etc. . .) – as positive. But it should not be forgotten:

   (i) that a global strategy of delocalization would necessarily accentuate the unequal development of the South. Nor should it be forgotten that Brazil's accelerated industrialization is concomitant with the de-industrialization of Argentina.

(ii) that this strategy is based on a repressive social policy. In every NIC the growth – prodigious though it may be – of the GDP and the industrial product has gone hand in hand with a stagnation or reduction in workers' wages and peasants' incomes. On the other hand, in the case of accelerated development at the hub of the system, such as in Spain, growth is seen to be accompanied by a parallel rise in wages and peasant revenues.

(iii) that for this reason, the peoples of the NICs scarcely appear favourable to the model proposed. The Shah of Iran was toppled at a time when the country's economy was expanding full tilt. South Korea denies pronouncements on so-called 'growth with redistribution'.

(iv) that, contrary to the model's claims, the alternative of giving priority to export industry does not improve the foreign balance. The proof: among the Third World countries it is the NICs which are most deeply in debt.

The Report accords a great deal of importance to immediate problems and in particular, the danger of a global financial crash which could result from world inflation and the staggering rise in certain countries' external debt.

André Gunder Frank goes so far as to assume that the report's real objective – and the principal aim of the proposed summit – might be precisely to study the ways and means of avoiding a financial crash.

The solution, envisaged many years ago and then abandoned, of establishing a 'link' between the issuing of international liquidity and development aid, is taken up again by the Report. Such a 'link' would make it possible to avoid the financial collapse of certain Third World countries whose external debt is jeopardizing the global balance. Herein, says Frank, lies the 'real arena of mutual interest, that of the states as a whole'. But can such a link actually be established?

The Report's general considerations concerning the international monetary system appear naive. It hopes for the establishment of an 'equitable international monetary system', which so far has never existed. To begin with there has only been a world monetary system during periods characterized by the the economic hegemony of a national centre. This was the case in the 19th century, until 1914, when the gold standard (sterling, in fact) coincided with British hegemony. This was again the case from 1944 (Bretton Woods) to 1971 (suspension of the dollar's convertibility) throughout the duration of American hegemony. On the other hand, during what is known as 'the thirty years' war' for the British succession, which pitted the United States and Germany against one another from 1914 to 1945, there was no international monetary system, but extreme chaos. It was not the lack of a world monetary system which caused this chaos, including the crash in 1929, but on the contrary, it was because of the lack of a hegemonic world power that it was impossible to have an international monetary system. Yet we have once again entered a period in which the succession to the United States is open to Europe (rather than Japan), at least on the scale of the capitalist system, whether global or that of the old hemisphere. The contest is underway.

Disorder necessarily leads to inflation. Undoubtedly inflation now has internal structural causes having to do with the strategy of the monopolies, which have refused competition through pricing and with the social order organized by 'collective contracts'. This is why inflation has continued to progress gradually since 1945. There can be no monetary cure for an illness when the currency is not the cause. Will the monetarists ever understand this?

Indeed, it is assumed that 'everybody suffers from inflation'. This is not the case. For the monopolies inflation pays, since unemployment conveniently exerts pressure on salaries and facilitates reorganization.

Now the imbalance of payments is structural and global, and a deficit in some countries is counterbalanced by a surplus in others. Such deficits can no longer be attributed to 'inadequate' national policies; they are the necessary counterpart of surpluses which are just as difficult, if not impossible, to reabsorb.

The international or regional monetary order – or more accurately, the monetary disorder, reflects the balance of powers, or the absence of a balance between the developed capitalist countries, and not North-South relations. Yet we have already claimed that what had actually changed were in fact relations between developed countries. This is why to talk of the 'specific needs of the developing countries', among other things, and 'the link', is naive. This is not the issue.

A final question: is the danger of a financial crash real or imagined? Major financial institutions can always be officially saved from collapse if the country's central bank is willing to come to their rescue (even at the price of nationalization) and accept the resulting inflation. In 1929 such a choice was impossible without suspending convertibility. Today things have changed. Naturally, a country's central bank might hesitate if it were alone in doing this because the ensuing speedup in national inflation would contribute to the deterioration of its currency in relation to others. But precautions would seem to have been taken already through the association into consortia of the lenders of the major financial institutions of all the lending countries for every international loan, whether large or small. In this case default on the part of a major borrower would threaten the whole system, which would be forced to react in a solitary way to avoid a crash.

But who are these borrowers? The Eastern countries and the newly industrializing countries of the Third World (NICs). With regard to the latter, we may recall that their swelling debt belies the traditional optimism of the World Bank which advocates export industries . . . But in fact the loans granted to these countries are never meant to be reimbursed. The reason for this is the supposed structural surplus of the lenders. These loans, although not always allotted to specific investments, constitute the latter-day form of foreign investment. They are intended to be profitable, and their relative interest rates will undoubtedly continue to increase. The result will be an increasing depletion of the Third World's real revenues, which is in fact the operation's very objective. This is why the danger of a crash seems less serious to me than it is generally thought to be. For either these countries will continue to alienate their independence (and their income) by indefinitely pursuing this pattern of development, and everything will go well, or else, following political changes, they will refuse to reimburse and will succeed in this inasmuch as historical precedents have shown – they may be the targets of retaliatory measures which will compel them to choose national or collective autarchy. And in this case the associated central banks of the lending centres will rush to the assistance of their 'victims' . . .

Rather, the danger of a crash will come from elsewhere: the erratic flows of liquid assets held by the transnationals (even more than by the petroleum states) which are governed only by the rules of short-term speculation. In this area, the advocates of flexible rates of exchange have done a service to the speculators, but only by compromising the collective interest of averting a disaster. This is perhaps why after the love affair with the Milton Friedman school, undoubtedly owing to the ideological alienation attached to the neo-liberal revival, the Western political and monetary authorities have begun to return to less absurd positions.

Three

What can be done? Strategy must be found to oppose to these plans, which are inconsistent, naive and unrealistic. Two major documents with sound propositions suggest the possibility of another course.

Four

Kenneth Dadzie's declaration to the Group of 77 (March, 1980)[7] is founded on realistic observations: (i) the incapacity of the system to provide effective management (ii) the shift in intra-Western relations, responsible for crisis of the dollar and the monetary system; (iii) the modification of East-West relations; and (iv) the North's refusal to make concessions to the South. The Director General draws the conclusion that the South must give priority to national, collective self-reliant development. The possibility of reform in the world system thus becomes secondary envisaged only, in the optimistic hypothesis, as a potential means of facilitating self-reliant development in the South.

These themes are taken up again in the programme of action of the Africa summit of the OAU (Lagos, April 1980): priority given to national and collective endogenous development, common action aimed at influencing the evolution of the world system and its increasing adaptation to the demands of self-reliant development among the African States.

For all of the Third World countries, whether more or less developed, NICs or petroleum producing states, the main problem is to bring about an agricultural revolution, and to this end, to reorganize (or build) industry so that it may serve agricultural development; to delink this industry from exportation and from the effective domestic demand of the privileged classes; and to initiate a process of promotion of technical creativity, thus permitting the development of adapted techniques which will gradually decrease dependence on imports of poorly adapted equipment.

Naturally, the forms and substance of the agrarian revolution cannot be the same in the 'labour reserve' countries and in those which have a vast potential for agricultural expansion. The forms taken by industry will obviously depend on a variety of factors (size of the economy, natural resources, energy, etc. . .) but also and above all, on the forms of agricultural development which industry is supposed to serve. In any area the fact that the overall objective and principles are the same does not exclude the multiplicity of concrete situations, points of departure and hence, of means; quite the contrary. Nevertheless, we are still a long way from embarking on such a course.

As a whole Latin America presents the characteristics of the newly industrializing countries (NICs). Furthermore, it appears to have been more successful in braving the impact of the crisis and maintained respectable growth rates throughout the 70's, while in both the developed capitalist world and in other Third World regions, Africa in particular, growth rates were tumbling. Latin America feels it can pursue this type of development by further supplementing its range of export industries with another range oriented toward the local, national and regional markets. It considers that to do so, it must continue to have recourse to the capital market and massive imports of technology. Accordingly, it has accepted increased dependence, particularly as it tends to align itself with the developed world on the question of energy policies.

While on the whole the Arab world (and Iran) exhibits a level of urbanization and industrialization similar to that of Latin America, it suffers the consequences of its massive but unevenly shared contribution to oil production. Low agricultural productivity (with a limited and unevenly distributed agricultural potential), the Palestinian question, conflict of the superpowers in the region and the deadlock of the political forces which have dominated the scene for 30 years, have played a part in creating a turmoil situation here, which is analyzed in another text[8].

The NICs of Eastern Asia are threatened by their lack of domestic markets and their extreme dependence on the world market, even more pronounced than in Latin America. It will undoubtedly prove impossible for them to pursue their model of development, and the ferment in South Korea is certainly not unrelated to the difficulties of a 'reconversion'. The countries of South and South-East Asia, like the whole of Africa, are already suffering from the massive transfer of the crisis' effects. The decline in growth and productive investments, like the accentuation of public and external financial debts, is already a familiar story.

But although the totality of Afro-Asian countries patently constitute the weakest links in the world system, not a single country in the group (not even Iran, nor Algeria, Angola, Ethiopia or Tanzania) has yet embarked systematically upon the path of a genuine, self-reliant development. At best, the embryonic and fragile development of some of the elements of such a strategy has been initiated and is being pursued.

Self-reliant development must first and foremost be national. Collective autonomy may facilitate this national choice, but cannot replace it. Under these circumstances, 'South-South cooperation' emerges as an extension of 'North-South cooperation', and contributes little that is new. The proposals of the Report in this regard conform to this conventional perspective, and the appeal for a triangular operation (OPEC finances and Northern technology to help the South) has elicited from some individuals the sarcastic but apt remark that 'the same thing is being done, but with somebody else's money'! The United Nations conferences (TCDC, ECDC . . .) are still less innovative, and what is more, have no resources! A critical assessment of OPEC and Arab aid, within the framework of Afro-Arab cooperation in particular, reveals that while the volume of financial transfers has grown, the projects proposed, like those requested moreover, continue to be conventional.

Yet the crisis seems precisely to offer the opportunity to launch a genuine strategy of collective autonomy which could offer compelling support for independent national strategies. Once the destination of the 'aid' allotted to development had been called into question, the new OPEC fund could foresee systematic actions to support a self-reliant industrialization. Iron and steel metallurgy provide an excellent example of what could be done. Indeed, the crisis in this sector has interrupted the process of delocalization toward the South of segments intended for export and dominated by the Northern monopolies. This let-up provides the golden opportunity to introduce a new strategy for this sector which would be oriented toward domestic needs. The uneven distribution among the countries of the South of iron ore deposits, domestic market requirements and capacities for financial and technological inputs should impel triangular South-South cooperation. In the area of energy as well, the development of oil substitute resources for the domestic consumption of non-petroleum producing developing countries should constitute a major feature of this new aid. Finally, with regard to the mining of ores, the development and exploitation of small deposits intended for small-scale local and regional consumption also calls for financial and technical assistance (including appropriate research); as do agricultural development, particularly in areas which require large investments (irrigation, mechanization, fertilizer production); and technological research, particularly as regards the development of industries oriented toward agricultural needs. It is interesting to note that trends in this direction have been favourably received by the OPEC Fund.

Furthermore, the crisis has already brought many countries to the point of financial ruin. Yet the system's response to this situation – submission to the IMF and the 'Club of Paris' – in the form of highly reactionary and inefficient formulas, can but extend the transfer of the crisis onto the weak partners: in the last analysis it is the poor, popular classes of the Third World which are made to pay, to raise the profit rate and maintain the levels of consumption and waste of the developed countries. It is interesting to remark that at the OPEC Fund there is an awareness of the need for short-term assistance, not to complement the pernicious action of the IMF, but to replace it with a different perspective. The IMF – which is responsible for contributing to the 'destabilization' of states which undertake an autonomous national, popular experience – in fact emerges as the Agency in charge of creating the immediate conditions which will pave the way for the transnationals to impose their global strategy. The new, short-term assistance would go specifically to those countries which, determined to set out upon an independent path, must resist these attempts to destabilize them.

Lastly, collective autonomy thus defined conveys the meaning which 'non-alignment' should have today. Originally a political solidarity movement intended to support national liberation struggles while remaining independent of the superpowers, non-alignment may today help broaden the scope of autonomy enjoyed by societies which refuse the tragic choice: Chile or Afghanistan.

Failing this option, the countries of Africa and Asia will inevitably slide into chaos and collapse in the coming crisis years. They will become the pawns of outside forces unless populist revolts unleash more basic changes.

Notes and References

1 The four articles on the crisis are the following:
   a) Towards a new structural crisis of the capitalist

system, *Socialist revolution*, n°1, 1975, San Francisco.

b) *Imperialism and unequal development*, chapter 5, Monthly Press, New York 1977.

c) Self Reliance and the NIEO, *Monthly review*, July–August 1977.

d) A propos du NOEI et de l'avenir des relations economiques internationales, *Africa development* n°4, 1978.

2 See the contribution of André G. Frank to this volume, page 329.

3 For the various colonial models involved (trading economy concessionary or labour reserve economies . . .) see S. Amin, Sous développement et dépendence en Afrique Noire, *Tiers monde*, n°52, 1972.

4 The way peoples are dealt with in the Brandt Report is reminiscent of the way the question of women is handled in most reports: a special chapter is devoted to them, with little concern for whether the content of that chapter contradicts what is said elsewhere! Yet it is now well known, owing in particular to the considerable efforts of feminist groups, that the conditions of non-remunerated domestic work (which is nonetheless productive of use values) impinge upon the values characteristic of the product of social labour (producing exchange values). In disregarding such work the Brandt Report, as concerns the 'informal sector', abandons itself to hollow platitudes.

5 Here we refer to the programme adopted by the Conference of non aligned nations in Dakar in 1975, which advocated the setting up of Third World producers' associations (and not combined associations of producers and consumers) and the creation of a common fund to provide support to these associations in the battles they are waging to see prices raised (and not a stabilization fund).

6 For the political economy of mining revenues see S. Amin. *The law of value and historical materialism*, chap. VI, Monthly Press 1978.

7 Reference is made here to the address delivered in March 1980 by Kenneth Dadzie to the Group of 77 in New York, (roneod doc.) U.N. 1980.

8 Samir Amin, *L'économie Arabe contemporaine*, Ed. de Minuit 1980.

AMILCAR O. HERRERA*

The present crisis is the reflection of the crisis in a way of life and a concept of the world, and cannot be resolved simply by way of economic growth and certain other palliative measures which do not go to the root of the problem.

Introduction

The Report of the Brandt Commission has the indisputable merit of being the first document to contain a concrete proposal regarding a new international economic order. Until now the so-called North-South dialogue has consisted of two totally disconnected monologues, and more especially of a refusal on the part of the countries of the North to take into account the basic claims of the developing countries. The Brandt Report represents the most advanced positions of the political leaders of the North, and consequently permits an evaluation of the possibility of establishing a more just international order, on the assumption that these progressive criteria would really be adopted by those responsible for the conduct of the developed countries.

It is impossible to present a detailed analysis of the proposals of the Report, with all their implications, in a few pages; consequently, the problem is to decide which is the most suitable approach for an examination which, without going into the technical merits of the solutions proposed for each of the problems identified, permits an assessment of the adequacy of the basic philosophy of the document towards the present world problem constellation. The Report consists of two fundamental parts: a diagnosis of the present situation – global and sectoral – and a collection of proposals, most of them sectoral, to resolve or alleviate the problems identified in the diagnosis. As is obvious, the validity of the solutions depends in great measure on the

* Argentina. Chaired the Bariloche Project on a Latin American World Model (intended as a 3rd World Alternative to the 'Limits to Growth' of the Club of Rome).

accuracy of the diagnosis; accordingly, our analysis will concentrate on the latter and will subsequently proceed to deal briefly with the recommendations.

As a starting point for a better understanding of the nature of the diagnosis and the proposed solutions, it is necessary to take into account the terms of reference which determined the composition and the work of the Commission. Firstly, the Commission was composed mainly of persons with political responsibility – at the present time and in the recent past – for decision-making in their own countries or in international organizations, persons, that is, whose view of problems was mainly formed through their participation in the activities of governmental organizations. Secondly, and partly on account of the very nature of its composition, the Commission attempted to propose solutions which were acceptable to governments, especially those of the developed countries. This implied that the proposals could not introduce modifications which might significantly affect the structure of world power or the concept of the world on which that structure is based.

The foregoing is not a criticism of the composition or the work of the Commission. The fact that the proposal in favour of a new international economic order arose in a resolution of the United Nations, that is to say, in an organization of governmental representations would seem to indicate that the proposal for the initiation of a North-South dialogue must be acceptable, at least in principle, to the governments involved. On the other hand, the objective of proposing realistic solutions, in the sense defined above, was not pursued with an excessively conservative or timid attitude on the part of the Commission; on the contrary, the solutions recommended, while remaining within the accepted limitations, take to the limit the possibilities of manoeuvring the system of world political and economic power. Consequently an analysis of the viability of the recommendations of the Report can give an indication of the point at which it is possible to establish a new, reasonably equitable international order without questioning the central principles on which the present world order is founded.

The Diagnosis

Let us begin our analysis with a brief review of the diagnosis of the situation of the Southern countries. The Report gives a detailed and realistic description of the deficiencies and problems of the underdeveloped countries in the sectors considered by the Report: population, food, energy, environment, natural resources, international trade, industrialization, etc. The description is essentially quantitative and includes information on current shortcomings and their effects on the standard of living of the local populations, and on the financial and human resources necessary to remedy these deficiencies and enable the populations of these countries to reach an acceptable standard of living in the course of the next two decades.

The description, although correct from the point of view of the magnitude of the shortcomings identified, nevertheless does not constitute a diagnosis because it refers to the consequences not the causes of poverty. Obviously, it is not possible to contend that the Commission should have made an exhaustive analysis of the structural causes of backwardness in most of the countries of the South; but it is no more possible to propose effective solutions if at least the most important elements of these structural factors are not taken into account. The implicit position of the Commission is that underdevelopment is an early stage of development and can be corrected simply by way of economic measures such as large-scale investment control, rationalization of production, and external aid to cover balance of payments deficits.

This position, despite some marginal references to political and social causes of poverty, is clearly evident in the nature of the solutions recommended. In all of them it is presumed that the governments will assume responsibility for deploying the resources arising from the proposed mechanisms of North-South cooperation. The underlying hypothesis is that in underdeveloped societies the mechanisms of wealth distribution are more or less similar to those operating in advanced capitalist countries; in the latter, there exists, in spite of the prevailing internal inequalities, a sufficient degree of social homogeneity and political participation of the public to ensure that the benefits of any increase in wealth reach, although in unequal form, all members of society. On the other hand, the characteristics of a productive system which is directed towards mass consumption ensure that it is in the interest of the possessing classes to raise the acquisitive capacity of all social strata.

Nevertheless, it is well known that the situation in most of the underdeveloped countries is totally different. The productive system is directed principally towards satisfying the needs of privileged minorities who have the same patterns of consumption as the upper and middle classes of advanced countries; this situation of privilege can only be maintained by means of oppression and exploitation of the masses, in the first instance the peasantry. The Report recommends that the governments of the poorer countries strengthen the power of the trade unions and encourage popular participation in the political and social decision-making process as a means of bringing about a more effective deployment of the resources stemming from ultimate North-South cooperation. This recommendation results from an amazing naivety, when one takes into account that even a superficial view of what is happening in the Third World reveals that the majority of the ruling classes resort to any means – in some cases, very well known in Latin America for example, even to the massive physical elimination of the opposition – precisely to avoid a popular participation which would mean the end of their privileges. To sum up, without going more deeply into a problem which is already well known, the poverty of the Third World largely depends on structural factors which have their own dynamics. Any proposal for solution which does not take these factors into account is doomed to failure at the outset.

Yet it is with the North that the weakness of the diagnosis is most evident. The Report makes the repeated error, in spite of its affirmations that the crisis is global, of assuming implicitly that the fundamental problems are in the South and that consequently it is in this part of the world that changes must be made; the North, certainly, must also modify some of its attitudes, mainly with regard to the undeveloped world, but its concept of the social and international organization which conditions in large measure the nature of the world crisis is not seriously questioned. Simply an illustration, for in this short commentary it is not possible to go deeply into such an issue, I shall draw attention to some of the points in the Brandt Report which demonstrate these shortcomings.

The Report refers to the world armaments race, especially in relation to its economic consequences, in pursuit of which resources are denied to other more productive ends; nevertheless, in spite of its sincere pacifist tone, the document fails to go to the root of the problem. Responsibility for this monstrous destructive nuclear apparatus which is capable of destroying humanity and a large part of the universe lies mainly with the United States, the Soviet Union, and Western Europe, although its lethal effects would reach the whole world. We cannot analyze here the direct and indirect mechanisms which condition the system, but it can no longer be ignored that if we persist in the present tendencies the possibility that the destructive apparatus will not ultimately reach the point of action is truly minimal.

There is no need for elaborate arguments to show that a 'defence' system which is based on Mutual Assured Destruction (MAD) is of a paranoiac irrationality incompatible with any notion of human solidarity; we wish nevertheless to refer to an aspect of the problem which strikingly highlights this absolute contempt for human values. In principle – and within its essential irrationality – there could be a certain logic in the assumption that the two opposing blocs will accept destruction before relinquishing their positions and privileges. After all, in their hands lies the taking or not of the final decision which unleashes the catastrophe; but the disaster will affect the whole world. In other words, the two thirds of humanity who do not take part in the confrontation nor have been consulted would also be destroyed as a mere 'by-product' of the conflict between the great nuclear powers. Furthermore, it becomes clearer each day that the destructive apparatus is largely conditioned on the one hand to the struggle of the two great power blocs for control of the Third World, and on the other to facing the threat to them posed by the growing dissatisfaction among the greater part of humanity with a world order which condemns it to backwardness and poverty. Whilst this situation exists it is not clear how the developed countries can, with any degree of credibility, refer to their concern for the well-being and the human dignity of the countries of the South. Another problem which, in spite of being a key issue in the Brandt Report, is not analyzed in its true significance is that of unemployment. The Report assumes that, apart from quantitative differences, the problem has the same essential characteristics in the North as in the South. In my opinion, because this assumption affects some of the Report's most important conclusions and recommendations it is one of the fundamental shortcomings of the document.

The developed countries possess a productive system capable of satisfying the needs of their inhabitants at a much higher level than that of the so-called basic needs. Nevertheless, an ever increasing part of the population fails to receive the benefits of that productive system because it fails to find a workplace within it. In addition to some concomitant, and as such essentially transitory factors, the principal long-term and irreversible cause of unemployment is the increasing efficiency of the production system, that is to say, the fact that technical progress ensures that less and less human effort is required for the same output. The advances in microelectronics, with the possibility of automating almost the entire system of production and services, will accelerate the diminution in the demand for labour. Thus we find ourselves in the paradoxical situation in which the complement of the old human aspiration for liberation from physical and routine labour has become a curse due to the incapacity of a social system to adjust itself to self-generated changes. If God had held the same views or the same subordination to interests created by the leaders of the North, Adam and Eve would have died of hunger in the Earthly Paradise because, in spite of the existence of a productive system sufficient for all their needs, they were unemployed in the sense of not having gainful employment.

Thus it is obvious that the present unemployment in the countries of the North is a new phenomenon which cannot be resolved with the same criteria as were used in the past. No longer is it a simple question of increasing investment for the creation of more sources of work; it is one of recognizing that the fundamental problem now focuses on the social distribution of the production more than on its indiscriminate increase. On the other hand, and this is even more difficult to admit, it is increasingly irrational to render access to the goods and services which are essential to a life worthy of human dignity subordinate to wages. I could enlarge on this theme; I simply wish to point out that unemployment in developed countries is, in a certain sense and in the form in which it exists, a false problem since its solution depends more on the creation of new forms of social organization than on the enlargement of the productive apparatus.

In the underdeveloped countries the nature of unemployment is very different; here, it stems primarily from the fact that the productive mechanism, by its reduced scale, absorbs little labour and is not capable of satisfying the basic needs of the population. At the same time, as we have already indicated, production is directed more towards satisfying the demand of the privileged strata than that of the deprived masses; in this case it is necessary to increase productive capacity and to modify the nature of production. It must be borne in mind, however, that if the same criteria are applied as at present prevail in the developed countries, unemployment in the South, even if the productive system is enlarged, will continue to increase. Technology which cannot absorb the labour of even the countries of the North obviously cannot employ a working population which is increasing at a rate two or three times greater. The solution cannot be the transfer of labour-intensive industries to the South: firstly, because this represents a division of labour which would tend to perpetuate the subordination of the South to the North and, secondly, because technological progress ensures that the comparative advantage of cheaper labour decreases from day to day. The real solution, just as in the North, lies in adapting the forms of social organization to a productive system which demands ever less human effort.

A point closely related to the foregoing is that regarding economic growth. The Report recognizes the new problems facing mankind in connection with the deterioration of the environment and the increasing pressure on renewable and non-renewable natural resources; however, it concludes that the best solution to the problems of the North, and indirectly to those of the South, is that the developed countries maintain high rates of economic growth. There is no intention to propound here the debated solution of zero growth, but there is no doubt that to propose as a long-term solution the continuation of economic growth as in the past reveals, at best, little imagination. The present crisis is the reflection of the crisis in a way of life and a concept of the world, and cannot be resolved simply by way of economic growth and certain other palliative measures which do not go to the root of the problem. The solution proposed is the natural consequence of failing to perceive that current unemployment is a new phenomenon which cannot be resolved by measures of the past, and of failing to question the system of values on which the prevailing manner of development is based.

The Proposed Solutions

The solutions proposed in the Report incorporate the defects which are to be expected from the nature of the diagnosis and the frame of reference within which the Commission worked. Basically, and to recapitulate the deficiencies of the diagnosis already indicated, it can be said that the Commission did not take into account the power structure which, as much at internal, national level as on the international plane, conditions the nature of the world crisis.

The measures recommended include an increase of international aid, especially to the poorest countries, but essentially propose mechanisms of financial transfers which allow the countries of the South to remain in debt. It is not disputed that the Report also proposes a policy of more just, or at least more stable values in international trade and a more effective participation of the countries of the South in international finance organizations. Nevertheless, since the power mechanisms and interests concerned are not taken sufficiently into account, it is not evident how these good intentions can be put into practice. Moreover, and even in the hypothetical case of the transfer of funds taking place, it is very doubtful whether, given the power structure currently prevailing in most of the countries of the South, its benefits would really reach the deprived masses.

On the other hand the Report bases the possibility of cooperation on the supposed existence of a mutual interest on the part of both North and South in the development of the South. Yet some difficulty is encountered in convincing the political leaders in the North of the validity of this argument, as recent events have clearly shown. Confronted by a crisis of recession, the reaction of the developed countries has been that of decreasing even more the already restricted area of action accessible to the countries of the Third World in the international context. In the economic field, the return to protectionism to the detriment of exports from the peripheral countries, the reduction of credit, and the further diminution of the already reduced aid allocations to the poor countries are no more than isolated indications of a persistence in the traditional attitude of myopic self-interest. In the political field, the end of the precarious détente between the two great power blocs and the acceleration of the arms race imply the return to a situation in which the destiny of the countries of the Third World is subordinated to the vicissitudes of a struggle for world hegemony.

The truth is that in the economic field and also as regards the exercise of power in the contemporary international structure, the interests of the South and the North are not complementary but conflicting. International inequality is no mere historical accident of economic and social development, but the product of a process with its own dynamics on which the privileged material situation of the countries of the North is in large measure based. To identify a plan of genuine mutual interest to both North and South, it is necessary to transcend immediate economic interests and begin to build a world order which assures the currently threatened survival of the human race. This calls for a radical revision of the premises on which the prevailing conception of harmonious and social development is based, but on its success depends the possibility of avoiding the ultimate catastrophe – the unleashing of the apparatus of destruction mounted by the great powers – and of building a world which is acceptable to all.

As I have pointed out, the foregoing criticisms do not deny the fact that the Report – within self-imposed limitations which essentially consist of not fundamentally questioning the values on which the present power structure is based – contains, in our opinion, the most progressive recommendations which a group of persons of good will can propose. That the proposed solutions may not be viable merely demonstrates that, with the retention of the basic elements of the present world order, the possibility of a genuine North-South dialogue is remote. In other words, what the countries of the South cannot do for themselves to resolve their problems, nobody else will do on their behalf.

Finally, this commentary on the Brandt Report may appear pessimistic. That is not so; it simply represents an objective viewpoint of reality in the contemporary world. The pessimism relates to the passive acceptance of that reality – or to the proposal of palliative measures which do not extend to the roots of the problem – on the implicit assumption of that reality being essentially unchangeable.

MAHDI ELMANDJRA*

> The South needs, above all, to realize that even if all the
> problems do not reside in the South, it is in the first instance
> in the South that almost all the solutions reside.

The Report of the Brandt Commission is an exercise in prospection: its recommendations relate to the 1980's and 1990's and Mr Willy Brandt emphasizes in his Introduction the need for 'a vision of the future without which no great task has ever been completed.' (p.10) It is an act of prospection inspired by highly honourable humanist principles, but one in which a number of concepts advanced during the 50's, 60's and 70's and not yet accepted by the North occupy a major part. An act of prospection in which retrospection does not consider itself to be out of place. This 300-page Report represents a positive step towards collective reflection on the problems of development. At the same time, it illustrates the temporal lapse which characterizes North-South relations viewed in terms of action.

If the Report had been published only five years ago it would have seemed like a revolutionary treatise to the South and a text of political fiction to the North. But how should one approach an acceleration of history and, above all, the increasing dissatisfaction of the peoples of the Third World where almost all – if not quite all – governments have shown themselves to be unable to meet the challenges of that history. The Report seeks to make up for the delays which have been incurred and of which it is evidently well aware, but it fails to forecast the delays of the future, not to mention their consequences.

*Morocco. Professor at the University of Rabat and President of the World Futures Studies Federation. Held several leading positions at UNESCO, among others Assistant Director-General for Social Sciences, Humanities and Culture, and for Planning and Pre-Programming. Member of many international scholarly institutions. Author of various studies on international relations and international development. This article originally appeared in *Futuribles*, No. 34, June 1980. Reprinted by permission of *Futuribles* and the author.

One of the recommendations which the Report claims to be an innovatory reform in international institutions refers to the creation of a World Development Fund (p.252). Yet in 1949 India proposed the creation of a United Nations administrative agency for development, while Chile took the initiative which subsequently led to a recommendation of the Economic and Social Council on 'the urgent problems of financing the economic development of underdeveloped countries.'

Thirty years later the Brandt Commission boldy proposes the establishment of an institution for development whose objectives would differ only marginally from those of the institution envisaged by the developing countries at the time of the debate on the Special United Nations Fund for Economic Development (SUNFED). The plea for a redistribution arrangement to replace the spirit of charity which, in the form of 'voluntary' contributions, finances the development programmes of the United Nations is indeed an audacious move.

Yet this boldness is largely mitigated by the number of decades which have had to pass before an initiative such as this could be found to appear acceptable to an international commission such as that presided over by Mr Willy Brandt. In this respect, we are far removed from the notions of anticipation and prospection.

A Report of this nature cannot be anything other than a compromise. The developing countries were effectively represented on the Commission by men who were familiar with the dossiers of the North-South dialogue. Their marks can be found throughout the Report in the argumentation presented and in the formulation of a number of recommendations. The preoccupations of the Third World are thus by no means absent in the Report – in some instances it is even possible to identify the author of a specific idea or a specific passage. The Report is the work of a team whose conductor, Mr Willy Brandt, sets the tone in his Introduction to the Report.

Mr Brandt clearly states the philosophy underlying his work when he refers (p.12) to the Ostpolitik which he encouraged in East-West relations and which contributed to bringing about political détente. He deems it possible to transpose this approach to North-South relations in an attempt to bring about economic détente. The Report is a political exercise, and because of its political nature it makes a global analysis, emphasizes universal objectives, and develops technical arguments, while minimizing or ignoring political obstacles.

This partly explains the discordance between the spirit of the ideas expounded in the Introduction and elsewhere in the Report on the one hand, and that underlying the concrete recommendations on the other. The latter are essentially economic, financial or monetary in nature; the practical implications of the preceding theoretical concepts are not always evident within them. For each of the criticisms which follow, it is easy to find phrases in the Report which could refute them. There nevertheless remains a certain discrepancy between the spirit of synthesis which governs the reflections and the analyses and the pragmatic, sectorial approach adopted in the recommendations.

Preoccupation with the political at the expense of the economic and the cultural restricts the approach to a static analysis and sheds no light on implications for the future of international relations. Furthermore, the results of the analysis are not explicitly transferred to the proposed programme of action, of which the primordial objective is the maximization of the mutual interests of North and South in the interest of survival. This is the interdependence strategy, that on which UNCTAD in Manila in 1979 and UNIDO in New Delhi founded their arguments with results which are familiar. In the history of decolonization, this concept of interdependence, always considered to be a limitation to independence, has in fact always proved to be the forerunner of independence.

Despite a laudable effort to integrate the sociocultural dimension into international relations, the Report commits the sin of allowing economics to reduce the restructuring of the international system to a series of sometimes very audacious economic and financial measures.

They are nonetheless reformist measures which depart from the assumption that the present system can adapt itself without undue difficulty by evading breakdowns and avoiding 'disorder.' Genuine changes necessarily provoke a certain amount of disorder in the transition from an old to a new order. There is nothing that will prevent this functional disorder, a disorder which, incidentally, has begun to make itself felt already. Where, in the plan of action presented by the Commission, are the value systems described in the foregoing analytical part of the Report? The most grave problem in the North-South dialogue is not economic in nature: it is one of mentality and an arrogant and ethnocentric cultural imperialism which makes genuine communication impossible. As we have seen, the Report does indeed refer to cultural imperialism, but what conclusions does it draw therefrom with respect to future action?

This non-integration of sociocultural aspects inevitably results in a linear and non-prospective vision which fails to incorporate all possible kinds of development. Such developments and mutations have already begun to take place and could gravely jolt or even destroy the scaffolding of any new 'order' which were to exclude them from its construct.

As the very concise and lucid analyses in the Report clearly show, the international system is characterized by enormous disequilibria with the large majority of the population living in a state of poverty unworthy of contemporary civilization. (One striking example cited in the Report is that of energy consumption: one American consumes as much energy as 1,072 Nepalese.) Yet it is not enough to direct the attack solely at the consequences of a system which generates inequality and inequity such as 'absolute poverty' (an expression coined by the World Bank which has been adopted for the purposes of this Report), political and cultural domination, monetary chaos, the industrial and commercial monopolies held by multinational companies, increased stockpiling of armaments, blackmail over foodstuffs, and the constant deterioration in the terms of trade. Mere palliatives will be the order of the day as long as no action is taken to deal with the causes of the dysfunctional and asymmetric operation of the system. And any such action would have to take the form of a transformation of the whole of the system, not that of successive adaptation measures taken too late for them to have any real impact.

Mr Brandt does indeed state that 'profound changes are required in international relations,' but the Commission's recommendations do not assist us in understanding how these are to be brought about. The transformation of international relations is already under way. It is the product of a conflict situation in which the confrontations between North and South are much more grave than one would like to admit.

The principal common interest of all humanity apart from survival – and survive we must without succumbing to resignation – is that of change by way of redistribution. Mr Brandt proposes priming such a redistribution process by levying an international tax, pointing out the limitations of concepts such as 'aid' and 'assistance.' On the other hand, he considers that 'whoever wants a bigger slice of the international economic cake cannot seriously want it to become smaller.' The distribution in question is one in which the 'economic health' of the industrial countries would enrich the poor without impoverishing the rich.

The lifestyles characteristic of the developed countries, which are among the causes of the present inequalities, and the wastage which they entail are not openly questioned in the Report. This is in stark contrast to the growing measure of doubt being expressed in this respect elsewhere within the developed countries themselves.

Although the Report does incorporate an identification of certain problems in North-South relations and an analysis of the 'grave global problems arising from the economic and social inequalities of the world community' in a spirit reminiscent of the Club of Rome (cf. p.19 – Towards a Globalization of Policies), the prospective element insofar as it refers to action based on anticipation of the possible and the desirable for the future is almost totally absent in the Report. This explains the only marginal place reserved for innovation. In fact, urgency is accorded to that which should have been done yesterday without too much reflection being devoted to its expedience for tomorrow. There is a need to restructure, but to restructure without losing sight of the tolerance levels for changing the contemporary system. 'Political realism' consists of not overstepping this tolerance level, the limit which no reformist effort, especially one with détente as its ultimate objective, can afford to ignore.

The objective of the whole exercise was in fact to find the ways and means of preventing a rupture. Whether or not we wish to accept the fact, this rupture is already present in a variety of forms within nations and among nations. It will sooner or later lead to the restructuring of mentalities without which it would be impossible to change the national systems of the Third World countries – a *sine qua non* for the construction of a new international system for the 21st century at whose portals we now find ourselves.

A new international economic order which would ensure that the basic needs of those living in absolute poverty were satisfied on the strength of a flight of generosity on the part of those whom these same impoverished individuals are enriching daily would only contribute towards consolidating the inequalities and the power relations which are the principal causes of that poverty. At a time when the notions of endogenous development and self-reliance are gaining ground in the Third World, it is very difficult to accept a brief phrase in the Report (p.43) affirming that 'the South needs, above all, finance.' The South needs, above all, to realize that even if all the problems do not reside in the South, it is in the first instance in the South that almost all the solutions reside.

Like political independence, economic independence, cultural identity and human dignity cannot be granted but have to be acquired at a high price. It is this which too many of the leaders of industrial and developing countries alike pretend not to understand; to do otherwise would defeat all their short-term calculations and present themselves with the prospect of a future in which no seats may be reserved.

The element of prospection enables us to anticipate new development models which will unseat mimicry, capital transfer, technology transfer, appropriate technologies, extraverted economics, and obsession with exporting. While awaiting the inauguration of these new models to foster dialogue between all men, irrespective of their cardinal differences, the reader of the Brandt Report will find it to be very informative and, despite a number of shortcomings which are inevitable in the work of a group representing such a wide range of viewpoints, a witness to the fact that there are still people who are full of goodwill and fired with idealism.